Robert Brandom

Philosophy Now

Series Editor: John Shand

This series of introductions to today's most read, discussed and important philosophers combines rigorous analysis with authoritative exposition to give clear, comprehensive and enthralling access to the ideas of those philosophers who have made a truly fundamental and original contribution to the subject. Together the volumes comprise a remarkable gallery of the thinkers who have been at the forefront of recent philosophical ideas.

Published

David Armstrong
Stephen Mumford

Donald Davidson
Marc Joseph

Nelson Goodman
Daniel Cohnitz & Marcus Rossberg

Saul Kripke
G. W. Fitch

David Lewis
Daniel Nolan

John McDowell
Tim Thornton

Hilary Putnam
Maximilian de Gaynesford

John Rawls
Catherine Audard

Wilfrid Sellars
Willem A. deVries

Peter Strawson
Clifford Brown

Bernard Williams
Mark P. Jenkins

Forthcoming

Thomas Nagel
Alan Thomas

Robert Brandom

Jeremy Wanderer

McGill-Queen's University Press
Montreal & Kingston • Ithaca

ISBN 978-0-7735-3485-8 (bound)
ISBN 978-0-7735-3486-5 (pbk)

Legal deposit third quarter 2008
Bibliothèque nationale du Québec

Published simultaneously in the United Kingdom by Acumen Publishing Limited and in North America by McGill-Queen's University Press

Library and Archives Canada Cataloguing in Publication

Wanderer, Jeremy, 1972–
Robert Brandom/by Jeremy Wanderer.

(Philosophy now)
Includes bibliographical references and index.
ISBN 978-0-7735-3485-8 (bound).—ISBN 978-0-7735-3486-5 (pbk.)

1. Brandom, Robert. I. Title. II. Series.

B945.B744W36 2008 191 C2008-902135-5

Typeset by Graphicraft Limited, Hong Kong.
Printed and bound by Cromwell Press, Trowbridge.

To Yoni

Contents

Acknowledgements

Robert Brandom's masterwork, *Making It Explicit*, is a strikingly impersonal tome. Apart from a brief appearance in a paragraph appended to the end of the Preface, Brandom himself remains, by and large, out of view in the book's 741 pages. There is a sense in which this style of writing exemplifies the kind of idealized Brandomian linguistic game discussed in the work: an I–Thou interchange between any author making claims and any reader keeping track on claims made, enjoined in a search to understand what is that joins them as a We, members of a community able to make and understand claims.

During the past few years, I have been one such reader. What follows is the result of this prolonged engagement with Brandom's rich and difficult body of work. While it has become commonplace in prefaces to books such as this to celebrate the collaborative nature of the process by which they came into being, writing this book has been a relatively solitary endeavour. (The singular form of both sides of the I–Thou relation should be taken seriously.) The end-product is, without doubt, idiosyncratic. Whether this should be regarded as a strength or a weakness (or both) is something that the reader can best judge.

That is not to say that I have not been well supported in the writing process, and I am indebted to conversations with Christian Barth, David Benatar, Dean Chapman, Greg Fried, Elisa Galgut, Cindy Gilbert, Ben Kotzee, Tony Holiday, Neil Horne, Jack Ritchie, Kevin Scharp and Bernhard Weiss. In particular, the outstanding copy-editing skills of Hinda Hoffman have ensured that the book is less idiosyncratic in style than it could have been and almost was. Thanks are also due to the editor and staff at Acumen, including the extremely patient Steven Gerrard, Sue Hadden and Elizabeth Teague.

My interest in all things Brandom dates back to the research undertaken for my doctoral thesis, written under the supervision of David-Hillel Ruben and Samuel Guttenplan. I owe a sincere debt of gratitude to them both for their encouragement and support over the years. My philosophical temperament is far from Rubenesque, while Sam undoubtedly thinks that I picked the wrong Pitt philosopher to take an interest in. Their influence on my thinking and teaching is far greater than this suggests, and I suspect than either of them realizes.

My parents, along with the various members of my extended Wanderer-Hoffman family, have always been an unending source of love, teasing and encouragement, without so much as even feigning an interest in the book's subject matter. They have both kept my feet firmly on the ground amidst my proclivities for *luftgescheft*, and provided the immensely fertile ground on which to keep them. Two family members deserve explicit mention, neither of whom were in my life when the project was first conceived, and both of whom are single-handedly responsible for delaying its completion. Adin has shown me the delights to be had in the works of quite another Bob the Builder, whilst Yoni continues to surprise me with delights of another kind entirely. The book is dedicated to her, for reasons best kept implicit (at least here).

JW
Cape Town
South Africa

Abbreviations

The following abbreviations for works by Robert Brandom have been used in the text.

AR *Articulating Reasons: An Introduction to Inferentialism*. Cambridge, MA: Harvard University Press, 2000.

BSD *Between Saying and Doing: Towards an Analytic Pragmatism*. Locke Lectures delivered in 2006 at the University of Oxford, forthcoming from Oxford University Press. Prior to publication, full text of the lectures is available online at http://www.pitt.edu/~brandom/locke/index.html. Citations in the book are from the online version of the lectures published immediately after the lectures were delivered. (In the text, BSD IV: 2 refers to page two of the fourth lecture).

FNNF "Facts, Norms, and Normative Facts: A Reply to Habermas", *European Journal of Philosophy* **8** (2000), 356–74.

KSOR "Knowledge and the Social Articulation of the Space of Reasons", *Philosophy and Phenomenological Research* **55** (1995), 895–908.

MIE *Making It Explicit: Reasoning, Representing and Discursive Commitment*. Cambridge, MA: Harvard University Press, 1994.

PP "Pragmatics and Pragmatisms". In *Hilary Putnam: Pragmatism and Realism*, James Conant & Urszula M. Zeglen (eds). London: Routledge, 2002.

RDAH "From a Critique of Cognitive Internalism to a Conception of Objective Spirit: Reflections on Descombes' Anthropological Holism", *Inquiry* **47** (2004), 236–53.

RPC "Replies", *Pragmatics and Cognition* **13** (2005), 227–49.

TOMD *Tales of the Mighty Dead: Historical Essays in the Metaphysics of Intentionality*. Cambridge, MA: Harvard University Press, 2002.

VP "Vocabularies of Pragmatism: Synthesizing Naturalism and Historicism". In *Rorty and his Critics*, R. Brandom (ed.). Oxford: Blackwell, 2000.

Introduction

Robert Brandom was born in New York in 1950. He completed undergraduate studies at Yale, and wrote his doctoral thesis at Princeton University under the direction of Richard Rorty. He is currently the Distinguished Professor of Philosophy at the University of Pittsburgh, where he has been a member of the philosophy faculty since 1976. Brandom is the author of four books, most notably *Making It Explicit* (henceforth MIE), and recently delivered the John Locke Lectures at the University of Oxford, entitled "Between Saying and Doing" (BSD). This book aims to provide a lucid introduction to Brandom's philosophy to date.

There are many reasons *not* to write such an introduction at this moment in time. Works of this nature are usually undertaken towards the end of a thinker's career, to provide a retrospective narrative that either outlines the development of the philosophy over time, or to reveal systematicity between parts of which the author was not consciously aware at first publication. This, however, does not apply to Brandom. First, he is relatively young, and at a stage when he is treated more as "the next big thing" than the finished product. Secondly, unlike many works rooted in the analytic tradition, Brandom's masterwork is a self-aware attempt at metaphysical system-building. Thirdly, Brandom's post-MIE writings, especially some of the essays in his *Tales of the Mighty Dead* (TOMD), already show signs of significant development of that system.[1]

One motivation for undertaking such a project nonetheless stems from a curious feature marking the reception of Brandom's work, hinted at in the comments that begin the review in the *Times Literary Supplement*, in response to MIE's paperback publication in 1999.

> Since its publication, beleaguered philosophers around the world have been muttering that they really must get round to reading [it]. Philosophy reading groups have sprung up in academic departments to provide security in numbers before taking it on, and PhD supervisors have settled for vicarious understanding and got their brightest students to read it for them . . . Despite being daunting, [MIE] has already developed a justified reputation as a contribution to philosophy of language.
>
> (Stout 1999: 35)

In a similar vein, the *London Review of Books* notes a year later that "[a]lthough it's famous, very few of my colleagues have read it either (I mean read it, not just bought it or dipped their toes in it)" (Oliver 2000: 35).

Seven years later, and well over a decade since MIE's initial publication, the situation remains by and large the same. Despite good intentions, philosophers still seem to be finding it difficult to get to grips with the detail and implications of this immense work, giving Brandom the rather paradoxical status of being both highly influential and little read.[2]

Brandom-philes place the blame firmly on the beleaguered philosophers themselves, who they claim have been intimidated by the sheer length of the book, and who are unwilling to seriously consider its novel philosophical orientation. Brandom-phobes, in contrast, blame the book, complaining that its length is due to constant repetition, irrelevant asides and the author's wordiness and predilection for rhetorical flourish. All of this, complains the phobe, serves to mask a basic lack of clarity surrounding many of MIE's central claims, so that the book's climax, heralded throughout, is frustratingly easy to miss, if present at all.

The phobe may well endorse the call for a middleman between Brandom and beleaguered philosophers in just the memorable manner recommended by Sydney Smith regarding the writings of Jeremy Bentham.

> [N]either gods, men, nor booksellers can doubt the necessity of a middleman between Mr. Bentham and the public. Mr. Bentham is long; Mr. Bentham is occasionally involved and obscure; Mr. Bentham invents new and alarming expressions; Mr. Bentham loves division and subdivision – and he loves method itself, more than its consequences. Those only, therefore, who know his originality, his knowledge, his vigour, and his boldness, will recur to

> the works themselves. The great mass of readers . . . will choose rather to become acquainted with Mr. Bentham . . . after that eminent philosopher has been washed, trimmed, shaved, and forced into clean linen.
>
> (Smith 1824/2001; cited in Lacey 2004: 297)

According to Smith, the goal of the middleman is, through astute selection and omission, to remove the need for reading the author in the original. Although I confess to moments of sympathy with the Brandom-phobe, especially when exploring some of the darker crannies of MIE, I resolutely do not wish to cast myself in the role of middleman here. The judicious pruning necessitated by the demands of an introductory volume not only chops away much of the detail, but also removes some of its most distinguished features. While I hope this book helps present and potential students of Brandom, beleaguered or otherwise, the following rider is meant seriously: it really is no substitute for reading and grappling with the original.

Instead, it is the frustrations of the phile, rather than the concerns of the phobe, that drive this project. Put off by its obvious demands, impatient readers often seem to have jumped to the part of the book perceived as most interesting, without fully discerning the broader structure within which that part is embedded. To use an example that will occupy us later, many critics of Brandom's inferentialist semantics seem to miss their target as the result of a failure to fully master the broader notion of a social linguistic practice, without which it cannot be understood. My overriding aspiration in what follows is to present a sympathetic account of Brandom's philosophical "edifice" (MIE: xii), in a manner that provides a glimpse of some fine detail, while having the broad contours clearly in view.

Whilst the constraints of this volume have forced inevitable omissions in content, I have tried to retain a sense of the spirit with which Brandom approaches philosophical concerns. Commentators have noted that part of the attraction of his work is the rare combination of attempting a grand-scale rethinking of the relationship between central philosophical concepts, while at the same time being prepared to be embroiled in the technicalities and minutiae necessary to see these lofty goals through. Less remarked upon, but to my mind even more attractive, is the spirit of intellectual inquisitiveness within which these lofty and lowly tasks are carried out. He approvingly describes, at one point, an approach to a particular philosophical problem as following "good Popperian methodology" that "adopts the stronger, more easily falsifiable hypothesis so as to see how far it can be pressed" (1997a: 189). Brandom, too, is prepared to conjecture boldly and then try to see what emerges from the attempt to follow through on this, asking us to judge the success of the "big bold conjecture" by the resultant product.[3] Our goal here is not so much to assess the resultant product, but to set out the system in enough technical detail to facilitate such an assessment.

To call Brandom's philosophy "systematic" is not just to say that he aspires to make the disparate parts of his philosophical thinking cohere. It goes beyond this. Like some of his heroes in the German idealist tradition, Brandom seems to see the creation of a unified system as some kind of distinctly philosophical goal.[4] This aspiration may seem strange for a thinker just identified as a student of Rorty, that arch-foe of metaphysical high theory, and especially for one who follows his teacher in saying "we pragmatists".[5] Brandom attempts a partial reconciliation by distinguishing between two types of metaphysical system-builders (VP: 180–81). The first type carefully attempts to construct a metavocabulary in which something can be said; insight is afforded by making explicit in this metavocabulary what is implicit in the contingent vocabularies of their time. The second type goes beyond this, and takes the metavocabulary constructed as the ultimate metaphysical vocabulary: it acts as the final arbiter in all disputes, so that what cannot be translated into this metavocabulary is dismissed as nonsense. Brandom sees himself as a metaphysical system-builder in the former sense, dismissing the latter group as "imperialist" or "maniacal". Unlike some of his idealist heroes, who aim to try to say absolutely everything about absolutely everything in their preferred metavocabulary, his (relatively!) modest aim can be seen as trying to develop a metavocabulary within which to say something about saying something.[6]

This points towards a core metaphilosophical difference between Brandom and other thinkers, such as Rorty, with whom he sympathizes. A common theme among such thinkers, and one that plays a pivotal role in Brandom's work, is the contention that thinking about thought and language must accord a centrality to the idea of a social linguistic *practice*, and should pay particular attention to the varied and ever-changing *use* to which the relevant parts of the practice are put. Appeal to terms such as *social practice* and *use* in this context is typically accompanied by a kind of theoretical quietism, based on the assumption that the essentially dynamic character of a social *practice*, and the novel and unsurveyable kinds of *uses* of expressions that arise as the practice develops, preclude the possibility of systematic theorizing in this area. Whilst Brandom embraces the essential dynamism of the practice, and the fact that it constantly changes in new directions that cannot be anticipated in advance, he rejects the suggestion that this undermines any attempt at systematic theorizing. One can – he contends – acknowledge, even embrace, contingency in all its various guises, without concluding that there is nothing philosophical to say, save therapeutic intervention for reasons of cultural politics.

Our focus in this book is on Brandom's inferentialist conception of rationality, as first set out in MIE and developed in more recent writings. A central part of this conception aims to specify the structure that a set of performances within a social practice must have (a) for the practitioners to count as sapient beings by virtue of their participation in the practice, and (b) for performances within the practice to have objective semantic content by virtue of their featuring within the practice.

These two goals provide the structure for this book. Part I, entitled "Sapience", uses gameplaying terminology to provide a structural model of linguistic practice, and considers various groups of potential participants ("Parrots" in Chapter 1, "Rational beings" in Chapter 2, "Logical beings" in Chapter 3 and, finally "Us" in Chapter 4) in terms of their relationships to this practice. Part II, entitled "Inferentialism", explores the meaning of the performances that are caught up in this gameplaying practice. Brandom's approach to semantics is outlined (at the "Sentential level" in Chapter 5, which is then extended to the "Subsentential level" in Chapter 6). Finally, the challenge that such an approach has in allowing for a representational dimension of language and thought is explored (looking at the problem of "Communication" in Chapter 7, and at the suspicion that the language-as-social-practice tradition must inevitably 'lose the world' in Chapter 8).[7]

Any metaphysical system-builder who does not harbour maniacal aspirations will acknowledge that the philosophical metavocabulary that they develop is (and, indeed, must be) incomplete and non-final. This, of course, applies to the inferentialist metavocabulary presented in the course of this book. As a result, an inferentialist is fully aware that this metavocabulary will require supplementation, even supplanting. Although Brandom may not be maniacal, he is a famously ambitious theorist. Some of his more recent writings suggest that he wishes to provide a successor to the inferentialist conception of rationality himself, by subsuming it within a broader historicist conception of rationality. (That it subsumes and not supplants ensures that the inferentialist conception is not – yet – obsolete.) This historicist conception of rationality has not been sufficiently developed by Brandom thus far to occupy centre-stage in this book, although it makes a brief appearance in the Conclusion, in the context of setting an agenda for further work.

Part I

Sapience

Introduction

Despite the many differences between you, the reader of this book, and me, its author, there is one thing that, necessarily, we both share. We, you and me, both belong to a community whose members all have cognitive capacities, in the broad sense of being able to reason and understand. There may also be other features and capacities that we share. We may, for example, both be mammals, and we may both be capable of some form of self-propulsion of parts of ourselves through space. While this may well be the case, the kind of interaction that is going on between us, communication via writing and reading with comprehension, requires that we share cognitive capacities. If, to the publisher's delight, this book finds unexpected readership on some alien planet, and you are one such alien reader, then there is an important sense in which you are not alien; you too are part of the "we" who share such capacities.

Brandom's work aims, in part, to give an account of this shared capacity, the sense in which we are both creatures that think, understand and are "subject to the peculiar force of the better reason" (MIE: 5). One may want to gloss this in terms of having a mind, a gloss however that needs to be treated with care. First, it is important not to think of the mind as some kind of thing, be it mental or physical, the possession of which is supposed to explain these capacities. Brandom's preferred vocabulary is to talk not of having a mind, but of "being minded" or of "mindedness", a way of talking that avoids the tendency towards reification. Secondly, he concedes that there is more to mindedness than having these cognitive capacities.

> Mindedness can be thought of coming in two flavors: sentience and sapience. Sentience is a matter of being aware in the sense of being awake that we share at least with our vertebrate cousins. Feelings of pain and sensations of red are paradigmatic sentient episodes. Sapient states, such as beliefs and intentions, and sapient episodes such as thinkings, by contrast, have propositional contents that are expressed in English by the use of "that" clauses with declarative sentences as complements. (RDAH: 238)

It appears, therefore, that the capacity in question is that flavour of mindedness that falls under the heading of sapience.

The "flavour" metaphor is somewhat misleading. While a focus on sapience as opposed to sentience may be a matter of intellectual interest and personal preference for some philosophers, Brandom's reasons for such a narrowed focus are, as we shall see, more principled. He does not have too much to say about sentience. Apart from when he perhaps treats it as an enabling condition for sapience,[1] this category is more or less ignored in much of his writing. For example, he distinguishes between reliable responding devices (those that are able to respond differentially to environmental stimuli) and sentient responders (those that are aware in the sense of being awake), and then proceeds to lump both together in one group that is contrasted with sapient responders (those possessing cognitive capacities).[2] The result is a more or less exclusive focus on the cognitive capacities characteristic of sapient beings.

We, you and I, are sapient beings. It is not just that "we" are members of a community who have this capacity in common, in the way one could refer to a community comprising those able to wiggle their ears or echolocate. In addition, we *recognize* each other as members of such a community. This recognition can be implicit as well as explicit. *Implicit recognition* is something we do by practically treating those with such a capacity as one of us; for example, by chatting with them. *Explicit recognition* involves a self-conscious awareness of community membership where this is capable of being expressed in the form of a claim; for example, by calling them sapient. A central Brandomian theme is that the implicit here has priority, so that one makes explicit what is already implicit in the demarcational practices of sapient beings through which we treat others as one of us. Those capable of implicitly recognizing and being recognized as sapient are those that Brandom calls *rational beings*. Those additionally capable of making such implicit recognition explicit are those that Brandom calls *logical beings*.

The recognition of sapience just considered was one-way recognition, from recognizer to recognized. Brandom goes a stage further, and talks of *mutual recognition* where this relationship goes both ways: I, in practice, recognize you, and you, in practice, recognize me. It is possible that those I recognize may not recognize me in turn. It is possible that I may not recognize those that so recognize me. When mutual recognition is achieved, and I am recognized in practice as sapient by those beings that I recognize in practice as sapient, there is yet an additional sense in which we can talk of "we" as a community of sapient beings.[3]

The aim of Part I of this book is to outline Brandom's account of sapience, by specifying the structure a social practice must have in order for practitioners to implicitly recognize and be recognized as rational beings, and to explore the relationship between rational beings and the logical beings capable of achieving explicit recognition of their sapience.

In Chapter 1, we begin by contrasting the verbal response of a *parrot* with the verbal response of a human being to the same stimulus. For parrots, read pariahs. We are not so much interested in investigating the verbal capabilities of actual parrots, as in exploring the possibility of someone having a kind of quasi-insider status in our sapient community.[4] Following this, in Chapter 2, we provide a model of a social practice that, it is claimed, includes all the conditions that are both necessary and sufficient for its practitioners to be *rational beings*. These rational beings are insiders in our sapient community, and have a distinctive kind of conscious awareness, although they have not yet achieved the kind of self-conscious awareness of logical beings. Chapter 3 explores the relationship between the self-awareness of *logical beings*, and the awareness of rational beings achieved in the previous stage. Finally, in Chapter 4, we consider the relationship between such logical beings and *ourselves*, in light of the challenge that the beings described are not recognizable by us as us, co-members of the community of sapient beings.

Chapter 1

Parrots

Introduction

On a number of occasions, Brandom introduces his particular conception of mind and language with the following question:

> What is the difference between a parrot who is disposed reliably to respond differentially to the presence of red things by saying "Raawk, that's red," and a human reporter who makes the same noise under the same circumstances? (KSOR: 897)[1]

In so doing, he forces the reader to focus on a purported discontinuity between the abilities of human adults and of parrots. Despite the similarity in the given descriptions of the behaviours, the vocal responses of the human adult and parrot reporter differ, as only the former *understands* her response. As a result of this difference, the human report is not only a *vocal* response, but also a *verbal* one.[2]

Although this starting point may seem chauvinistic in the extreme, the intention is not to catalogue purported deficiencies designed to elevate the status of man over beast. Rather the aim is to understand the criteria implicit in the performances that we, sapient beings, use in demarcating those whom we treat in practice as "we", shared members of the community of sapient beings. Without doubt, this demarcational starting point forces attention on our own case, but such reflection is not anthropocentric *per se*, and not all self-regard need be dismissed as excessive.

The difference between human talk and parrot talk also provides the starting point for John Locke's celebrated discussion of language at the beginning of Book III of his *An Essay Concerning Human Understanding* (henceforth E – Locke 1689/1915). According to Locke, humans are able to produce "articulate sounds, which we call words. But this was not enough to produce language; for parrots, and several other birds, will be taught to make articulate sounds distinct enough, which yet by no means are capable of language" (E: 3.1.1). Locke's starting point also focuses attention on a purported difference in ability between human adults and other creatures. Despite the descriptive similarities in behaviour between the parrot and the adult human reporter, they differ in a basic sense, as only the latter *understands* her response. As a result of this difference, parrots can produce *words*, but not *language*.[3]

Locke's concern here also need not be read as unabashed anthropocentrism. Earlier in the *Essay*, he considers a report of "a very intelligent rational parrot", able to "discourse, reason, and philosophize" (E: 2.27.8). The very possibility of such a creature, who presumably understands the words uttered, reveals that Locke is not concerned with difference between species *per se*. Rather, he is using what he considers to be a widely accepted example to discern the difference between the production of articulate sounds and linguistic behaviour.[4]

The similarity between Locke and Brandom extends no further than the use of a common exemplar and shared demarcational starting point; in almost every other aspect, it is hard to imagine two more different and opposed conceptions of mind and language. Outlining these differences, by considering their differing ways of distinguishing between human and parrot talk, is the primary aim of this chapter. Brandom's account of sapience is built upon a number of underlying assumptions, and the contrast with Locke not only affords a useful entry point into the account, but also provides a way of bringing these assumptions to the surface.

Taken individually, many of these underlying assumptions are not unique to Brandom, and the goal here is to orient, rather than to defend. It would be disingenuous, however, to overstress the evaluative neutrality of the exercise, not least due to the fact that the Lockean account is often treated as the paradigm of an erroneous conception of language, so that any attempted contrast serves to flatter the Brandomian alternative by association. There is, however, more to such a contrastive strategy than the salesperson's crass technique of inflating the perceived value of his goods by forced comparison with even shoddier alternatives. While many contemporary accounts of mind and language claim to have overcome the deficiencies of the Lockean picture, some nonetheless share certain features with Locke that are rejected by Brandom. The contrast with Locke in this chapter will provide a tacit contrast with these contemporary accounts too, thereby providing an introduction to Brandom's genuinely non-Lockean alternative.

Brandom on parrot talk

There are many similarities between the vocal responses of the human adult and the parrot in the case just described. Both responses are the result of reliable dispositions to respond differentially to red things. Further, there is a sense in which both responses can be said to be classificatory: because human adults and parrots respond differentially to red things, those red things are responded to in a like manner; thereby red things are treated as being of a particular type and as distinguished from other types. Further still, both responses have potential significance for others, in the sense that others can respond to these vocal performances in ways that reveal them to be informative.[5]

What then is the difference between the response of the parrot and the response of the adult human, in virtue of which the latter but not the former is a verbal performance? At the core of Brandom's reply is the claim that the parrot's response is not part of a specific norm-governed *social practice* called *linguistic practice*. Not every social interaction between sentient beings is a social practice, and not every social practice is linguistic. What makes a social interaction between beings a social practice is that it involves the exchange of socially significant performances that are governed by norms recognized in some sense by the participants. What makes a social practice a specifically linguistic one is that the practice includes the speech act of asserting among its possible performances. We shall develop each of these in turn.

Social practice

Early in MIE, Brandom proffers the following answer to the demarcational question:

> What is special about us is the sort of grasp or uptake of normative significance that we are capable of. To be one of us in this sense of "us" is to be the subject of normative *attitudes*, to be capable of acknowledging proprieties and improprieties of conduct, to be able to treat a performance as correct or incorrect.
> (MIE: 32)

It is one thing to do something; it is another for that doing to have the *normative status* of being appropriate or inappropriate. According to Brandom's answer, what demarcates the practices of us sapient beings is that we are able to acknowledge what ought, and what ought not, to be done. This acknowledging is taking a *normative attitude* towards a norm-governed performance.

It is possible to distinguish between two very different ways of acknowledging norms: acknowledging a norm by being subject to it; and by being sensitive to it. The former is to acknowledge a norm by obeying it in practice. In this sense every happening in nature involves implicitly acknowledging a norm: an acid ought to turn litmus paper red under certain specified conditions, and in so doing it can be said to implicitly acknowledge this norm. The latter, in contrast, is to acknowledge a norm by grasping and understanding it. In this sense one acknowledges a norm by taking a normative attitude towards it.[6]

A core difference between acknowledgement by being subject to the norm and acknowledgement by being sensitive to the norm is that only the latter allows for the possibility of error (MIE: 30–31). It is not possible for the acid to be bound by the norm mentioned above and yet not turn litmus paper red in the circumstances specified. If this occurs, then the acid is not bound by that norm, but by another one that it obeys on this occasion. When acknowledgement of the norm involves adopting an attitude towards a performance, however, it is possible for that norm to be binding and yet to be disobeyed in practice. It is only in this second case that we can talk of the normative status of a performance at all: one could say that the performance of the acid was expected in the sense of conforming to a regularity, but it is strange to talk of a performance of turning the litmus paper red as being appropriate or even correct, for there is no possibility of it being inappropriate or being incorrect. As used here, taking a normative attitude towards a norm-governed performance involves acknowledging a norm by being sensitive to it.

In order to interpret a set of performances as being part of a norm-governed social practice, therefore, the key is to be able to interpret some of the performances as the taking of normative attitudes towards other socially significant performances. Taking such a normative attitude involves acknowledging the normative status of certain other performances, treating them as appropriate or inappropriate. Taking a normative attitude towards another performance is something that a social practitioner does; that is, it is an assessing performance. This assessing performance must be separate from the performances being assessed, or else it fails to provide the possibility of doing anything else but acknowledging a norm in the sense of obedience.

On some occasions, assessing performances could take an explicit form, such as by saying that the performance is inappropriate. This, however, is not the only form that assessing performances can take. As the following example shows, it is possible for the taking of normative attitudes to be implicit in assessing performances.

Placing my signature on a job contract a few years ago significantly altered the normative status of my subsequent doings, and thus my normative status. As a result, I am currently *obligated* to undertake other performances, such as teaching the courses specified in the contract and undertaking endless administrative duties. As a result, I am currently *entitled* to other performances, such as parking my car in staff parking bays and signing-off on certain course-related forms. As a result, I am currently *precluded* from other performances, such as lying in bed on particular mornings. These are normative statuses, since it is appropriate for me to do what I am obligated and entitled to do, and inappropriate for me to do what I am precluded from doing.

Certain others, such as my head of department (HOD), recognize the norms that now govern my performances, so that if I decide to stay at home on a morning when I am supposed to be invigilating an exam, he will take a con-attitude towards that performance; that is, he will treat it as inappropriate. Taking a con-attitude towards my performance is something that the HOD could do explicitly, such as by sending me an email stating that my performance was inappropriate. It is also possible for such a normative attitude to be implicit in his responsive performances. He could, for example, respond to my staying at home with a negative sanction that classifies my performance as inappropriate. The point is not that the HOD aims to punish my performance because of his prior grasp of the inappropriateness of my performance, but that the sanctioning performance itself is his adopting a normative attitude towards my performance, which could be made explicit by his thinking or saying that my performance is inappropriate. The sanctioning performance is his implicit acknowledgement of the impropriety of my staying at home.

The easiest way to think of such sanctioning practices is in terms of positive and negative reinforcement. In response to this dereliction of my duties as a lecturer, my HOD responds by increasing my work load, and by removing my rights to a staff parking bay. Assuming that this is undesirable, the negative sanction will have the effect of reducing the likelihood of a repeat performance. What makes my HOD's responsive performance a sanction is that it is a performance that results in the negative reinforcement of certain performances, as seen in the subsequent reduction of similarly inappropriate behaviours.

If the only way to identify sanctioning performances were in terms of the subsequent reduction of inappropriate performances, then my HOD's response would only count as a sanctioning performance if it actually resulted in such a reduction. This does not seem to be correct, however, since his response can be seen as a sanction even if it has absolutely no effect on my subsequent performance. What makes it a sanction is that it alters the normative status of my subsequent doings. Before my no-show at the examination venue, I was treated by the HOD as entitled to certain things, including staff parking rights, and obligated to undertake a certain work load. Subsequent to my no-show, he treats me as entitled to less and obligated to more. In this case, a performance can be a sanction even if it has no effect on my subsequent behaviours, as long as it involves an alteration of my normative status. It may not be possible to spell out such an alteration of my normative status in terms of my subsequent behaviour, as I may well not perform as now obligated, or desist from performing in ways that I am now not permitted.

Brandom calls responsive performances that can be classified as a negative sanction in terms that make no reference to the norm system in question, such as those that result in the negative reinforcement of performances as seen in the subsequent reduction of similarly inappropriate behaviours, *external sanctions*. In contrast, responsive performances that can be classified as a negative sanction only in terms of the norm system in question, those that are specified by their altering the normative status of the performer, are called *internal sanctions* (MIE: 44).

On some occasions, internal sanctions can themselves depend on external sanctions. If, for example, I continue to park in a staff bay, my HOD may respond by physically removing me from the campus, and thereby force compliance. On other occasions, such internal sanctions can themselves be understood in terms of further internal sanctions. For example, continuing to park in a staff bay could be responded to by further alterations in my normative status, such as the removal of further rights and the imposition of greater fines. Indeed, it is possible for there to be a system of sanctions that are all internal, in the sense that what makes a performance a sanction is entirely specified in terms of the alteration of the normative statuses of subsequent performances. Although not all social practices are like this, the linguistic practice that will be our focus here is an example of a social practice in which all sanctions are internal.

For a set of performances to be part of a social practice is, on this account, for there to be a distinction in perspectives between performing and assessing the performances. The "basic building-block" of a social practice is, therefore, the relation between a performer who is the subject of normative statuses and an audience taking a normative attitude towards the performer's norm-governed performances (MIE: 508). An account of social practice that accords primacy to this building-block is one that Brandom calls an "I–Thou" approach to the social. This contrasts with an "I–We" approach, which takes some shared set of communal norms set by a "We" as the building-block in an account of social practice. The term "social" in "social practice" as used in this chapter is in the I–Thou sense. The concept of a community, a We, is built out of this basic interactive I–Thou relationship.

Simple and interpreting practitioners

Until now we have considered the question of when a set of responsive performances should be considered part of a norm-governed social practice. It has been proposed that the set must include performances interpretable as the adoption of normative attitudes towards other performances, so that the performers within the social practice can be the subject of normative attitudes.

Even if this proposal is accepted, one can still ask a more local question regarding the status of an individual performance and performer within the practice. After all, a social practice is composed of many different performances produced by many different performers. Does each and every performance within the up-and-running social practice need to be produced by practitioners who are themselves capable of undertaking such normative attitudes in order for it to be part of the social practice?

Brandom's response to this local question is that it is possible for a performance in a social practice to be socially significant even if its performer is incapable of being the subject of normative attitudes, provided that the practice as a whole includes performers capable of undertaking normative attitudes towards it. This suggests a division between two types of practitioners in a social practice: interpreting performers and simple performers.[7] An *interpreting performer* is capable of being the subject of normative attitudes, so that her performances are interpreted as involving both normative attitudes and normative statuses. Such a performer is able to both produce socially significant performances, and to be sensitive, at least implicitly, to the norms governing such a performance. A *simple performer* is one whose performances can be treated as having a normative status, such as being appropriate, but cannot be the subject of normative attitudes, and is thus insensitive to the normative status of her performance.

In order to develop this point, it is useful to highlight a key, though contentious, aspect of Brandom's account of the relationship between normative attitude and normative status which has been obscured in the discussion until now. In being the subject of normative attitudes, a performer in a social practice has been said to acknowledge (in the sense of being sensitive to) norms governing performances within the practice. Such talk may give the impression that these norms transcend the practice, so that performances have a normative status irrespective of whether anyone takes a normative attitude towards them, and that taking a normative attitude involves the recognition of such practice-transcendent norms and statuses. Brandom, however, has no wish to invoke practice-transcendent norms and normative statuses, and contends that normative attitudes should be seen as *instituting* the normative status of the performances assessed (e.g. MIE: 48, 161–7, 623–8).

This may be easier to understand if we return to our example of a social practice. In sanctioning my performance, my HOD adopts a normative attitude towards that performance. He treats it as a performance for which I am responsible, in a distinctive sense of responsibility that invokes norms to which I am bound. In this case, the norms are clearly not practice-transcendent norms existing in some noumenal realm beyond the phenomenal realm of everyday performances. They are the products of, and maintained and developed by, the decisions made by certain members of the university to which I have agreed to bind myself, by signing the job contract. The practical normative attitudes of the relevant authorities can be said to institute the norms in light of which my performance becomes inappropriate. A basic Brandomian commitment is that such social institution of norms is not a mere idiosyncrasy of the example chosen; normative statuses are always social statuses, and are constituted, maintained and developed by the normative attitudes of practitioners.

Precisely how to understand the claim that such statuses are instituted by normative attitudes, and how this claim coheres with his commitment to the objectivity of some norms so that it must be possible for any and all practitioners to be mistaken in their assessments of what the norms require, will be the subject of much discussion later on. Regardless of how this claim is understood, it has implications for the distinction between simple and interpreting performers. In particular, it precludes the possibility of there being a social practice comprising just simple performers incapable of being subjects of normative attitudes. If all the performers in a practice were simple performers, there would be no norms in play, and none of the performances would have a normative status such as being appropriate. There can, however, be a social practice that combines simple performers with interpreting performers. In such a "mixed" practice, the interpreting performers are capable of undertaking normative attitudes towards the performances of both interpreting performers and simple performers, treating these as appropriate or otherwise. In this "mixed" practice, it is possible for the performance of a simple performer to have a normative status, and, therefore, to have significance within the social practice, even though the simple performer herself cannot be the subject of normative attitudes.

This distinction between simple and interpreting performers is important in the context of Brandom's response to the demarcational question. Let us assume for the moment that we do not treat parrots as the subject of normative attitudes. A parrot, therefore, is not treated as an interpreting performer. I, an interpreting performer, can nonetheless treat the reliably trained parrot's uttering "Raawk, that's red", as having the normative status of being appropriate; after all, in the description of this case, I am told that the parrot is a reliable reporter. I therefore adopt a normative attitude towards its performance, treating it as appropriate. A parrot is, therefore, a simple performer in a social practice. Its vocal performances are socially significant, although the parrot is not the subject of normative attitudes. The significance of the vocal performance is derived from the acknowledgement of the norms governing the performance by other interpreting practitioners.

Linguistic practice

As the case of the lecturer highlights, not all social practices are linguistic.[8] For Brandom, a linguistic practice is any social practice whose structure includes the speech act of *asserting*.[9]

Why privilege asserting among all other speech acts? One defence he proffers is that all other speech acts depend on asserting (e.g. MIE: 172; BSD II: 17; AR: 81). Take, for example, the speech act of ordering, such as ordering someone to close the door. Brandom contends that no one could be said to perform such a speech act unless one is also capable of asserting that the door is closed. In contrast, asserting is a speech act that one is able to perform without necessarily being able to perform any others.

Even if one could defend the claim that all speech acts depend on asserting in this manner, further argument is still required to conclude that we should treat the inclusion of asserting within a social practice as a necessary and sufficient condition for that practice to be a linguistic one. At this stage, it is best to treat Brandom's commitment as stemming from a general rationalist, philosophical outlook, rather than as the result of a specific argument. Loosely, asserting involves staking a claim which can stand as a reason for other claims, and which stands in need of reasons itself. Intimately connected with asserting is inferring, in the sense of treating one claim as a reason for another.[10] To privilege both asserting and inferring in this manner is to treat such reason-giving and reason-taking practices as *the* defining feature of our sapience. While the term "linguistic" may pick out an array of different and unrelated things in ordinary parlance, the rationalist outlook ensures that we are interested primarily in whatever it is that makes a social practice a discursive rational practice. The focus on the speech act of asserting is plausible when seen in this context.

For a performance to be treated as an act of asserting, the asserter must have some mastery over the role of that assertion in "the game of giving and asking for reasons"; that is, what other claims it gives reasons for and what claims are reasons for it. According to Brandom, the vocal performance of a parrot is not treated as an act of asserting, since the parrot is treated as lacking such mastery.

> A parrot . . . can produce an utterance perceptually indistinguishable from an assertion of "The swatch is red". Our nonetheless not taking it to have asserted that sentence, not to have made a move in that game, *is* our taking it that, unaware as it is of the inferential involvements of the claim that it would be expressing . . . , it has not thereby succeeded in committing itself to anything. (AR: 191)

The claim that "the swatch is red" has other claims, such as "the swatch is coloured", is an inferential consequence. Further, the claim itself is an inferential consequence of other claims, such as the claim "the swatch is scarlet". A claim thus occupies a position in a network of inferential relations to other claims, relations that capture the inferential involvements of that claim. Understanding a claim involves the practical ability of mastering some of the inferential involvements of the claim, so that one can, by and large, use this claim appropriately in asserting and inferring performances. Asserting requires some understanding of the asserted claim; that is, having some practical mastery over some of the inferential involvements of what is claimed.

One need not have grasped all the inferential involvements of a claim in order to be able to assert it. How much mastery over the inferential involvements of a claim is required? Consider, for example, being forced to play a game of soccer with a child.[11] If the child is rushing around after the ball in a haphazard and crazy manner, so that it is apparent that she has no understanding of any of the rules, then one may play along, but one will not treat any of her haphazard doings as the making of a move in the game of soccer. On the other hand, if the child appears to have some mastery over the rules of the game – perhaps she knows not to handle the ball outside the penalty area, to kick the ball in the right direction and appears to be trying to score a goal – then one will treat her as a soccer player, and treat her performances as moves, even if she makes mistakes and displays no grasp of the offside rule. There are no hard-and-fast answers as to how many of the right moves one must have mastered in order to be treated as a soccer player, but some mastery is required. Similarly, some practical mastery over the inferential involvements of a claim is required for a person to be treated as understanding the claim and for their vocal utterances to be treated as verbal assertings.

In responding to the question, "what makes a social practice a linguistic one?" we have invoked two interrelated features. The first is the inclusion of the speech act of asserting within the social practice. The second focuses not on the act of assert*ing* but on what is assert*ed*; that is, the position that the asserted claim (in the sense of what is claim*ed*) plays in a network of inferential relations to other claims (again in the sense of what is claim*ed*). These two features are linked by Brandom's contention that to perform the act of asserting one has to have some mastery over the inferential involvements of what is asserted. The first feature, privileging asserting over and above all other things we can do with words, reflects Brandom's "*logocentrism*";[12] the second feature, providing an account of what is asserted in terms of its role in reasoning (rather than its origin in experience, for example), reflects Brandom's commitment to an *inferentialist semantics*. Brandom further asserts the explanatory primacy of the former over the latter, so that we are to understand what is claim*ed* in terms of the act of claim*ing*. This prioritizing of *knowing how* to do something in explaining what it is to *say that* something is the case is a third fundamental Brandomian commitment to a form of *pragmatism* about the linguistic.

A two-ply account of observation reports

Let us summarize Brandom's overall response to the demarcational question which emerges from this discussion. A parrot may be able to classify, in the sense of reliably distinguishing red things from others in its responses. It is not, however, treated as having sufficient practical mastery of the consequences of the application of the concept RED, nor what such applicability follows from, for its response to be treated by linguistic practitioners as the making of a verbal, as opposed to a vocal, claim. Linguistic practitioners may attribute a normative status to its performances in light of their own sensitivity to the inferentially articulated norms governing linguistic practice, but they do not treat the parrot as the subject of such normative attitudes.

We can recast this response to the demarcational question using the terminology provided by Brandom's "two-ply account of observation".[13] This requires us to briefly outline the two-ply account, before applying it to the case of parrots. This effort should prove useful, as it will allow the ideas and terminology introduced to feature in the ensuing discussion.

According to the two-ply account, making an observation report, such as claiming that "the swatch is red", involves an exercise of two distinct practical capacities.[14] The first is the ability to respond differentially to some stimulus, and the second is the ability to make a move in a linguistic practice. These two abilities are sufficient for the report to be (a claim to) observational knowledge.

Any system that has the ability to respond differentially to stimuli could be called a "reactive system".[15] A reactive system is capable of "reading", that is the ability to discriminate certain kinds of stimulus inputs, and "writing", that is the ability to differentially produce certain types of response outputs. In some cases, reading and writing are integrated into a "read/write cycle", so that the system can write a token of a specific type, and then read it as the type of token that it is.[16] The stimulus types are the set of all token inputs that the system can read, and the response types are the set of all token outputs that can be written. If the system has the ability to reliably respond differentially to instances of red by saying "red", then it has the ability to read red stimulation-kinds, and to write red performance-kinds in response. If the system has the ability to respond differentially to the presence of muons in cloud chambers by citing a particular equation in particle physics, then it has the ability to read muon instances and to write particular equations in particle physics.[17] Any reactive system capable of reading and writing has what Brandom calls Reliable Differential Responsive Dispositions, or RDRDs for short. The first ply in Brandom's two-ply account of observation reports invokes these RDRD abilities.

The second ply invokes the ability to make a move in the game of giving and asking for reasons. It may seem strange to call this an *ability*, since making such a move is tied to the notion of a social practice, and abilities and practices differ. There is, for example, a distinct sense in which abilities, such as the ability to write your name or the ability to reliably differentially produce certain verbal sounds, can be said to manifest themselves in an individual, while performances in a practice, on the other hand, such as the acceptance of a job offer or the making of a claim, require a consideration of the social normative context that includes the judgement of other practitioners about the doings of the individual in question. Practices and abilities, however, are intimately related in at least two important ways. First, in order for a person to be treated as a participant within a social practice, the person must be treated as having some ability to produce certain performances under certain circumstances, even if this ability is not perfectly exercised in every instance. Secondly, one performance, such as signing a signature at the bottom of a job contract or producing a verbal sound, can at once be *both* an exercise of that ability and a performance in the social practice. The difference between the two is the vocabulary used to specify the performance: one is the "naturalistic, physicalistic" vocabulary of responsive abilities; and the other is the normative vocabulary of social practice (TOMD: 350).

The second ply, therefore, points to another distinctive ability: to have mastered enough of the inferential role of the response for that response to be treated as a move in the game. If the performance is recognized as such, the very same doing which is an RDRD can be treated as a move within a linguistic practice by shifting to another vocabulary. In virtue of being so treated, those non-inferentially elicited observational judgements that are "wrung from us", as a result of "being properly trained and wired up" (Brandom 1998: 372), become assertings through their inferential engagement with other judgements, and thus susceptible to rational critique and justification.

Brandom's use of the term "ply" indicates that these two plies are somehow intertwined. It is important to highlight one way *not* to understand the relationship between these two plies, namely any understanding that falls prey to the Myth of the Given.[18] In this context, the erroneous understanding would be that the output of the first ply somehow imposes some sort of rational constraint on the second. Brandom provides the following diagram to illustrate this:

> Physical objects → Sensings of Sense Contents →
> Noninferential beliefs → Inferential Beliefs.[19]

The things to focus on in this diagram are the arrows. Reading from left to right, the first arrow is a causal one that "relates particulars describable in a non-normative vocabulary"; the last arrow is a justificatory one, "an inferential notion" (Brandom 1997c: 127). To fall prey to the Myth of the Given would be to treat the middle arrow as anything but causal; to do otherwise would involve a failure to keep causal and justificatory considerations separate. For Brandom, the content of beliefs consists in their inferential articulation, and thus their potential justificatory relations to other such beliefs. The erroneous conception of the relationship between the two plies would be to think that this inferential articulation, part-mastery of which is required for the second ply, is somehow *given* by the first ply (cf. Rödl 2005: 97–100). According to Brandom, we avoid the Myth of the Given "by seeing nothing non-judgemental that could serve to *justify* perceptual judgements, rather than just to *cause* them" (Brandom 2002a: 93–4). (We shall return to these issues in depth in Chapter 8, where we consider what a positive account of this intertwining between the two plies would be.)

Recast in the language provided by his two-ply account of observation, Brandom's response to the demarcation question is as follows. Parrots have mastered the first ply; that is, they have the RDRD abilities to read red stimuli and write "Raawk, that's red" in response. Parrots have not, however, mastered the second ply; that is, they do not have sufficient mastery over the inferential involvements of what is claimed by that sentence for their vocal response to be treated as an asserting. Linguistic practitioners who are aware of the parrot's RDRD abilities (the first ply) can use this to learn from the utterance, but this is very different from the way in which they would learn from the assertings of others able to make moves in the game of giving and asking for reasons (the second ply).

These claims require, and will receive, further clarification and evaluation. At this stage, however, let us consider Locke's alternative response to the demarcation challenge.

Locke on parrot talk

Locke begins his discussion of language by noting that human beings are social creatures, and that such fellowship requires communication so that one's ideas can be made known to other human beings.

> Besides articulate sounds, therefore, it was further necessary that he should be able to use these sounds as signs of internal conceptions; and to make them stand as marks for the ideas within his own mind, whereby they might be made known to others, and the thoughts of men's minds be conveyed from one to another. (E: 3.1.2)

Given their private nature, Lockean ideas cannot be conveyed as they are. Instead, we human beings use publicly available sounds as signs of these ideas in order to communicate with each other. Although parrots may also articulate sounds, this is not language, claims Locke, for these sounds are not used as signs of ideas in their minds.

Unlike the way in which we treat human sounds, we treat the parrot's cry as "nothing but so much insignificant noise" (E: 3.2.7). Is such differential treatment rooted in a perceived deficit in parrot talk, or in a perceived underlying deficit in parrot thought? Put differently, when a parrot says "red" in the presence of a red thing, is the reason that we treat these sounds as words and not language a result of the fact that we treat the parrot as unable to entertain the idea of red, and therefore cannot treat its sounds as signs of ideas, or is it a result of the fact that, while it can entertain the idea of red, there is no connection between that idea and its vocalization?

Locke would certainly reject the claim that parrots lack an inner life entirely.[20] He is quite clear that non-human animals can have ideas in perception.[21] His subsequent discussion of the active operations of the mind involved in thinking, such as retention, discerning, comparing and compounding, implies that some members of the animal kingdom not only perceive, but also are able to engage in active thinking, albeit to different degrees.[22] There is, however, a difference between the minds of "man and brute". Noting that non-human animals lack general terms, Locke claims this to be evidence that "[b]rutes abstract not" (E: 2.10.10), and thus do not have general ideas, ideas that are arrived at through processes such as abstraction from simple ideas. Although Locke makes much of this difference, calling the ability to abstract "a perfect distinction betwixt man and brute" (E: 2.11.10), he concedes that brutes are able to reason.

> For if they have any ideas at all, and are not bare machines, (as some would have them,) we cannot deny them to have some reason. It seems as evident to me, that they do some of them in certain instances reason, as that they have sense; but it is only in particular ideas, just as they received them from their senses. (E: 2.11.11)

What the brute lacks, therefore, is the ability to abstract, and thus have general ideas, although it is able to engage in a type of reasoning, reasoning with particulars.[23]

Parrots, therefore, can have an idea of red from sensation, but are unable to form general ideas via abstraction. This, however, does not answer the question about the status of parrot talk raised above. That question was not whether the inner life of parrots differs from that of human beings, but whether the reason for the differential treatment of parrot sounds and human sounds that Locke assumes is based on such a perceived difference. Locke's answer seems to be that the source of the differential treatment lies not in a particular conception of parrot thought, but in the way in which we relate to the sounds themselves.[24] This is clearest in a passage later on in the *Essay* where Locke notes that there are occasions on which the words of human beings are, like parrots, not language:

> Before a man makes any proposition, he is supposed to understand the terms he uses in it, or else he talks like a parrot, only making a noise by imitation, and framing certain sounds, which he has learnt of others; but not as a rational creature, using them for signs of ideas which he has in his mind. (E: 4.8.7)

Imitation is seen as a process in which we produce articulate sounds by copying others; speaking a language, on the other hand, involves the voluntary use of a sound as an arbitrary sign of an idea, for the purposes of communication.[25]

The reason for Locke's distinction between the words of the parrot and the language of the adult human being, therefore, is not based on a distinction between their minds *per se*, but rather in the perceived connection between their mind and the words produced. While human beings and parrots differ in their capacity to reason, both are reasoning creatures who have ideas. The difference between parrot sounds and human language is that we treat parrot sounds as produced by imitation, and thus as disconnected from their ideas, whereas we treat human sounds, on most occasions, as deliberately produced with communicative intent, and thus as language.

Brandom on mindedness: some unLockean assumptions

An extended compare-and-contrast exercise of the approaches of Locke and Brandom to the demarcational question is rendered otiose by the obvious chasm separating their responses. For Brandom, the vocal response of the parrot is not a verbal one, as it is not treated as a socially significant performance within a norm-governed linguistic practice, even if it may be accorded a normative significance by practitioners. For Locke, however, the parrot produces words and not language, since the sounds are not produced by the parrot with the intent to communicate an idea to an audience.

I shall, nonetheless, isolate four central differences that emerge from the previous discussion as a way of highlighting certain assumptions guiding Brandom's response.[26] In slogan form, these differences are:

- Locke treats mind as independent of, and prior to, language; Brandom proffers a linguistic conception of mindedness.
- Locke's conception of mind is individualistic; Brandom's is social.
- Locke bases his account of thought in experience; Brandom bases his in reasoning.
- Locke takes an atomistic approach to thinking; Brandom takes a holistic approach.

A relational linguistic approach to mindedness

Even if Locke's *Essay* is sometimes treated as "the first modern treatise devoted specifically to philosophy of language" (Kretzmann 1968: 175), in it language occupies a secondary status relative to that of mind. Language is thought of instrumentally, in terms of its purposes in communicating ideas between people. It is a response to the need for sociality between already minded creatures, and is only discussed after a complete description of mindedness has been undertaken. This is not, of course, the case for Brandom, for whom language plays an ineliminable role in his conception of mindedness. As we saw in the discussion of simple and interpreting performers, even if we can attribute claims and beliefs to non-linguistic creatures such as parrots, this is dependent on the fact that the creatures doing the attributing are full participants within a linguistic practice.

Brandom does not, however, simply invert the Lockean primacy of mind over language by treating language as primary. Instead, he adopts a relational approach. One does not explain what it means to claim that the swatch is red as the public expression of the conceptually more basic believing that the swatch is red, nor explain the latter as the internalization of the more basic former. For him, believing and claiming are "two sides of one coin, . . . neither . . . activity . . . can be made sense of independently of the other" (AR: 6). This is a relational linguistic approach to the mind, as neither mind nor language is treated as independent of, nor temporally or conceptually prior to, the other.

A perspectival, vehicleless approach to mindedness

Locke's conception of mind can be said to be individualistic in two senses. First, whilst he concurs that minded beings were created with the inclination for social interaction, social interaction plays no essential role in constituting mindedness. Secondly, Locke conceives of the mind in broadly epistemic terms, so that mental states are seen as essentially private, in that one can only have first-personal access to such states. A mind can thus only be directly known by the individual whose mind it is. Brandom, in contrast, proffers an explicitly social conception of mindedness. "Social" here is to be viewed through perspectival I–Thou lenses, whereby "linguistic practice and therefore intentionality [is] essentially social only in the sense that it can be made intelligible only in the context of mutual interpretation" (MIE: 659, n. 50). This is to be contrasted with I–We accounts whereby the performance of an individual is given meaning only by being linked to some wider notion of a community that collectively or distributively assesses norms.

In addition to these two "Lockean" senses of individualism about the mental, it is possible to highlight a third. According to this, even if some descriptions of mind may make reference to the individual's social context, there is a basic level of description that can pick out such states that makes no reference to anything that is external to that individual, no matter how the boundaries of the individual are conceived. Consider this parallel: squiggles on a page, such as the ink marks that make up this sentence, can be fully specified using vocabulary that does not mention what the sentence means. In this sense, a meaningful sentence can be said to have a non-intentionally specifiable vehicle. This third sense of individualism about the mental claims that for every mental state there is some non-intentionally specifiable vehicle, and that such a vehicle is quite literally inside the physical confines of the individual to whom the state is attributed.

By conceiving the mental in the normative terms of attitudes and statuses, Brandom can be seen to reject this third sense of individualism about the mental. As he puts it:

> [t]hinking of our cognitive dealings with the world in terms of commitments construed as social normative statuses is an intelligible alternative to thinking of them in terms of inner states. Commitments can be undertaken oneself and attributed to others by the production of public performances. But the commitment

> themselves – what is undertaken or attributed – need have no non-intentionally specifiable vehicles. (RDAH: 251)

Consider again my change in normative status as the result of signing a job contract. My current normative status, captured by the network of obligations, entitlements and preclusions, is something for which there does not seem to be a non-intentionally specifiable vehicle. The case involves a change in normative status, and not in some inner state. Brandom models beliefs on normative statuses, thereby moving us towards a vehicleless conception of mindedness. It is because of this unusual way of thinking about beliefs that Brandom prefers not to use the term "belief" in the formal setting out of his system. (As he puts it, "I do not officially believe in beliefs" (AR: 174).) The resultant conception of mindedness is resolutely social in all three senses.

A rationalist approach to mindedness

Empiricism is the most common of the various "isms" attributed to Locke. Sensory experience plays a dual role in his account of mind. First, it furnishes us with the raw materials for cognition, so that increasingly abstract ideas are derived, via processes such as abstraction, from the data just given in sensation. Secondly, this sensory experience is accorded a core epistemic role, as the foundation upon which all justification stands. For present purposes, Locke's empiricism consists in taking this raw material provided in sensation as the basis of both mind and knowledge (see AR: 24).

Sensory experience does not play a central role in Brandom's response to the demarcational question. He goes so far as to allow for the possibility that there could be a full linguistic practice, complete with contentful utterances and thoughts, in which none of these utterances or thoughts has specifically empirical content (e.g. MIE: 221). In this sense, our starting point in this chapter, with the observational reports of human reporters, is a poor choice, as it may give the erroneous impression that this is an essential feature of any Brandomian linguistic practice. It is, however, possible for there to be a Brandomian linguistic practice in which reasons are given for claims and claims are given as reasons, although no performances are accorded the status of being observational reports.

Our own linguistic practice is, of course, not like this, and in our case Brandom is prepared to affirm what he terms "platitudinous" or "stripped-down" empiricism, which is the claim that "knowledge of the empirical world depends essentially on the capacity of knowing organisms to respond differentially to distinct environmental stimuli".[27] If one thinks of experience as a learning process rather than as a state or episode, one could say that experience does play a role in Brandom's account, when applied to those linguistic practices with empirical content. This sense of experience, however, is far removed from the kind of conception of experience used as the raw material for cognition by an empiricist such as Locke. Indeed, it is far removed from the notion of experience invoked by almost anyone who accords sensory experience a central role in semantics or epistemology. Brandom simply rejects the claim that there are any epistemically or semantically significant intermediaries

> between perceptible facts and reports of them that are noninferentially elicited by the exercise of reliable differential responsive dispositions. There are, of course, many *causal* intermediaries, since the noninferential observation report . . . stands at the end of a whole causal chain of . . . events, including a cascade of neurophysiological ones. But I do not see that any of these has any particular conceptual or (therefore) cognitive or semantic significance. (AR: 206, n. 7)

In rejecting the need for sensory experiences as intermediaries in this sense, Brandom is correct when he states "'[e]xperience' is not one of my words" (*ibid.*: 205).

An inferentialist approach to mindedness

A guiding trope of Brandom's work involves the rejection of representationalist semantics, replacing it with his own alternative, called inferentialism. (Calling it "semantics" serves to indicate that it is, in the first instance, an account of what is claim*ed* in the act of claim*ing* something.) Representationalists attempt to account for the semantic content of linguistic expressions and mental states by invoking various forms of word–object relations (such as those between singular terms and objects, predicates and sets of objects), and use these relations as the building-blocks for an account of the truth conditions and inferential relations of the sentences in which these words are involved. Representationalists thus tend to take a building-block approach to semantic explanation; beginning with basic blocks that are independent of any others (*atomism*), they proceed to show how such blocks can be combined to account for more complex judgements (*bottom-up*).

Whilst there is a sense in which such semantic concerns are removed from Lockean thinking,[28] there are certain features of the representationalist way of thinking that have echoes in our account of Locke.[29] Locke's conception of thinking is a building-block picture. It begins with simple atoms that can be grasped independently from all others, and moves upwards towards an account of our judgements. In other words, even if Locke does not share the semantic concerns of the representationalist tradition narrowly conceived, his account has both the atomism and bottom-up tendencies that are the hallmarks of the building-block approach of this representationalist tradition. Brandom's approach, in contrast, stresses the inferential involvements between sentential claims (*holism*), and treats subsentential parts, such as singular terms, in terms of their potential contribution to these inferential involvements (*top-down*).

Summary

By focusing on the specific question of the difference between the verbal performance of the parrot and the vocal performance of the human reporter, we have been able to consider some of Brandom's more basic commitments in theorizing about mind and language.

In terms of the specific question, it has been claimed that a parrot vocalization is not treated by participants in a linguistic practice as making a move in the practice, since the parrot lacks sufficient mastery over the inferential involvements of the sentence vocalized. Whilst these vocalizations or signals can be treated as meaningful by linguistic practitioners based on their own understanding of the response, and can thus be accorded a normative status in the practice, the parrots themselves are not treated as fellow practitioners because of this lack of understanding.

In outlining Brandom's response to the demarcational question, we have noted that Brandom rejects four broad assumptions that often guide thinking about mind and language: the primacy of mind over language; individualism about the mind; empiricism; and representationalism. Whilst all four are found in an extreme form in Locke, weaker versions of each can be seen as still pervasive in contemporary theorizing. In this regard, Brandom's whole orientation to thinking about mindedness alienates him from many others working in this area.

Chapter 2

Rational beings

Introduction

It is possible to distinguish between three different questions that can be asked about the notion of a linguistic practice:

1. What are the criteria that must be satisfied for a social practice to be a linguistic one?
2. What structure must a set of performances within a social practice have to fulfill those criteria?
3. When should an interpreter treat a specific set of performances as having that structure?

Chapter 1 focused on the first of these questions, claiming that a social practice is a linguistic one when the practice includes the speech act of asserting. This chapter considers in detail Brandom's response to the second question. The third question will be addressed in Chapter 4.

One way of answering the second question is to provide a model of a social practice that contains the minimal structural components that are both necessary and sufficient for it to be a linguistic one. A social practice is made up of the norm-governed performances of the practitioners: performances that are the making of a move within the practice, and performances that are the assessing of those performances as appropriate according to the norms. As a result, linguistic practitioners must have certain move-making and move-assessing abilities. In providing a model of a linguistic practice, therefore, we need to specify a certain set of practical abilities displayed by individuals, part-mastery of which is treated by fellow practitioners as both necessary and sufficient for being a rational being.

The most familiar framework to use for these purposes is that of a game.[1] Among the characteristics identified in demarcating the discursive performances of the adult human being from the responsive performances of parrots, in virtue of which the former are verbal and not just vocal, were that the performances must be subject to normative assessment and have consequences for the normative statuses of other performances. Moves in a game are governed by rules that make certain performances by the gameplayers appropriate or inappropriate at a certain stage in the game. Furthermore, in most games moves are not idle: a performance has consequences for the appropriateness or otherwise of other moves, and alters the normative status of the gameplayers themselves as described by the rules of the game.

The main section of this chapter, therefore, will describe in detail the bare bones of a social practice, a kind of norm-governed game. Brandom's bold claim, made in the final sections, is that we should see this game described as a model of a linguistic practice. Use of the term "model" is not to imply that the playing of the game is a model of something else that is thereby modelled. What we shall offer here is a description of a game that, if played, would be a linguistic practice. That, at least, is the "big bold conjecture" on offer (RPC: 238). In the first section, we will set out in more detail various constraints on the way in which the game is described, so as to clarify both what the game is supposed to be a model of, and the kind of theoretical insight it is supposed to afford.

Motivating the gameplaying model

A description of a set of gameplaying performances is sensitive to the vocabulary used to articulate it. In describing the game, Brandom places a number of constraints on the vocabulary used. The first (C1) is that the vocabulary used should not include intentional or semantic terms. The second (C2) is that the vocabulary used should include normative terms.[2] These two constraints interact to produce a third (C3); the normative terms invoked in describing the game as a result of (C2) must be graspable independently of the intentional or semantic terms ruled out in (C1).[3]

The constraints (C1–C3) assume that we can divide the terms that comprise a language into different fragments that are called vocabularies. One could divide the terms of a language into such fragments in an infinite number of ways, with each way of so dividing motivated by various pragmatic interests. One could, for example, talk of a mathematical vocabulary, a soccer vocabulary or a vocabulary comprising four-letter words. A particular claim made in a language belongs to the fragment in question by virtue of the claim containing terms that fall within the fragment.

The constraints on the description of our gameplaying practice mention two such vocabularies: intentional or semantic and normative vocabularies. It would be folly at this stage to enter into a detailed discussion of precisely what makes a term fall within these two fragments for Brandom. Instead, we shall make do with a gesture and some examples of each. Intentional or semantic vocabulary involves terms that relate to contentful mental or linguistic attitudes (acts or states), or to the contents of such attitudes. Examples include terms such as "asserting" and "thinking", "meaning" and "thought". Normative vocabulary involves terms that are fraught with ought. Examples include terms such as "correct", "should", "good", "permissible", "obligatory" and "right".[4]

Most commentators assume that constraints (C1–C3) are motivated by the explanatory ambitions that they treat Brandom as having here: achieving a *reductive explanation* of linguistic practice.[5] Although this will be questioned in Chapter 4, we will follow them with this assumption for the time being. In an ideal reductive explanation, the *explanandum* (the thing being explained) is fully captured in the language of the *explanans* (the thing doing the explaining). The gameplaying model is, on this reading, the *explanans* to which a linguistic practice is explanatorily reduced. Before outlining the model, let us specify more carefully just what the relevant *explanans* and *explanandum* are supposed to be, as well as outlining just what is involved in such a reductive explanation.

Reductive explanation

Philosophical puzzlement is sometimes directed at vocabularies that are treated as problematic. Such puzzlement could take at least two forms: a lack of understanding regarding how to use the vocabulary ("I don't know my way about') or a perceived failure of the vocabulary to cohere with another vocabulary that is treated as privileged in some principled sense. In either case, philosophical illumination may take the form of domestication or elimination. Domestication involves the drawing of theoretical links between the puzzling vocabulary and a more familiar, and usually privileged, vocabulary. Elimination involves accepting that the puzzlement is genuine and showing the philosophical enquirer how to live without it.

Explanation is a form of domestication in which the *explanans* is formulated in a vocabulary which the explainer understands in full, and the *explanandum* is explained using this already mastered vocabulary (FNNF: 373). In a *reductive* explanation the vocabulary used in the *explanans* is independent from the vocabulary used in the *explanandum*; in a *non-reductive* explanation there is a relation of dependence between the vocabularies.[6] One way of developing this notion of (in)dependence is to move to a pragmatic key, and to look at what one must do in order to deploy the vocabularies in question, that is the abilities required to make claims involving the terms that comprise the vocabulary. The *explanandum* would not be independent of the *explanans* if the practical abilities required to deploy the vocabulary used in the *explanandum* were necessary for the practical ability to deploy the vocabulary used in the *explanans*. In such a case, one could not have a grasp of the vocabulary doing the explaining prior to a grasp of the vocabulary to be explained. In a reductive explanation, the *explanandum* is explained in an antecedently intelligible vocabulary that comprises the *explanans*. A non-reductive explanation, in contrast, would involve tracing the systematic links between two dependent vocabularies so as to make both of them intelligible at once.

Outlining the notions of reductive explanation and independence of vocabularies in terms of the abilities used to deploy them, as we have done here, is not to imply that all reductive explanation should be construed in such pragmatic terms. It is, however, a central Brandomian insight that this kind of explanation in terms of the abilities required to deploy the vocabularies is available and potentially illuminating.[7] From such a pragmatic viewpoint, there is a kind of domestication by reductive explanation that is achieved when we specify in one vocabulary, whose use we have fully mastered, what needs to be done to be able to deploy another vocabulary.[8]

The point of the description of the gameplaying practice in this chapter is to domesticate semantic or intentional vocabulary, by explanatorily reducing it to a description of a practice that makes no use of such a vocabulary (C1), but makes extensive use of a normative vocabulary (C2) that is practically independent of intentional or semantic vocabulary in the sense just outlined (C3). (C1) and (C3) stem from Brandom's explanatory reductive ambitions.[9] The second constraint stems from Brandom's contention, noted in the previous chapter, that it is simply not possible to capture the essential normative dimension of any social practice using a vocabulary that ostensibly eschews all normative talk.

What motivates Brandom's explanatory ambitions here seems to be neither of the two sources of philosophical puzzlement regarding vocabularies just identified. He appears to find neither intentional nor semantic vocabulary unclear, and does not find either particularly difficult to fit into a privileged vocabulary set. (This is, in part, because of a relaxed metaphysical orientation in which no vocabulary set is being treated as privileged.) The motivation, rather, seems to stem from what was identified earlier as a kind of genuine intellectual curiosity. The success of this "big bold conjecture" is to be judged by the resultant explanatory insight it affords.

The explanans

The thing doing the explaining – the *explanans* – is a gameplaying model described using a normative vocabulary. (C3) requires that the normative vocabulary invoked in describing the model be graspable independent of the grasp of intentional or semantic vocabulary. Although Brandom is not explicit about this, fulfilling this constraint requires him to use a distinctive and unfamiliar type of normative vocabulary.[10]

The reason is the following. A social practice is one in which certain performances have the normative status of being appropriate or inappropriate. Appropriateness is a normative term, and thus claims containing this term can be incorporated into the *explanans* in a reductive explanation of intentional or semantic vocabulary. We do not, however, talk of appropriateness *simpliciter* in everyday discourse. That is, we operate with a tacit qualification relating the sense of appropriateness in question to the relevant context, talking more fully of, say, rational appropriateness and moral appropriateness or appropriateness relative to pursuing a particular goal.[11] It is important that the notion of appropriateness used in the description of the gameplaying model is not the notion of rational appropriateness, for it seems that this does not have the requisite independence of intentional or semantic vocabulary required by (C3). In the course of conversations, for example, we frequently chastise people for making claims that are rationally inappropriate given other things they believe, or urge people to see the rational consequences of their claims. It would be extremely strange, to the point of incomprehension, for someone to have an understanding of these concepts of appropriateness without at the same time understanding that these notions apply to assertings. As a result, the normative vocabulary deployed in the *explanans* cannot be the familiar vocabulary of rational appropriateness.

Using the notion of a game to describe linguistic practice is overused in philosophy, and Brandom himself prefers to talk of "practice" rather than "game", as the latter has the tendency to suggest something playful and not serious (FNNF: 361). I have, nonetheless, persisted with the gameplaying terminology in outlining Brandom's model. One reason is that the notion of a game helps capture the unfamiliar notion of appropriateness used in the *explanans*. As we have been using the term, a game is a structured set of interactive social performances that necessarily involve implicit normative assessments of those performances as appropriate or not. This is the undifferentiated notion of appropriateness that is shared by all the kinds of games that interest us. Specific games have highly differentiated norms associated with them which distinguish them as the kind of game that they are. The normative statuses of appropriateness to be used in the gameplaying terminology here should be treated as the undifferentiated notion of appropriateness, and not the more familiar differentiated notion of rational appropriateness.[12] This unfamiliar notion of normative appropriateness does have the independence of intentional or semantic vocabularies required by (C3).

The explanandum

Having just said something in clarification of the *explanans* (i.e. normative vocabulary), let us say something in clarification of the *explanandum* (i.e. intentional or semantic vocabulary).

There is a narrower and a broader sense in which the *explanandum* could be understood. In the narrower sense, the things to be explained are claims that specifically invoke intentional or semantic terms. In this sense, we are trying to domesticate, via reductive explanation, claims such as: "Henry believes that p", "'p' means p", "it is rationally appropriate to assert that p if and only if p". These claims fall within the scope of the *explanandum* in this narrow sense since, as a matter of their content, they invoke specifically intentional or semantic terms. In a broader sense, all contentful claims, and the acts of claiming them, fall within the scope of the *explanandum*, whether or not they specifically invoke intentional or semantic terms. In this sense, claims such as “Polly put the kettle on” and “Suki took it off again”, or the acts of asserting or desiring this, are also part of the thing to be explained. The target of the reductive explanation under consideration is the broader one: we are trying to model, in terms of a game described in normative vocabulary, what it is to perform any linguistically significant performance or meaningful utterance, irrespective of whether these contain specifically intentional or semantic terms.

This wider sense of the *explanandum* appears to lead to the problematic situation in which normative vocabulary now features in both *explanans* and *explanandum*. The *explanans* is formulated using normative claims which themselves are part of the language to be explained, in the wider sense of the *explanandum* just canvassed. But this circularity is something that will beset any attempt to specify in language what it is to use a language: the attempt will have to specify what it is to use the language in which the attempt is formulated. (Brandom calls this “achieving expressive completeness”.) Theorists use a normative vocabulary in modelling a linguistic practice. The practitioners themselves need not have mastered the normative vocabulary that the theorists are using. A full reductive explanation should be able, first, to capture any linguistic practice in the gameplaying model described, and, secondly, to introduce into this game the very normative vocabulary that is used by the theorists to describe the game. A full reductive explanation comprising both these stages is inevitably circular, but it is not a circularity that should worry us.

This can be illuminated by the Brandomian idea of an *autonomous discursive practice*. Typically, a vocabulary is some fragment of a language, such as a normative vocabulary or a vocabulary of four-letter words. For some such fragments, it is possible for someone to speak a language, in the sense of having the ability to make meaningful claims, but for that person not to have mastered any of these specific fragments. I presume this is the case for “four-letter-word” vocabularies. Brandom argues, as we shall see, that this is the case for normative vocabularies. An autonomous vocabulary is one that one must be able to use if one is to be able to make any claim whatsoever. Brandom calls such autonomous vocabularies *languages*, so that when we talk of linguistic abilities without further qualification (i.e. without restricting them to the ability to deploy a particular vocabulary fragment) we are referring to these autonomous vocabularies. The practice involving the ability to use such autonomous vocabularies is an autonomous discursive practice – "a language game that one could play though one could play no other" (BSD II: 15). Using this terminology, we can say that our *explanandum* is an autonomous discursive practice. The normative vocabulary that plays an ineliminable role in the *explanans* need not feature in the *explanandum*. If it does feature, then it becomes part of the content of the claims made that are to be explained.

One final caveat before beginning the description of the game. The gameplaying model practice is the *explanans* in a reductive explanation of intentional or semantic vocabulary in the broad sense. That is, it describes, in independent normative vocabulary, what it is to perform rational acts or to be in rational states, and what it is for those acts or states to possess the specific conceptual content that they have. Explaining what it is for a performance to be an asserting is an example of a reductive explanation of the intentional, whilst explaining what it is to possess the content expressed by claims such as "the swatch is red" is an example of a reductive explanation of the semantic. In the remainder of Part I, I shall, for expository purposes, limit myself to considering the reductive explanation of the intentional, and not the semantic. More specifically, given the pride of place that Brandom accords the speech act of asserting in an account of the intentional, I shall limit myself to the matter of providing a gameplaying account of what it is to perform an assertoric speech act. Although some semantic concerns will be addressed indirectly as they arise, semantics remains in the background until Part II.

Gameplay

Let us consider a simple game involving two players and a set of counters. Although all the counters are similar in that they bear the trademark™ of the game, some of the counters differ from others in a whole host of other respects. Token counters can be divided into types, so that each type includes all and only those that are identical to each other in all relevant respects.[13] Unlike some other games, this one does not come in a box with a finite number of counters.

Basic moves: commitments

A basic move in this game involves one *gameplayer* placing a counter in front of her. When this is done, all counters of that type are said to "belong" to that player. In the language of the game, these are the counters to which she is *committed*; they are her *commitments*.[14] One could depict this in a diagram, by drawing a box labelled "commitments" next to the name of each gameplayer, and noting down the counter-types to which she is committed at any stage of the game by placing them in her commitment-box. Further, the playing of one counter in this manner has consequences: by placing it in front of her, she not only becomes committed to counters of that type, but she also becomes committed to certain other types of counters. These additional counters are said to be the *committive consequences* of the former; one *inherits a commitment* to these additional counters from a commitment to the others. In the diagram, these additional counter-types are also to be added to the commitment-box as a result of playing a counter.

At any stage of the game one can divide counter-types into two categories: those to which the gameplayer is committed, and those to which she is not. Those counter-types that "belong" to a player at a given stage of the game, those that feature in her commitment-box, can be said to (part-) constitute that player's score. Players keep track of their scores, as well as the scores of others. Participants in this game, therefore, play both the roles of gameplayers and *score-keepers*. In keeping score on a particular individual, one is said to *attribute* commitments to that individual.

A scorekeeper can place a counter-type in a gameplayer's commitment-box either because that person undertakes a commitment to that counter-type, or because the counter-type that is added to the commitment-box is a committive consequence of another counter to which the gameplayer is committed. Since the scorekeeper's take on what are the committive consequences of an undertaking may differ from that of the gameplayer, the scorekeeper can attribute two different scores to the gameplayer: the first is the score that the score-keeper thinks the gameplayer would acknowledge ("*the acknowledged score*") and the second is the score that the scorekeeper thinks the gameplayer ought to acknowledge ("*the score*").

In keeping score on oneself, of course, one cannot make such a distinction, for the score that is acknowledged is what is taken to be the score. In attributing a score to oneself, therefore, one attributes only one score – "the score". Crucially, *undertaking* a commitment differs from such acknowledgement. In attributing a score to oneself, one attributes those commitments that one acknowledges. In undertaking a commitment, one adds to one's score both the commitment itself and those commitments that are its committive consequences. It is possible (and likely) that one will not acknowledge all such consequences even though one should. In undertaking a commitment, unlike in *acknowledging* a commitment, one is binding oneself beyond that which one currently recognizes as the committive consequences of the undertaking.

In addition to undertaking and attributing commitments, let us introduce two more moves that scorekeepers and gameplayers can make. The first involves the removal of a counter that had been placed before one. In so doing, a gameplayer *disavows* a commitment; she withdraws her commitment to a counter to which she had previously committed herself. Under certain circumstances, the scorekeeper will respond by removing from that gameplayer's commitment-box both the counter and those that are its committive consequences. The circumstances when this will not happen are cases where those counters are the committive consequence of another commitment that still features in the gameplayer's commitment-box, and has not also been disavowed. The second involves a scorekeeper waving a counter in the air so that it attracts the attention of a gameplayer. In so doing, the scorekeeper is said to *query* whether that counter features in the gameplayer's commitment-box. If the gameplayer's *response* to the query is to take the counter and place it in front of her, then the gameplayer has undertaken a commitment, and that counter should be added to the box.[15]

Basic moves: entitlements

Thus far the account of the game has been developed to include a description of the performances of a gameplayer and a scorekeeper, so that the gameplayer can, in her performances, undertake, disavow and acknowledge commitments, and the scorekeeper, in his performances, can attribute and query acknowledged and consequential commitments. It is important to introduce another normative status that a gameplayer can have in this game, the status of being *entitled*.

Among those counters that a scorekeeper places in the commitment-box, he distinguishes those to which he treats the gameplayer as entitled. In diagrammatic terms, one can talk of the scorekeeper drawing another box next to the gameplayer's name, a box labelled "entitlements", into which those counter-types so entitled are placed.

As in the case of commitments, placing a counter in the gameplayer's entitlement-box has consequences: she not only becomes entitled to counters of that type, but also to certain other types of counters as well. These additional counters are said to be the *permissive consequences* of the former; one *inherits an entitlement* to these counters from an entitlement to the former.[16] As was the case with the attribution of a commitment, not all such permissive consequences will be acknowledged by the gameplayer, so the scorekeeper must distinguish between acknowledged and attributed permissive entitlements.

There is a basic difference between commitments and entitlements. A counter-type gets added to that gameplayer's commitment-box in one of two ways: either through that counter-type being placed by the gameplayer in front of her, or by the inheritance of the commitment to that counter-type as the committive consequence of another counter-type that has been played. A counter-type can only be added to the entitlement-box, however, in one way: through the inheritance of the entitlement to that counter-type, as the permissive consequence of another counter-type to which one is entitled. There are no moves in the game whose entitlement is basic, in the sense of not inherited.

In order for entitlement to enter into the game being played, the game must have what could be called "*a default and challenge structure*". In most cases, at the same time as adding a counter-type to the commitment-box, the scorekeeper will also add that counter-type to the entitlement-box. Such commitments have the default status of being entitled, although it is a status that is open to *challenge* by the scorekeeper, and can be removed if the gameplayer is unable to *answer* the challenge.[17] For the moment, let us say that a challenge involves the scorekeeper placing the challenged counter in between player and scorekeeper, and a response to such a challenge by the gameplayer involves placing another token in front of her (acknowledging another commitment) for which the challenged token is a permissive consequence. In a situation in which no such challenge has been issued by the scorekeeper, the assumption is that the gameplayer could provide an answer to a challenge if it were made. The scorekeeper, therefore, treats the undertaking of a commitment by the gameplayer as a move to which the gameplayer is *prima facie entitled*, and as a result, adds that counter-type to the gameplayer's entitlement-box.

Some counter-types will feature only in the commitment-box but not in the entitlement-box: the playing of such a counter was, according to the scorekeeper, one to which the gameplayer was not entitled. Some counter-types will feature only in the entitlement-box but not in the commitment-box: although the gameplayer is entitled to play the counter, she has not.[18] Some counter-types will feature in both the commitment- and the entitlement-boxes associated with that player by the scorekeeper. At this stage, the important point to note is that the same performance, the placing of a counter by a gameplayer in front of her, involves *both* the undertaking of certain commitments and the provision of certain entitlements.

Further moves: incompatibility

Thus far, commitments and entitlements attributed to the gameplayer have been treated as independent of each other; placing a counter in front of the gameplayer results in the scorekeeper making changes to both the commitment and entitlement-boxes associated with that player, without considering the effect of the change in one box on the other. In this section, we shall develop the game to include interactions between commitments and entitlements.

In this development, placing a counter before the gameplayer has an additional effect over and above adding various counter-types to the commitment- and entitlement-boxes. It also involves the removal of certain counter-types. Specifically, the addition of a counter-type to the commitment-box requires the removal of certain other types from the entitlement-box. The counter-types that ought to be removed from the entitlement-box as a result of adding other counter-types to the commitment-box are said to be *incompatible* with each other.[19]

As a result of such scorekeeping practices, counter-types can be said to stand in three different relationships to each other. If the addition of a counter-type to a gameplayer's commitment-box results, according to the scorekeeper, in the addition of other counter-types to that gameplayer's commitment-box, then those counter-types are said to stand in *a committive relationship*: commitment to one involves commitment to the other. If the addition of a counter-type to a gameplayer's entitlement-box results, according to the scorekeeper, in the addition of other counter-types to that gameplayer's entitlement-box, then those counter-types are said to stand in *a permissive relationship*: entitlement to one involves entitlement to the other. If the addition of a counter-type to a gameplayer's commitment-box results, according to the scorekeeper, in the removal of other counter-types from that gameplayer's entitlement-box, then the counter-types are said to be *incompatible*: commitment to one precludes entitlement to the other. (These relationships form the core of Brandom's inferentialist semantic theory, and are examined in Chapter 5.)

Let us spell out what is involved in keeping the score following this introduction of incompatibility. When the gameplayer places a counter of a certain type before her, the scorekeeper responds in the following manner.

(a) The scorekeeper adds counters of that type to the commitment-box associated with that gameplayer, as well as other counter-types that stand in committive relations to it, as determined by the scorekeeper.[20]
(b) The scorekeeper subtracts from the gameplayer's entitlement-box all those counter-types incompatible with each of those added to the commitment-box.
(c) The scorekeeper adds counter-types to the entitlement-box that are all committive consequences of the counters that remain in the entitlement-box, following the removal of incompatible counter-types.
(d) The scorekeeper adds that counter-type to the gameplayer's entitlement-box, together with other counter-types that stand in permissive relations, providing that these are not incompatible with the commitments already added.[21]

Further moves: the interpersonal dimension

One should not identify the two players in this game exclusively with the roles of gameplayer and scorekeeper. Each player undertakes and attributes commitments and entitlements to him/herself and to each other; each player is both a scorekeeper and a gameplayer. The interaction between the two goes beyond such mutual scorekeeping, however, for the commitments and entitlements attributed to a gameplayer by a scorekeeper have an effect on the commitments and entitlements undertaken by the scorekeeper himself. Modelling this involves providing an account not only of the *intrapersonal inheritance of commitments and entitlements* (of how the addition of a counter-type to the commitment- and/or entitlement-box of an individual results in the addition or subtraction of other counter-types to those boxes), but also *the interpersonal inheritance of commitments and entitlements* (of how the addition of a counter-type in the commitment- and/or entitlement-box of an individual results in the addition or subtraction of counter-types to the commitment- and/or entitlement-boxes associated with other gameplayers).

Under certain circumstances, placing a counter in front of the gameplayer not only involves the addition of that counter (and other related counter-types) to that gameplayer's commitment-box, but also entitles the scorekeeper to play the same counter-type (and other related counter-types). This happens when the same counter-type features, according to the scorekeeper, in the commitment- and entitlement-boxes of the gameplayer, and there are no incompatible counter-types in the commitment-box of the scorekeeper. As a result of keeping the score on other players, therefore, one is able to alter one's own score. Placing a counter in front of one person entitles, in certain circumstances, the other person to place that counter in front of themselves too.[22]

One can, therefore, inherit an entitlement to a counter-type in one of two ways (or both). First, the entitlement is inherited from other counter-types in one's own entitlement-box that stand in a permissive relationship to this one (and is not incompatible with other counter-types in one's commitment-box). Secondly, that counter-type features in the commitment- and entitlement-boxes of another player on whom you are keeping score (and is not incompatible with other counter-types in one's commitment-box).

There is an important difference between these two ways of inheriting an entitlement. Recall that one can attribute a default entitlement to a gameplayer on the assumption that she could defend the challenge by providing another counter from which the default entitlement is a permissive consequence. As a result, in adding a counter to one's own entitlement-box based on its featuring in the boxes of another player, one is relying on the other's undertaking the responsibility of defending this if challenged. This results in two ways in which one can demonstrate entitlement to a commitment if challenged to do so. One can either demonstrate one's entitlement by placing, in front of one, a counter-type that stands in permissive relations to the counter-type under challenge, or by deferring (perhaps through pointing) to the gameplayer in question.

Indeed, this interpersonal dimension to the gameplaying practice allows for additional ways to spell out what is involved not only in responding to a query, but also in ways in which a scorekeeper can challenge a gameplayer. Earlier a challenge was described in terms of the scorekeeper placing the challenged counter in between player and scorekeeper. In light of the interpersonal inheritance of normative statuses described here, we do not need to introduce this description of a challenge. The scorekeeper can challenge the gameplayer's entitlement to an assertion by simply placing before him a counter that he treats as incompatible with one attributed to the gameplayer. In so doing, he demonstrates his refusal to recognize the gameplayer's entitlement to the commitment, something he would be doing if he were to play the same counter as the gameplayer; that is, by undertaking the commitment himself.

Commitments and entitlements revisited

Before turning to the question of just what kind of game this is, let us pause and consider an objection that the sceptical reader may harbour regarding the description of the game thus far. The objection stems from the suspicion that the gameplaying terminology, italicized in the text above, illicitly sneaks into the game features that are congenial to treating it as a model for linguistic practice.[23] In particular, a normative dimension of the game seems to have been incorporated into the description merely by labelling certain moves, and the resultant scorekeeping boxes, with the terms "commitments" and "entitlements".

Consider, for example, the manner in which commitments were introduced into our description of the game. As expressed above, following the placing of a counter before a gameplayer, all counters of that type are said to "belong" to that player. In the language of the game, these are the counters "to which she is *committed* . . .".[24] The problematic transition from *belonging* to *commitment* in these two sentences was intended to be provocative. It is relatively clear what it could mean for a counter-type to belong to someone, and how one could capture this in diagrammatic terms by means of possession-boxes that record what counters belong to a person at a given stage, and how these possessions are altered over time in light of various changes. It is far less clear what it could mean to say that one is committed to a counter-type: commitments are normally thought of in terms of a commitment *to do* something, whilst here we are talking of a commitment to something. Replacing commitment with possession removes this awkwardness, as we normally speak of possessing something. Indeed, it barely alters our grasp of the gameplay as described if talk of commitment-boxes is replaced with talk of possession-boxes. The point of this suggestion is to highlight the sceptic's concern that, whilst the language of the game may talk of commitments and entitlements, it is not really commitments and entitlements that are actually being labelled.

If it is to be more than a cheap terminological trick, we need to understand what it is to be committed or entitled to a counter-type. When they are first introduced, Brandom asks us to think of commitments and entitlements in terms of obligations and permissions. The only reason these more familiar terms are not used is that they have a tendency to be thought of in terms of the authority of a commander imposing these statuses (MIE: 169). If we resist such a tendency, and speak of permissions and obligations instead of commitments and entitlements, we do seem to have the normativity sought after, although we now need to understand what it is to be obligated or permitted to a counter-type. Perhaps here we need to talk of being obligated or permitted to do something, but then the issue becomes: obligated or permitted to do what?

In any case, traditional talk of obligations and permissions does not seem to function in the same manner as Brandomian commitments and entitlements. For example, it is widely assumed that being obligated entails being permitted: having the normative status of being obligated to fast on a particular religious occasion entails having the normative status of being entitled to fast on that religious occasion. In our gameplaying model, being committed to p does not similarly entail being entitled to p; one can be committed to something to which one is not entitled.

In a revealing analogy, Brandom compares normative statuses, such as commitments, to strikes and balls in baseball, such that "[d]eontic statuses are just something to keep score with, as balls and strikes are just statuses that performances can be treated as having for scorekeeping purposes" (MIE: 194). As MacFarlane points out, deeming a performance to be a strike or a ball in the game of baseball is not, on its own, saying anything about the obligations and permissions of the batter (MacFarlane forthcoming). Its connections with performing proprieties are indirect, mediated as it were through the effect that the attribution of the strike or ball has on the gameplaying score. For example, according a performance the status of a strike means that a strike is added to the score associated with that batter. If, as a result of doing this, the batter now has three strikes, he is out and not entitled to run to first base.

By analogy, continues MacFarlane, the normative statuses in our game, such as commitment or entitlement, are only indirectly linked to performing proprieties of the gameplayer, where these are mediated through the effect that the attribution of the deontic status has on the gameplaying score. For example, according a performance the status of the undertaking of a commitment means that a commitment will be added to the commitment-box so that the performer is now, according to the scorekeeper, precluded from being entitled to commitments that are incompatible with this one, and thus ought not (is not entitled to) put the incompatible counter in front of her. On this understanding it would seem that, despite the terminology, Brandom concedes that what is attributed to the gameplayer, that is, a commitment or an entitlement, is not itself a commitment or entitlement for the gameplayer to do something. Rather, it is an expedient utilized in the practice of keeping score: "an artificial scorekeeping device".[25]

To elaborate, let us switch focus from normative statuses to scorekeeping attitudes. Scorekeeping is a doing: it involves the performances of a scorekeeper that are the adoptings of normative attitudes towards other performances. In other words, it involves responsive performances that treat other performances as appropriate or inappropriate in light of the players' scores. Scorekeeping thus involves sanctioning performances, which could be thought of in the carrot-and-stick terms of external sanctions such as beatings or – as is more apposite – in terms of internal sanctions that involve the alterations of the normative status of the gameplayer in light of their performances. Although nothing has been done in the description of the game to discourage the picture of scorekeeping as involving little more than updating actual scorecards in response to various performances, it is important to treat the alteration of the normative status associated with the player as sanctioning performances by the scorekeeper that serve to partition the gameplayer's performances into those that are, and those that are not, appropriate.

A basic idea in the scorekeeping account involves the practical recognition of two different senses in which a performance can be appropriate, so that performing "as committed is appropriate in one sense" and performing "as entitled is appropriate in another" (MIE:

159). In such a practice, the attribution of entitlements is distinguished from the attribution of commitments in terms of which performances are sanctioned: one sanctions a current performance that is not entitled, whilst which future performances are sanctioned is altered by the attribution of a commitment. In keeping score, thus, the scorekeeper practically treats certain performances as appropriate or inappropriate in light of the score associated with that gameplayer (and with her own).

The thrust of this response is, therefore, to concede something to the sceptical reader. Commitments and entitlements are not commitments and entitlements to do something. On the other hand, the sceptic is not correct in claiming that a normative dimension has simply been sneaked into the description by a case of deliberately misleading labelling, for there are systematic connections between such statuses and the proprieties of scorekeeping performances in the form of keeping score. Whilst we may use these terms in our everyday discourse ("he is committed to lecturing on Monday morning"; "you are entitled to enter the cinema"), these everyday uses are directly linked to commitments and entitlements to perform in various ways. In contrast, the technical deployment of these concepts here should be distinguished from such everyday usage; normative statuses of commitments and entitlements are to be treated as artificial scorekeeping devices whose connection to proprieties of actual performances is indirect.

The defining move

What distinguishes this particular game from others is that it involves the recognition of a certain kind of performance by the scorekeeper, which we shall, for the moment (and not quite at random), call A'ing. To say that the scorekeeper recognizes such a move is to treat it in practice as an A'ing.

In treating the gameplayer's placing of a counter before her as an A'ing, the scorekeeper does a number of things. He treats it:

1. as the undertaking of a commitment and related commitments by the gameplayer (that is, as licensing the attribution to that gameplayer of commitment to that and related counter-types – that is, placing those counter-types in her commitment-box);
2. as entitling that gameplayer and other gameplayers to that and related commitments (that is, as licensing the attribution to the

gameplayer of a default entitlement to that and related counter-types, and licensing other gameplayers to undertake commitments to that and related counter-types – that is, placing those counter-types in all their entitlement-boxes);

3. as the undertaking, by the gameplayer, of a responsibility to provide, by making another appropriate move, the entitlement to that commitment if appropriately challenged to do so by another gameplayer (that is, as licensing the removal of the entitlement to that counter-type upon failure to appropriately respond to an appropriate challenge, and licensing others to discharge their own responsibility for their commitment to that counter-type by deferring to the gameplayer).

In recognizing a performance as having this tripartite structure, the scorekeeper treats the gameplayer as A'ing.

A'ing makes appropriate certain practical responses of the gameplayer and other gameplayers which were not appropriate prior to the A'ing. One could say that A'ing authorizes certain other moves. This authorization, however, depends on the gameplayer discharging her responsibility to demonstrate her entitlement to the move if challenged. Were she to fail to do so, in the eyes of a scorekeeper, then her A'ing does not authorize or license other moves. A'ing, therefore, involves a combination of *authority* (authorizing further moves) and *responsibility* (a conditional task-responsibility to perform appropriately if challenged to do so).[26] All A'ings share this mixture of authority and responsibility captured in the tripartite structure just outlined. What distinguishes one A'ing from another is the particular alteration of score as a result of playing that counter-type. The effect of a particular A'ing performance, according to a scorekeeper, can be fully captured by comparing the game's score according to that scorekeeper, both before and after the performance.

Brandom's "big bold conjecture" lies in the identification of A'ing with the act of asserting, so that the game just described is a linguistic practice, one that should be seen as the *game of giving and asking for reasons.* In light of this conjecture, an asserting performance (the placing of a counter in front of her) plays a dual role: one could say that it entitles other assertions and is entitled by other assertions, or one could say it provides *reasons* for other assertions and has reasons provided for it.

Many games involve a structure of commitments and entitlements with consequential relations operating between them. Many involve a practice of scorekeeping, the taking of normative attitudes towards gameplaying performances. Many involve a mixture of authority and responsibility, so that one move authorizes others depending on the undertaking of responsibility of that performer. Linguistic practices are, according to Brandom, those in which some of the performances have the significance of making claims (assertings), and those in which some of these claims provide reasons for others (inferrings). The extremely bold conjecture is that, appearances to the contrary, the gameplaying practice just described contains just such performances.[27]

In saying "appearances to the contrary", I do not just mean that the game described lacks some of the surface features typically associated with linguistic practice. It is, for example, correct that the game is small, there are no specifically *speech* acts, the counters do not have compositional structure and it only involves two players. In light of the bold conjecture, all this shows is that none of these features is actually required for a linguistic practice. The point is that the gameplay seems to lack just those features highlighted as essential to any linguistic practice, in that it seems possible to imagine people playing just the game outlined in full, and yet not to treat them as asserting and inferring things. Brandom's conjecture is that the impression that these people were engaged in another game would be a misunderstanding of what it is that these people were doing.

The conjecture is indeed big and bold. Brandom's defence is best considered once we have developed the model further, and this will be the focus of Chapter 4. Although Brandom's primary reason for describing the gameplay rests on this bold conjecture, the discussion here is of philosophical interest even if the conjecture is rejected. In the remainder of this chapter we shall explore aspects of this model that do not depend on the success of the bold conjecture.

Is assertion social?

A seminal aspect of Brandom's model is the specific account of asserting that it provides. This account need not rely either on acceptance of the bold conjecture nor on the logocentric assumption that the presence of such an act is both necessary and sufficient for a social practice to be a linguistic one. It has, therefore, potential appeal even among those not persuaded by, or interested in, the reductive explanatory project detailed in this chapter.

An account of assertion, as used here, is neither an account of the intentions or other propositional attitudes associated with asserter and assertee under idealized circumstances, nor of the conventional–institutional setting in which the speech act occurs. Rather, an account of asserting specifies the idealized function of that speech act within an up-and-running discursive practice. This is done by describing, in structural terms (i.e. in terms of its authority and responsibility structure broadly construed), the ideal outcome of a successful instance of the act in the context of its performance in an up-and-running instance of such a practice. The function described is idealized in the sense that it specifies the ideal outcome of a successful instance of asserting. This is to concede that some instances of asserting may not have a successful outcome, while other speech acts may achieve the same outcome by mimicking this speech act. (Lying, for example, may have the same outcome as asserting; even though it is not the same act, its success deliberately relies on the prior existence of asserting within a social practice.)

We shall consider one aspect of Brandom's account of asserting highlighted in a recent paper by Peter Pagin, entitled: "Is assertion social?" (Pagin 2004). Pagin defends a negative answer to this question and argues, among other things, that Brandom's account of asserting is mistaken as it would return a positive answer. Pagin does not deny that an act of asserting is social in the relatively trivial sense that performing the act affects, in a systematic manner, the normative status of both asserter and audience (*ibid.*: 835). What he denies is that a description of the systematic alteration of normative statuses uniquely associated with a successful instance of the act provides a complete account of the speech act of asserting.

Here is Pagin's proposed refutation of Brandom's account in full:

> According to Brandom, the nature of assertion consists in the fact that the speaker achieves two different normative results at the same time: on the one hand he authorizes the audience to claim anything that follows from what is asserted and on the other he undertakes the responsibility of justifying it. This can be summed up in:
>
> > [α] To assert that p is to authorize the audience to claim whatever follows from p and to undertake the responsibility of justifying p.
>
> It is not hard to produce [a] counterexample, i.e. a sentence giving rise to a non-standard way of discharging these tasks:

> [β] I hereby authorize you to claim whatever follows from p and undertake the responsibility of justifying p.

> If it is within the power of the speaker to authorize the audience to make assertions, then she can surely do so by way of making the authorization explicit. In that case, by means of a sincere utterance of [β] I can indeed authorize you to claim whatever follows from p and undertake the responsibility of justifying p. Still, I [have not] asserted that p. What I say is fully compatible with the falsity of p. So Brandom's analysis isn't acceptable.
> (Pagin, 2004: 839–40; minor modifications added)

Pagin's claim is that an account of the speech act of asserting is not exhausted by an account of its social significance, and is therefore, *pace* Brandom, not a social act.

Pagin is correct to highlight the Brandomian contention that asserting essentially functions to alter the normative status of participants in a practice, so that an account of this social significance is an account of asserting. Indeed, a central feature of his conception of linguistic practice is that *all* speech acts are social in this sense. Giving an account of a speech act thus requires one to outline the distinctive pattern of changes of normative status that result from a successful instance of performing it. Pagin is also correct that [α] above does not provide an exhaustive account of asserting. This is not, however, because asserting is not a social act, but because [α] fails to capture the distinctive social function of asserting.[28]

Different speech acts are structured so that they target different types of audiences. A basic distinction is between person-specific and non-person-specific audiences.[29] For example, a promise targets the person or people to whom the promise is made, whilst an assertion targets anyone and everyone who might come to overhear the assertion, whenever and wherever they do.[30] Different speech acts are structured so that they have different types of entitlements to perform associated with them. Again, a basic distinction is between person-specific and non-person-specific entitlements to perform. For example, the entitlement to assert is not tied to that particular asserter in the way in which the entitlement to promise is tied to that promiser; that it is a specific so-and-so that is making the assertion is irrelevant to the entitlement in a way in which it is not the case for the act of promising.

To treat a performance as an assertion is, on this account, for the audience to treat it as a reassertion licence. The authority for the licence is the responsibility undertaken by the asserter to show entitlement to this if appropriately challenged to do so. In a successful instance of this act, the audience will thus be disposed to assert the same claim under certain conditions and thereby themselves issue a reassertion licence so that others too are entitled to assert this on the say-so of the original asserter. An act of reassertion is thus the audience's practical recognition of the performance as a successful instance of the speech act of asserting. A central part of what is recognized in this way is the person-non-specificity of the asserter's entitlement and audience; in practically recognizing this, the audience becomes entitled to reassert the claim to anyone. Even though audience members are relying on the authority of the particular asserter for their justification, they are holding him responsible for providing a non-person-specific entitlement for the claim that allows them to reassert it to anyone. Contrast this with the case of a promise: because of the person-specificity of the entitlement and the audience, I am not able to "repromise" in the same manner.

In treating an act of asserting that p as having been successful, the scorekeeper attributes to the gameplayer a commitment and entitlement to p, and undertakes the commitment herself. In a successful instance of assertion, the audience thus undertakes a commitment based on recognizing the authority that is implicitly claimed in asserting. In ordinary parlance, we would say that the audience takes the claim to be true. In Brandom's account, taking a claim to be true is not the attribution of something, but rather an undertaking of a claim oneself. (This is developed more formally in Part II.) In an unsuccessful instance of assertion, one may treat the asserter as committed to the claim and entitled to the claim, but nonetheless not undertake the commitment oneself. In ordinary parlance, we would say that the claim is false. Taking an asserted claim to be false involves the audience undertaking a commitment that precludes its entitlement to reassertion. In other words, it removes the authority involved in an act of asserting.

Pagin asks "Is assertion a social act?" Brandom's answer is a qualified "yes". Assertion is social in both the relatively trite sense that the act of asserting systematically alters the normative status of asserter and audience, and the stronger sense that a description of this systematic alteration delivers an exhaustive account of the speech act.[31] Both of these are social in an I–Thou sense, based on a distinction of perspectives between asserter and assessor, between the practical attitudes of attributing and undertaking normative statuses. The account is not social in an I–We sense that refers to a broader community with regard to which the performances of an asserter are assessed.

Summary

One overall aim of Brandom's work is to provide an account of sapience, by specifying the structure that a set of performances within a social practice must have in order for its practitioners to be sapient (read: rational) beings. This chapter has attempted to outline such a structure, deploying a distinctive kind of normative terminology to describe a distinctive kind of game. The normative terminology is distinctive in the sense that it can be fully grasped without having mastered any intentional or semantic vocabulary. The game is distinctive in that it involves the attribution of two kinds of normative statuses (commitments and entitlements) to gameplayers, so that keeping track of the alterations of these statuses as the practice proceeds requires keeping track, in practice, of the consequential relations between different performances having these normative statuses.

A defining feature of the game described is the recognition by gameplayers of a particular kind of move, an A'ing. Brandom's bold conjecture is that any practice that includes A'ing (a.k.a. asserting) should be treated as the game of giving and asking for reasons, and participants in this practice are rational beings. If the bold conjecture is successful, the gameplaying model delivers an explanatory reduction of linguistic practice.

No reason has yet been given to endorse this bold conjecture, as its defence is best considered once logical, and not just rational, beings have been brought into explicit focus. Such logical beings are the subject of Chapter 3; defence of the conjecture follows in Chapter 4.

Chapter 3

Logical beings

Introduction

It is possible to be able to do something, yet not be able to say exactly what it is that one is able to do. You may, for example, have bicycle-riding abilities, but not have mastered the vocabulary that a technical writer would need in order to describe precisely what is being done. The converse is also possible. You may be able to say what is required to be able to do something, without having the ability to do that thing yourself. A skilled golf coach may be able to tell his charge precisely what she needs to do to improve her swing without having that ability himself (BSD I: 31).

It may be thought that neither of these possibilities applies where the abilities in question are those required to deploy a language. "If you can talk, then you can talk about talking, and if you can talk about talking, then you can talk", goes the thought. Brandom denies the first half of this claim, at least one understanding of it. Whilst the abilities required to talk are required to be able to say what you need to do when talking, the converse is not the case. It is possible for someone to be able to talk, yet not be able to deploy a vocabulary that allows her to make these linguistic abilities explicit in the form of claims.

The vocabulary required to make linguistic abilities explicit will be called *logical vocabulary* and those able to deploy logical vocabulary will be called *logical beings*. Although Brandom concedes that there is an intimate connection between rationality and logic (captured in the relationship between the implicit and the explicit), he rejects a blanket identification of these abilities. A logical being is also a rational being, although one can be a rational being but not a logical one.

If the bold conjecture of Chapter 2 is correct (and we shall assume throughout this chapter that it is), the gameplayers of the preceding chapter are rational beings even though they may not have mastered the ability to deploy any logical vocabulary. Logical beings are, additionally, able to make explicit what they are already able to do in the form of statable principles. With regard to the abilities to ride a bicycle or to drive a golf ball, one could debate whether it is possible to capture all that the cyclist or golfer knows how to do into a knowing-that form. In the case of a linguistic practice, however, there is nothing that is, in principle, immune from such codification, given suitable explicating vocabulary.

This chapter focuses on the differences between logical and rational beings. It aims to spell out in detail what is meant by the explicating role of logical vocabulary, and to explore what difference the mastery of such logical vocabulary makes to the rational beings considered in Chapter 2.

The LX relation

Logical vocabulary, and the abilities required to deploy it, can be said to stand in a dual relationship to an autonomous discursive practice: a relationship of elaboration and explication (or an LX relation, for short – BSD II: 23). First, the abilities required to deploy a logical vocabulary can be *elaborated* from the abilities required to deploy a language. Secondly, once acquired, these abilities allow the practitioner to *make explicit* features of the discursive practice from which it is elaborated. Brandom thus adopts a quasi-pragmatic approach to demarcating logic: any locution that stands in an LX relation to an autonomous discursive practice is a logical locution.

Elaboration

Elaboration is a relation between two practical abilities. Although we are most interested here in such a relation where both of the practical abilities in question are linguistic, for illustrative purposes it is useful to focus first on instances where this is not the case.

Consider, for example, the relationship between the following two practical abilities: the ability to do multiplication and subtraction (P1), and the ability to do long division (P2) (BSD I: 35–6). P1 abilities seem to be primitive with regard to P2, in the sense that P2 abilities seem to involve elaboration on P1 abilities. In fact, the relationship between P1 and P2 is even stronger than that captured by the generic notion of elaboration. Performing P2 just involves performing P1 abilities in a particular sequence under particular circumstances. So whilst, in practice, it is possible for someone to have mastered P1 but not P2, there is a distinct sense in which anyone who has P1 abilities has, *in principle*, everything they need to have P2 abilities.

One way of capturing this idea of *in principle* is via the idea of an algorithm, a step-by-step set of instructions that specify precisely how P1 abilities can be combined to achieve P2. A simple kind of algorithm is a straight-schedule algorithm: a list of instructions telling the system to perform one primitive ability followed by another followed by another . . .[1] Any reactive system that can read a stimulus and write a response can be said to follow a straight-schedule algorithm (the idea of a reactive system was introduced in Chapter 1). All that is needed to move from P1 to P2 are the read–write abilities needed to follow an algorithm. An algorithm can, on the one hand, be said to show how to elaborate simple abilities into complex ones, and, on the other, provides a pragmatic analysis of the complex abilities into simpler ones.

Contrast this relationship between P1 and P2 with the relationship between the ability to draw a passable picture of a stick-figure man (P3) and the ability to draw a passable picture of a human face (P4). Here too there are two distinct abilities that seem to stand in a relation of elaboration. It does not, however, seem to be a relationship of algorithmic elaboration, but rather a relationship that Brandom terms "elaboration by training".[2] Whilst there may be a training regimen that can move someone from P3 to P4, we cannot articulate precisely what that extra is that needs to be done from the comfort of our philosophical armchairs. In other words, what is needed to move from P3 to P4 are not just algorithmic-elaborating abilities (abilities that can be specified from the philosopher's, or at least the automaton-theorist's, armchair) that *precisely* capture *all* that needs to be added to the primitive abilities to achieve the complex one. This is not to say, of course, that such a transition cannot be achieved: people do learn to draw faces, and this is often achieved by attending training courses that attempt to develop primitive drawing abilities into complex ones. The difference, however, is that the ability needed to master P4 from P3 is not something that can be perfectly articulated in advance across all cases, as in the transition from P1 to P2. The training course is developed contingently, from past trial and error, and may well differ from case to case.

The last point is worth elaborating. The difference between the transitions from P1 to P2 and from P3 to P4 is not that everyone with P1 abilities must be able to achieve P2 abilities, but that not everyone with P3 abilities must be able to achieve P4 abilities. Even in the former transition, all sorts of idealizations are involved that may not be realized in each and every case, ensuring that some practitioners may not be able to achieve abilities P2 from P1 and algorithmic abilities. For example, one idealization is what Brandom terms "response substitution", so that reading and writing abilities required to follow the algorithm can be responsively linked in any arbitrary combination. (If I can read a 0 and in response write a 0, and if I can read a 1 and in response write a 1, the idealization is that these abilities can be elaborated so that I am able to read a 0 and write a 1 in response.) When considering this idea in such abstract terms, the idealization does not seem difficult to realize; when considering its implementation in real beings, however, it is obvious that this may not be possible. (If I can respond to hash browns by saying "yum" and to marzipan by saying "yuck", I may not be able to develop the ability to say "yum" in response to marzipan.) The difference between the transition from P1 to P2 and from P3 to P4 is that in the former (algorithmic elaboration) one can state precisely all that needs to be done by anyone and everyone to achieve the transition, given certain specifiable idealizations, something that cannot be done for the latter (elaboration by training).

With this distinction between two forms of elaboration, we can turn to the question of the relation between the abilities of rational and logical beings. In this case, it is a relation between (P5) the practical ability that is both necessary and sufficient for deploying a language (the minimal set of abilities needed to be able to make an assertion) and (P6) the practical ability sufficient for deploying a logical vocabulary (making claims that incorporate distinctively logical terms). Brandom contends that the relation between P5 and P6 is that of algorithmic elaboration, as it is possible to specify precisely all that needs to be added to the rational abilities in order that, given certain statable idealizations, anyone with rational abilities can acquire logical ones. Rational beings are thus *in principle* capable of doing everything that logical beings can do, although before undertaking this algorithmically specified tooling-up process they have not yet actualized this potential.

Explication

Elaboration is a process by which one acquires the ability to do one thing from the ability to do another. As is clear from the manner in which this was introduced, using the example of algorithmic elaboration of the abilities to do long division from the abilities to multiply and subtract, elaboration is not limited to linguistic abilities. A variety of practical abilities can be said to be elaborated from the ability to perform others.

The same seems true of explication.[3] Even though we shall be considering cases where what is made explicit is the ability to deploy a language, it seems possible to make explicit what is implicit in various non-linguistic abilities too. For example, we mentioned earlier the abilities of a technical writer to make explicit in the form of words what is involved in the ability to ride a bicycle, or the abilities of a coach to say what is involved in swinging a golf club. These are both cases in which non-linguistic abilities are made explicit. Explicating, in this general sense, means codifying in the form of principles some instance of practical knowing-how. Of course, the abilities required to make something explicit are specifically linguistic; they involve *saying* what it is to do something. This does not mean, however, that every instance of explication only applies to cases in which the abilities explicated are linguistic. One could thus have a 'logic' of a practical ability that specifies in explicit terms what it is to perform something non-linguistic, such as riding a bike or swinging a golf club. The 'scare quotes' are used to highlight that such a vocabulary is not a logical vocabulary in our sense, as it is not an LX vocabulary: it is not elaborated from the selfsame practices it explicates. It would be an example of explication nonetheless, as it codifies what is implicit in a doing in the form of an explicit claim that can act as a reason for something, and for which reasons are asked.

There is a particular kind of explication that takes place when what is explicated is a social practice and not just an ability. The former, but not the latter, requires consideration of the social normative context, in which an exercise of the practical abilities by an individual is treated by others as a socially significant performance, a move in the game. When the target of the explication is a social practice, what are made explicit are normative proprieties that are implicit in the socially significant performances that are explicated.

When what is explicated is a social practice, it becomes possible to distinguish between codifying the norms actually followed by participants in the practice, and codifying the proprieties of norms that ought to be followed by participants in the practice. Whilst it may be tempting to think of this in terms of a descriptive–prescriptive difference, I think this should be resisted when trying to get a handle on the Brandomian notion of explication. For a claim to be said to *codify* a practice, the claim must be warranted by some feature of the *existing* practice that is codified. Even on a subtle conception of normative prescription, according to which issuing a prescriptive is not just issuing an injunction but makes a tentative proposal as to how best to carry on in the future that is itself subject to criticism from within the norms of the practice explicated, the prescription ceases to be a form of codification.[4] This is because the warrant for the prescriptive claim is not derived solely from features of the existing practice that is codified. Instead, the relevant difference here is not between the descriptive and the prescriptive, but between descriptive claims that codify what participants do in practice and descriptive claims that codify norms governing what participants ought to do in practice according to proprieties implicit in their practical doings. The latter is not a prescription of what people ought to do, but a codification of what people appropriately sanction as appropriate within that practice.[5]

We have claimed, thus far, that explication involves the codification of practical knowing-how in a set of claimable principles. We have further noted that there is a specific kind of explication when the target of explication is a social practice, so that what is explicated are the normative proprieties of performing implicit in the performances within that practice. Explicating a linguistic practice is a unique case even within this particular kind of codification of social practice. This uniqueness arises from the fact that what is doing the explicating and what is being explicated are both linguistic abilities – the abilities needed to be able to make claims. Both feature within the selfsame practice and are subject to the same proprieties and sanctions. The LX relation, that special case where the ability required to explicate a doing is algorithmically elaborated from that very selfsame doing, is limited to the case in which both the doings in question are linguistic. Although the remainder of this chapter explores this unique case, the point here is that what makes this case special stems from the target of the explication, and not the very idea of explication itself. As I understand it, any attempt at codifying practical know-how is engaging in the process of explication, whether or not the practice explicated is linguistic, and whether or not the explication involves proprieties of performance.

LX vocabulary: retail considerations

Logical locutions are terms whose function it is to explicate linguistic practice. This section provides some examples of this broader category of logical locutions, in order to answer two key questions about the notions of elaboration (L) and explication (X). The (L) question asks "Just how is it possible to introduce, via algorithmic elaboration, the ability to deploy logical vocabulary from the ability to deploy rational vocabulary?" The (X) question asks "What does mastery of this explicating tool allow rational beings to do that they could not do otherwise?" Both (L) and (X) questions admit two readings: retail and wholesale. The retail version considers each logical locution in turn, to consider both how it could be elaborated from rational abilities, and what particular feature of linguistic practice it explicates. The wholesale version generalizes from these instances to provide a broader account of the relation between rational and logical beings. Contrary to sound business practice, we shall consider retail matters first.

Consider a highly contrived instance of the game described in the previous chapter involving three gameplayers, A, B and C, and four counter-types that we could label p, q, r and s. In this mini-game, when A places p before her, B treats this move as an appropriate performance, and now treats A as committed not only to counters of type p, but also to counters of type q that are, according to B, consequential commitments of type p. B also treats A as entitled to counter-type r as well, which is, according to B, a permissive consequence of q. Additionally, B treats A as no longer entitled to s, which is, according to B, incompatible with q. Finally, in response, B places counter-types p, q and r before him. Following B, C also places counter-types p and r before her, but not q, which is, according to C, incompatible with other commitments she holds.

One must not be misled by such use of ps and qs into considering A, B and C as having logical abilities. A, B and C are examples of the gameplayers of Chapter 2 who lack the locutions required to have explicitly grasped the logical relations between the propositions p, q, r and s. Even the very talk of counters themselves is shorthand for talk of equivalence classes of possible tokening performances. In other words, they are rational beings able to practically adopt normative attitudes towards the consequential performances of others.

The conditional

Let us first consider the introduction of that paradigm of logical locutions, the conditional, into this practice. Prior to the elaborative process, B can practically treat A as consequentially committed to q if he is committed to p. Introducing the conditional "if . . . then" into B's repertoire allows him to make this explicit in the form of a statable claim: "if p then q".

The relationship between the rational ability to deploy a language and the logical ability to deploy this new locution is one of algorithmic elaboration. Prior to the elaborative process, B can respond differentially to the performances of A. For example, if the performance-type is the putting forward of p, B responds – among other things – by putting q in A's commitment-box. These abilities, reading p-type stimuli and writing q-type responses, are sufficient, given certain idealizations, for the introduction of conditionals. All that one needs to add to these abilities is a form of response substitution: to be able to produce a token "if p then q" in the circumstances that previously elicited the writing of a q-type response, and to be able to respond to a token of "if p then q" with consequences previously elicited by reading a p-type response.[6] In this sense, logical abilities can be algorithmically elaborated from rational ones.[7]

Before the introduction of this logical locution, rational beings make claims in the context of their discursive practices and alter those claims in light of inferential relations with other claims. They are, however, unable to criticize and alter those inferential relations themselves, as this would require the ability to consider, in an explicit form, a particular conditional claim. With the introduction of the conditional, one can state these inferential relations in explicit form, so that the relations can themselves become part of these discursive practices and can be rejected or accepted as part of the discussion. Adding this logical locution to one's repertoire as a result of this elaborative process thus allows one to bring inferential relations into the discursive enterprise in the form of explicit claims, such that they can become the target of critical evaluation.

". . . is committed to . . ." and ". . . says . . ."

The previous example involved locutions that are typically treated as logical. The range of locutions that Brandom treats as logical is far from typical. The reason is this. Logical locutions are those whose function it is to make explicit implicit features of linguistic practice. Linguistic practice includes both acts of claiming (the pragmatic dimension of linguistic practice) and the contents claimed (the semantic dimension of linguistic practice). As a result, we require two kinds of logical locutions. Some logical locutions, such as the conditional, serve to make explicit semantic dimensions implicit in rational practice. Others, such as the "is committed to . . ." locution, serve to make explicit pragmatic features implicit in rational practice. In this section we consider two examples from the latter group.

In the contrived game introduced above, B practically treats A as committed to counter-type p. Introducing the "is committed to . . ." locution into B's repertoire allows him to make this explicit in the form of a statable claim: "A is committed to p". Prior to the introduction of this locution, B can be said to practically recognize (read) circumstances in which A is committed to p, and respond (write) to such circumstances by adding that commitment and consequential commitments to A's score-box. To introduce the "is committed to . . ." locution that can make this explicit, there needs to be a form of response substitution: one now asserts "A is committed to p" in the circumstances previously recognized, and respond to "A is committed to p" with the consequences previously performed. It is thus a straightforward case in which the ability sufficient to deploy a language can be algorithmically elaborated into the ability sufficient to deploy the "is committed to . . ." locution.

Consider the related ascriptional locution of the form "says . . ." (which will be treated as interchangeable with "asserts . . .").[8] "says . . ." and "is committed to . . ." differ: A may be treated by B as committed to things that she has not asserted and would not be prepared to assert. Prior to the introduction of this locution, B can treat A's placing a counter of type p before her as an asserting of p by responding to it, in practice, in a manner that respects the tripartite account of asserting outlined. When the "says . . ." locution is introduced into the language, B can make this explicit by saying "A says p".

As a result of mastering these locutions, B can now achieve certain things in his scorekeeping practices that he could not do before. Prior to its introduction, for example, B's attributing in practice that commitment to A was a response elicited by his perceiving A place the counter before her, in much the same way as the human reporter's response "the swatch is red" is elicited by his perceiving a red swatch.

Following the introduction, B can now say that "A says p" in a manner that allows C to attribute such a commitment to A even though C did not actually perceive A's performance. Further, mastery of the "says" locution allows such ascriptions to be embedded in one another, and thus iterated. Having mastered the locution, C can make claims such as "B says A says p".[9] Embedded claims of this sort only become possible with the introduction of the "says . . ." locution, and are of central importance for anyone trying to interpret a practice involving multiple scorekeepers.

LX vocabulary: wholesale considerations

In the examples previously considered, it is clear that adding logical vocabulary to a rational discourse does not alter that discourse, but rather makes explicit what was already implicit in it. Brandom goes so far as to stipulate an aspect of this as an explicit condition: the introduction of logical locutions must be inferentially conservative, so that, following their introduction, one would not treat as good inferences involving the non-logical vocabulary what were not good inferences prior to the introduction of the logical vocabulary.[10] If by adding a particular locution to an inferential practice one now endorses claims made in vocabulary available in the original practice that one would not have endorsed prior to the introduction of such vocabulary, then the locution added was not a logical one.[11] Given this essentially conservative role of logical vocabulary, the wholesale question demands an answer: what can logical beings do that rational beings cannot?

The examples discussed thus far suggest that the function of logical vocabulary is to allow practitioners to codify aspects of the scorekeeping practice for themselves. As a result, these aspects become explicit as claims that can serve as reasons, and for which reasons can be demanded.

> Logic transforms semantic practices into principles. By providing the expressive tools permitting us to endorse in what we say what before we could endorse only in what we did, logic makes it possible for the development of the concepts by which we conceive our world and our plans (and so ourselves) to rise in part above the indistinct realm of mere tradition, of evolution according to the results of the thoughtless jostling of the habitual

> and the fortuitous, and enter the comparatively well-lit discursive market place, where reasons are sought and proffered, and every endorsement is liable to be put on the scales and found wanting. (MIE: 402–3)

Let us highlight three aspects of these heady sentiments. The first is *codification*: mastery of logical vocabulary allows codification in the form of explicit principles of otherwise implicit rational practices. The second is *critique*: having codified the norms governing their practices, practitioners can now use these principles as reasons for other claims, and reasons can be asked for them. The third is *self-awareness*: in making such discursive practices explicit, we become self-consciously aware of ourselves and others as rational beings.

Rational beings can engage in discursive practices; they are able to recognize implicitly, the norms governing their discursive practices, and to revise their own commitments on the basis of inferential connections between these. Logical beings can, in addition, discourse about such practices, and are able to criticize the inferential connections themselves. One cannot, of course, make explicit all of their rational practices at the same time, and there is no end to such an ongoing process of critique and revision. In piecemeal fashion, however, logical vocabulary provides the tools needed to engage in this unending process of discovering, repairing and developing inferential commitments.

It is the very conservativeness of logical vocabulary gestured towards above that allows it to play such a role in this process. In characterizing the nature of logical locutions through the twin processes of elaborating and explicating, Brandom allows us to think of such locutions in terms of the difference between potential and actual (BSD II: 34). On the one hand, any rational being able to deploy a language can potentially use logical locutions, as they can be algorithmically elaborated from such practices. On the other hand, such potential needs to be actualized, so that having mastered the abilities sufficient to deploy logical vocabulary, one is able to explicate what is implicit in linguistic practice. On this conception, logic does not afford some special epistemic insight, such as being able to prove certain truths. It is a tool that functions to make *explicit* features that are implicit in any linguistic practice.

This wholesale question asks what it is that logical beings can do that rational beings cannot. The answer is captured in the

Brandomian slogan that "logic is the organ of semantic self-consciousness" (MIE: xix). Rational beings are conscious, but have not yet achieved the self-consciousness that comes with the mastery of logical locutions. Consciousness here is not some sentient awareness in the sense of being awake or the "turning on of a Cartesian light" (MIE: 120), but rather a sapient awareness that comes through being able to do something.[12] In the case of rational beings, this doing involves mastering the practical ability to assert and infer. Having mastered this ability, rational beings are able to deploy a language and make explicit claims. Through such doings, conscious rational beings can implicitly recognize themselves and others as conscious rational beings. Like consciousness, self-consciousness too is something we do. It is a concrete, dynamic process involving asserting and inferring, where these doings additionally involve making claims about the assertings and inferrings of rational beings. Self-conscious logical beings not only implicitly recognize themselves and others as logical beings, but can also make such recognition explicit in the form of claims.

A layer-cake picture of sapience

What has been presented thus far in this chapter is a layer-cake picture of sapience (cf. TOMD: 328–9), whereby rational beings need not be logical, but all logical beings are rational. As Brandom puts this,

> we can make sense of creatures who are *rational*, in the sense that they make claims and give and ask for reasons for them (engage in practices of assertion-and-inference), but are not yet *logical*, in that *all* the inferences they endorse are *material* inferences and no expressions are yet in use that play the inference-explicitating role characteristic of *logical* vocabulary.
>
> (RPC: 241)

Rational beings are those beings able to make claims. Logical beings are those who have the additional abilities required to render these rational practices explicit.

It is possible to distinguish between two different ways of understanding the point of identifying such a layer-cake structure. The first is that doing so reveals a particular structure internal to our full-blown linguistic practice, by separating out certain linguistic abilities as complex relative to others (L), abilities capable of making the less complex ones explicit (X). The second is the contention that the first layer of the cake, the doings of rational beings, constitutes an independently available linguistic base level. The difference between these is whether there could be rational beings that are not logical. It is enough for the first understanding that the identification of the first layer is a kind of abstraction from one cake, even if it could not exist independently as a rational practice. The second way of understanding the layer-cake structure is committed to the possibility of the existence of an independently available rational layer.

Brandom intends both. Not only is he trying to provide an insight into the organization of our own up-and-running linguistic practice, but he also claims that "[t]here is nothing incoherent about a language or stage in the development of a language in which the only vocabulary in play is nonlogical" (MIE: 384). That is, Brandom contends that there could be a group of beings giving and asking for reasons that have not achieved semantic self-consciousness as they lack any logical locutions.

That there are no obvious actual instances of rational but not logical beings, or that such instances are hard to imagine, need not undermine the second way of understanding the layer-cake picture of sapience. It may well engender a sceptical attitude towards it nonetheless. This sceptical attitude is shared by some of the critics of Brandom's layer cake, who find it hard to swallow the suggestion that beings lacking the capacity for self-correction could be said to reason and claim.[13] Rational beings are supposed to be those "who live and move and have our being in the space of reasons", those "subject to the peculiar force of the better reason" (MIE: 5). Part of what makes the force of the better reason peculiar is that being under its control is not a kind of brute, external diktat of something other than us. Reasons are something that we can and do interrogate and critique from within. Brandom's rational but not logical beings lack the critical ability that is essential to being in the space of reasons. The objection is that until and unless one can make reasons explicit as reasons, and so criticize them, one is not really reasoning or claiming at all.[14]

The sceptical train of thought just canvassed depends on a general conception of the peculiar character of rational force. Daniel Laurier provides a version of this objection to Brandom's layer-cake picture that draws on particular features of Brandom's own system.[15] Ascriptional locutions, such as the "says . . ." and "is committed to . . ." locutions, are logical locutions not mastered by Brandom's rational beings. Without such locutions, notes Laurier, rational beings are unable to treat someone as a scorekeeper, as opposed to just keeping score on them. In other words, rational beings can attribute normative statuses to others, but not normative attitudes. Furthermore, lacking such locutions, rational beings are unable to mark in practice the distinction between *their own* normative status and normative attitude, especially in the present tense. In other words, rational beings have no mastery over the distinction between what they are committed to now (their normative status) and what they treat themselves as being committed to now (their normative attitude). Unable to mark such a distinction means that rational beings not only lack ascriptional locutions, but also lack practical mastery over the concept of a "belief". The reason for this is that mastering the concept of "belief" requires grasping the possibility of a difference between what one believes and the truth, and this is a difference that rational beings would be unable to master without the use of ascriptional locutions.[16] Since there are good reasons for thinking that to be a believer one must have mastery over the concept "belief",[17] Laurier concludes that there are good reasons for doubting that there can be rational beings (believers) lacking logical locutions as Brandom contends.[18]

Both of these objections target the second, and bolder, understanding of the point of the layer-cake conception noted above. Apart from a general predilection for the bolder conjecture, why does Brandom endorse it? This question is all the more poignant given that it is remarkable just how little of the explanatory and structural features of Brandom's model are disrupted by endorsing the weaker understanding. Even if one rejects the claim that there can be rational but not logical beings, one can still distinguish between rational and logical locutions, and understand the relation between the abilities to deploy these in terms of the LX relation, and distinguish between the kind of consciousness afforded by mastery of rational locutions and self-consciousness afforded by mastery over logical ones. According to this weaker understanding, rational and logical abilities are *independent* though *interdependent* aspects of our sapience. Not every exercise of rationality, even inferring, need involve the deployment of distinctively logical locutions (they are independent). But unless one has some logical capabilities that could be deployed, thereby allowing for critical self-reflection upon such an exercise, these exercises would not be instances of rationality (they are interdependent). Both logical and rational abilities are jointly needed for a practice to be a sapient one. Brandom's version of the layer-cake model rejects this claim of interdependence between rational and logical; the lower levels of his layer cake can stand independently of the upper ones. It is hard to see why.

Exploiting the LX relation as a philosophical tool

The conjecture just considered, that is, the claim that there can be rational beings that are not logical beings, is different from what we earlier dubbed "Brandom's bold conjecture" – the claim that the gameplayers of Chapter 2 are rational beings and that the game is a linguistic practice. If we grant the bold conjecture, then this chapter can be said to have afforded insight into the relationship between rational and logical beings. More specifically, the process of algorithmic elaboration has revealed just what is required to develop logical abilities from these rational ones, and the process of explication has revealed just what logical beings who have mastered such locutions can do that rational beings cannot. If one does not grant the bold conjecture, and we have as yet to provide reasons for so doing, one can legitimately wonder what has been achieved here. After all, without the bold conjecture, we have managed to describe nothing more than a game. The locutions introduced in this chapter are, therefore, just more gameplaying terminology, and their apparent similarity to our own logical locutions is, at best, coincidental and, at worst, deliberately manipulated to create this false appearance.

The concern is not just that unless the game can be identified as a linguistic practice there seems little point for taking an interest in it ("just a game"). There is an additional concern as to whether, in the absence of the identification, one can make sense of the very distinction between logical and non-logical locutions. Some non-logical locutions themselves can be elaborated from others, so one cannot use the mere possibility of algorithmic elaboration alone to distinguish the logical from non-logical ones. What is needed is to be able to identify the logical abilities as those that are elaborated from, and are explicative of, the abilities required to deploy a language. This requires prior identification of the abilities needed to deploy a language, a task that seems impossible unless one already has some conception of the broad character of the practice in question that is able to provide some constraint on what is, and what is not, included among such abilities. If, for example, we are able to say that the practice is a discursive one, then this at least provides some constraint on what to include as a basic ability which any discursive practitioner must have, and we can then use this base to identify logical locutions as being elaborated from and explicative of these basic abilities. In contrast, if the only characterization of the base practice is that this is "a game", this does not impose any similar constraint on identifying the base abilities; without this, it becomes unclear what makes the LX locutions different from the basic gameplaying ones.

This is not to imply that the conception of logical locutions as an LX vocabulary is of no elucidatory value whatsoever, unless one accepts Brandom's bold conjecture. The methodology employed here – one that considers how the ability to deploy certain locutions can be introduced via a process of elaboration from, and to provide insight by explication of, another set of linguistic abilities – can be used to provide philosophical illumination, even if one rejects both the conjecture and the layer-cake conception of the relation between logical and rational abilities. In the remainder of this section, it will be shown how to use Brandom's account of elaboration and explication as a new tool for philosophical analysis and domestication, even if one rejects his bold conjecture.

To illustrate this, we return to the mini-game described earlier, but this time we shall treat it as a description of what is clearly an up-and-running discursive practice. The putting forward of counter-types should be thought of as making genuine claims and inferrings, ps and qs are to be treated as propositions, and the practitioners are to be treated as having mastered the logical abilities required to talk about the logical relations between these. The only difference between this practice and our own is that, despite having some logical abilities, we are to imagine that these discursive beings lack certain philosophically interesting locutions: those relating to the concepts "knowledge" and "norms". Adapting Brandom's methodology to this case, let us consider how to introduce such locutions into the practice and what aspects of the practice they are able to make explicit.

Knowledge

In this updated version of the mini-practice, B comes to undertake a commitment to p as a result of A asserting that p. In such a situation, B does not just treat A as having claimed that p but he is also treating A's asserting as a successful one. As we saw in Chapter 2, assertings have a distinct interaction of authority and responsibility associated with them. In this case, B treats A as having been successful in both of these respects. That is, B treats A as committed to p, as entitled to that commitment, and B undertakes that commitment himself. This trio of practical responses comprises B's practical recognition of the authority of A's asserting. C, in contrast, does not respond to B's putting forward a counter-type by placing the same counter-type in front of her. That is, C does not recognize the authority of A's asserting that p.

B can make such practical recognition explicit in the form of a claim by saying that A knows that p. This is yet another instance of algorithmic elaboration. Prior to elaboration, A can recognize and respond to "knowing circumstances"; response substitution allows the introduction of the "knows that . . ." locution in those same circumstances and with those same consequences. Once B has mastered the "knows that . . ." locution, this can be theorized and argued about, so that the issue of the epistemic goals of the game of giving and asking for reasons itself can become a topic of critical discussion within that game.

This example highlights an important aspect of Brandom's explanatory methodology. Philosophers have long attempted to provide an analysis of the conditions that are individually necessary and jointly sufficient to say that S knows that p, for any subject S and any proposition p. The classical answer has a tripartite structure, such that S knows that p if and only if S believes that p, S is justified in believing that p and p is true. The account of the "knows that . . ." locution proffered here also has a tripartite structure that mirrors this classical account. Attributing knowledge involves doing three things: attributing a commitment (corresponding to the belief condition), attributing an entitlement to that commitment (corresponding to the justified condition) and undertaking that commitment (corresponding to the truth condition).

There is an important difference of approach, however, despite such similarities. Rather than asking what the property is that we are ascribing when we say that a subject knows something, as in the classical account, the strategy here is to give an account of what it is that we are doing when we attribute knowledge to someone; that is, what the practical significance of the performance of attributing knowledge is. The focus is on the doings of the attributor, on the social and normative significance of acts of attributing knowledge, rather than on the property attributed.[19] In addition to providing a clear-cut methodology for approaching such complex issues, this approach has an important advantage in terms of the parsimony of its metaphysical assumptions.[20] In the classical account we treat attributions of knowledge as describing some property that is independent of such attributions, and the aim is to provide an account of this property. By contrast, on our account, attributing is not describing something but doing something, and the aim is to provide an account of what this doing is. We need not worry about the additional property over and above the doing described in the account.[21]

Beyond the specific insight into the concept of "knowledge" afforded by the analysis, the example reveals the philosophical value of approaching troubling philosophical concepts through the question of how to introduce them into a practice and what the addition of this new locution allows practitioners to do that they could not do before. The LX tool provides a clear sense of the precise circumstances in which the concept can be deployed, and a clear sense of the consequences of so doing. Whilst such a methodology is not unique to Brandom, viewing such locutions through the prism of elaboration and explication affords a rigour to the methodology that promises to yield greater philosophical insight.[22] It provides the lost philosophical puzzler with a way of finding a path back to familiar terrain.

Norms

Normative vocabulary is usually treated as a primary example of a puzzling vocabulary. The reason for the puzzlement stems from familiar Humean concerns with regard to fitting such norms into the set of concepts that form part of an empiricist worldview. Cast as an epistemic problem, the puzzlement is this: how can observations regarding how things are give a subject any justification for judging how things ought to be? The puzzlement here takes the second of the two forms identified in Chapter 2: it stems from a perceived failure of judgements involving normative concepts to cohere with a privileged set of judgements involving concepts that together comprise part of an accepted empiricist worldview. Philosophers have traditionally attempted to provide philosophical illumination of puzzling normative concepts by domestication (by, for example, showing how to translate statements involving norms into statements that are empirically respectable) or by elimination (attempting to show how we can make do without them).

Brandom's methodology suggests a novel way of domesticating normative concepts: in showing that normative concepts can be elaborated from, and explicative of, discursive abilities, he shows that the puzzlement need not arise at all.

> In order to be able to talk at all . . . one must already know how to do everything necessary in principle to deploy . . . normative vocabulary. If so, one cannot be stuck in the position Hume took himself to be in: understanding ordinary empirical, descriptive vocabulary, but with that providing no grip on the use of . . . normative vocabulary. (BSD IV: 33)

The point is that if one is able to deploy any vocabulary at all, then one is already able, in principle, to do everything that is needed to apply normative vocabulary.

Normative vocabulary can be introduced into the discourse in much the same way as the concept of knowledge, via algorithmic elaboration. By way of example, consider how to introduce the terms "commitment and entitlement" into the mini-practice described. Prior to the introduction of these locutions, B is able, for example, to practically treat A as committed to p and/or entitled to p. All that is needed to introduce normative vocabulary here is response substitution: B must learn to say that A is committed/entitled to p in just those circumstances where he would have practically treated A as committed/entitled to p, and with the consequences that whenever one says that A is committed/entitled to p, B treats A in practice as having such a commitment/entitlement. As a result of the introduction of such normative vocabulary, B becomes able to say that an act of asserting is permissible or that is an act that A *ought* to perform.[23]

The cursory remarks here are not meant as a vindication of the attempted domestication of normative vocabulary. Rather, the point is the illustration of a novel approach to traditional philosophical problems. Here we have an example of the domestication of philosophical puzzling concepts by showing their relationship to another set of concepts that are deemed less puzzling. The relationship between them is not one of translation, reduction or supervenience. Rather, philosophical illumination is provided by revealing the relationship between the practical abilities required to deploy these sets of concepts. The term "domestication" is particularly appropriate in this case, as it picks out both a sense of taming something wild and making it feel at home. As a result of the domestication, normative concepts cannot be puzzling for they are ones that we were, in principle, at home with all along.

Summary

Algorithmic elaboration is a relation between two practical doings, whereby it is possible, in principle, to specify everything that is needed to perform one complex doing in terms of another primitive one. Explication involves the codification in the form of principles of what is implicit in a doing. When the practical doings being explicated are linguistic, then we have a special kind of relationship between the explicating performances and the explicated performances: an LX relation. This relation obtains where the abilities sufficient to explicate one vocabulary can be algorithmically elaborated from the abilities sufficient to produce that same vocabulary. Where this obtains, a linguistic practitioner is able not only to make claims in one vocabulary, but also to explicate aspects of the performances of claiming, and of what is thereby claimed. The practitioner is not merely a rational being, but also a logical one, having achieved the semantic self-consciousness that accompanies mastery of logical locutions.

Brandom's bold conjecture is that the gameplaying practice described in the previous chapter is a linguistic practice, and that the locutions elaborated from, and explicative of, this gameplaying practice are logical locutions. Drawing on his seminal account of the speech act of asserting, we ended Chapter 2 by demonstrating that Brandom's gameplaying model can yield philosophical insight even without accepting the bold conjecture that motivated the development of the model. Using the examples of the concepts "knowledge" and "norms", we end this chapter on a similar note: showing how an account of logical beings and their relationship to rational beings can be used to domesticate philosophically problematic concepts even without accepting the bold conjecture. It is high time that we cease this strategy of avoiding the central question: what reason do we have for thinking that Brandom's bold conjecture is successful? Why should we think that we could treat "them" as "us"?

Chapter 4
Us

Introduction

Our discussion of linguistic practice has identified three types of being with regard to the gameplaying practice: simple, rational and logical beings. Simple practitioners, exemplified by the parrots of Chapter 1, are outsiders to the practice, although some of their performances can be treated by practitioners as having significance within the practice. Rational beings, the gameplayers-cum-scorekeepers of Chapter 2, are insiders to the practice, as they are able to practically treat both their own performances and the performances of others as significant moves within the practice. Logical beings, considered in Chapter 3, are rational beings who have additionally mastered the vocabulary that allows them to be self-consciously aware of the role played by such performances within this linguistic practice.

There is yet a fourth type of being that has been lurking in the wings of this discussion, and even emerging into the limelight on occasion: ourselves, the author and reader of this book. It was we who interpreted the gameplaying practice described in Chapter 2, and it was we who interpreted the doings of logical beings in Chapter 3. Indeed, we were the first type of being introduced into the discussion, on the assumption that its goal is to make sense of ourselves as sapient beings.

How are we to understand the relationship between ourselves and the rational and logical beings considered until now? According to Brandom's bold conjecture put forward towards the end of Chapter 2, the relationship is straightforward: we should not treat ourselves as an additional type of being, over and above logical beings. If we come across a social practice that we interpret as including performances with the combination of authority and responsibility characteristic of asserting (in the precise sense outlined in gameplaying terms in Chapter 2), then we ought to treat the practitioners as sapient beings like ourselves. This bold conjecture is central to the whole account of linguistic practice advanced thus far; without it, there is little reason to be interested in the details of the particular gameplaying practice described.

The aim of this chapter is to consider Brandom's defence of this bold conjecture. After outlining a way of understanding the conjecture and the central challenge it faces, we consider two possible Brandomian ways of defending the conjecture, one stronger than the other. It is argued that the stronger response to this challenge is unsuccessful, while the weaker response is both incomplete and unlikely to persuade those unsympathetic to the enterprise. In the final section, I suggest a modified version of the conjecture that is more easily defensible, although it falls short of the reductive explanatory ambitions ascribed to Brandom.

The conjecture: interpretive equilibrium and the collapse of levels

One way of outlining the bold conjecture begins by considering the notion of interpretation. In the discussion of linguistic practice, we have considered what structure a set of doings must have for them to be interpretable as being part of a linguistic practice. Interpreting itself is a doing, so one can ask a similar question about the performance of interpreting rather than about the performances interpreted. What is it that an interpreter needs to be able to do to be able to interpret performers as simple, rational beings or logical beings?

The answer differs depending on the performer being interpreted. If one is interpreting the performances of simple performers, then the interpreter herself needs to be at least capable of being the subject of rational, normative attitudes – that is, capable of treating certain performances as rationally appropriate. In other words, in order to be able to interpret simple performers, the interpreter herself must be a rational being.

If one is interpreting the performances of rational beings, then the interpreter herself also needs to be capable of treating those interpreted as scorekeepers. To treat someone as a scorekeeper requires the ability to deploy ascriptional locutions, such as "says" or "asserts". For example, treating someone as a scorekeeper requires the ability to attribute ascriptions and acknowledgements to them, and to embed one ascription in another so that they can be iterated. As we saw, this ability only comes with the ability to make attributions explicit using ascriptional locutions. Ascriptional locutions are part of logical locutions broadly conceived. In other words, in order to be able to interpret rational beings, the interpreter herself must be a logical being.

In both of these cases there is a disparity between the doings of the interpreter and the doings of the interpreted: one must be a rational being to interpret simple practitioners and a logical being to interpret rational beings. If one is interpreting the performances of logical beings, such disparity falls away and an "interpretive equilibrium" is reached (MIE: 642). The interpreter needs to have mastered the same logical locutions required to explicate the practices as the logical players themselves have mastered. Of course, there may be disparities in logical competence, as some are better at interpreting than others. But logical abilities, the abilities required to deploy logical locutions, suffice to fully characterize the performances of logical beings. In other words, in order to be able to interpret logical beings, the interpreter herself must be a logical being.

For the moment, all that is meant by the phrase "interpretive equilibrium" is that there is parity between the abilities of interpreter and interpreted with regard to the practice. Crucially, this is a weak understanding of the notion of an interpretive equilibrium, as it is consistent with there still being an important disparity between interpreter and interpreted. This disparity may have been masked by our having utilized the terms ^{s}logical^{s} and ^{s}rational^{s} in describing the performances of the interpreteds. On this weak understanding of the phrase "interpretive equilibrium", it is possible for the interpreter to have mastered all the locutions required for keeping score and playing the game, but not relate the activities interpreted using such locutions to her own rational and logical abilities. Even once interpretive equilibrium is reached, one is able to fully interpret ^{s}logical^{s} and ^{s}rational^{s} beings and yet not treat them as logical and rational. In such a case, one interprets practitioners as being able to keep score in a game and be self-aware of such scorekeeping abilities, while not treating the game that is being played as one of giving and asking for reasons.

This possibility highlights the fact that even once we have reached (this weak sense of) interpretive equilibrium, there is one further level that we can go in describing the relationship between interpreter and interpreted. In this further level, the interpreter relates her own logical and rational abilities to the abilities of the logical and rational beings interpreted. In such a case, it is not really us interpreting them, but rather a regular case of conversation. Here, a "collapse of levels" occurs between external interpreting and internal scorekeeping, as we fully recognize them as us (MIE: 644).

I have portrayed achieving an interpretive equilibrium and the occurrence of a collapse of levels as two separate stages. According to Brandom's bold conjecture, however, they are not. Indeed, he uses the two phrases to refer to the same thing.

> [A]t the highest levels of we-saying, interpretive equilibrium is achieved . . . Finally, the sort of scorekeeping that is – according to the interpreter outside the community – internal to and constitutive of the community being interpreted comes to coincide with the scorekeeping of the interpreter . . . External interpretation collapses into internal scorekeeping. (MIE: 644)

If we are able to interpret a group of performances as part of a gameplaying practice having the structure described, with the practitioners having mastered the ability to make this structure explicit so that we too have mastered this ability, then not only have we achieved an interpretive equilibrium, but this should be accompanied by a collapse of levels also. In such a case, we should cease to think of it as we, sapient beings, interpreting them, ^{s}logical^{s} and ^{s}rational^{s} beings. We need to drop the scare quotes and engage in conversation.

The challenge: the possibility of conversation

As we have seen, it is possible, in theory, to distinguish the idea of achieving interpretive equilibrium from the idea of achieving a collapse of levels. What is needed is a defence of the bold conjecture that treats the two as coming together. Why should an interpreter who has fully mastered the gameplaying and scorekeeping abilities see these gameplayers as trafficking in reasons as opposed to playing a funny kind of game?

John McDowell dramatizes just this question by asking us to consider a community of Martian anthropologists encountering our gameplayers. Suppose these

> Martians convey information to one another in a way extremely unlike ours – so much so that the hypothesis that human vocalizations are, among other things, our way of doing that does not immediately suggest itself to Martian anthropologists. And Martians have a rich repertoire of not necessarily competitive games: rule governed behaviour with no external point that they engage in just for fun. Perhaps the fun lies in the intellectual challenge of keeping track of the players. Now suppose that they see human vocal behaviours as just such a game. It does not occur to them that the behaviour has a meaning, except in the sense in which, say, chess moves have meaning . . . They do not see the moves in the games as assertions . . . But they miss nothing about linguistic behaviour that is capturable with the concepts of commitments, entitlements and practice-sanctioned consequence. (McDowell 2005: 128)

There does seem to be an intuitive difference between playing a non-competitive game for the fun of keeping track of the alterations of gameplayers' scores in light of their moves, on the one hand, and the practice of asserting, on the other. According to Brandom's bold conjecture, if these anthropologists came across beings playing a game that had the structure described in Chapter 2, then they ought to treat it as the latter. The challenge is to say why.

The description of the anthropologists implies that they have their own discursive practices. This suggests a way of conceiving the difference between treating the gameplaying practice as "just a game", as opposed to treating it as "the game of giving and asking for reasons". It is the difference between keeping score on them and conversing with them, where the latter involves mapping the scores kept in that game onto the anthropologists' own discursive performances, so that a move made by a gameplayer alters, for example, the things the anthropologist himself is prepared to assert. What reason, then, do we have for accepting the identification of A'ing and asserting, so that the anthropologists are able to converse with our gameplayers?

The challenge is a critical one for the Brandomian programme, although it is one that needs to be articulated with some care if it is not to be dismissed out of hand. Specifically, it should not be read as a concern about projection: a worry that the conjecture only looks plausible when we unwittingly and, more to the point, unjustifiably, project our own rational practices onto the model. This way of understanding the challenge trades on the applicability of a "making/finding" distinction with regard to rationality, a distinction that Brandom rejects.

> [T]o say that some behaviour by others is rational is roughly to say that it can be mapped onto *our* linguistic behaviour in ways that make it possible for us to converse with them – at least to draw inferences from their claims, to use them as premises in our own reasoning . . . Rationality, then, is by definition what *we*'ve got, and interpretability by us is its definition and measure.
>
> (TOMD: 4)[1]

As the end of the quotation suggests, this is not just a methodological point regarding how one identifies rationality ("its measure"), but a point about what rationality is ("its definition"). According to this, if our anthropologists are able to converse with such gameplayers, then those players are, "by definition", rational beings. As such, the concern that we are merely projecting our practices onto theirs should not even arise: if we can converse with them, they are rational.

Let us capture this conception of rationality in the following conditional:

> [INT] *If any set of performances within a social practice is interpretable by us, in the sense that it can be mapped onto our own linguistic performances so as to make conversation possible, then the social practice interpreted is a rational practice.*

[INT] provides a way of articulating the challenge facing Brandom, even once we have rejected the applicability of the making/finding distinction. The challenge is to demonstrate that the antecedent of the conditional obtains in our case, by showing that performances in the gameplaying practice described in Chapter 2 can be mapped onto our discursive performances to allow for conversation between us.

This challenge is *not* the same as the local question when, in practice, a specific interpreter should treat a specific set of performances as having fulfilled the criteria identified for those performances to be part of a rational practice.[2] Brandom's approach to this local question is "latitudinarian . . . one *ought* to adopt the discursive scorekeeping stance whenever one *can* adopt it" (MIE: 644). Such a latitudinarian response to demarcational issues may be sound strategic advice on a local level, but is of little relevance to our concerns. The question here is not under what practical circumstances we should treat others as one of us by having a conversation with them, but whether, when faced with the gameplayers of Chapter 2, we could do so even if we were to take such a latitudinarian approach. What is needed is a demonstration that such a mapping is possible in the case of our gameplayers.

It is unclear what form such a demonstration could take. In what follows, I consider two possible approaches derived from Brandom's writings: a stronger one that attempts to provide the required demonstration, and a weaker one that settles for plausibility.

The stronger defence: interpretive equilibrium requires the collapse of levels

The stronger defence denies a basic assumption made in the challenge as outlined, namely that it is possible for the anthropologist to fully master the gameplaying practice and yet not interpret it as a rational one. According to the defence, the very act of mastering the gameplaying practice requires the interpreter to deploy his/her own rational and logical abilities in interpreting the game, since it is not possible to interpret these gameplaying performances without drawing on one's own rational and logical resources. If so, achieving interpretive equilibrium brings with it the collapse of levels, and the challenge itself falls away.

Why should interpretation of our gameplayers require the utilization of our own rational and logical resources? It may seem that a claim to this effect is made by Brandom towards the end of MIE, where he argues that any act of interpreting must begin "at home", with the interpreter's own norms.

> We are always already inside the game of giving and asking for reasons. We inhabit a normative space, and it is from within those implicitly normative practices that we frame our questions, interpret each other and assess proprieties of the application of concepts . . . The structure of those practices can be elucidated, but always from *within normative space, from within our normative practices of giving and asking for reasons.*
>
> (MIE: 648, 649, italics added)

At first blush, this seems a promising route to pursue in developing a defence of the bold conjecture. If we can prove that interpretation must begin at home, then this does seem to rule out the possibility of an outside anthropologist who is able to fully master the scorekeeping practices of our gameplayers without relating them to their own discursive performances.

Why does Brandom think that interpretation begins at home? One reason is that this is the only way of overcoming a problem facing any account of social practice – the so-called "gerrymandering problem".[3] This notorious problem stems from the fact that any specification of a set of behaviours in non-normative terminology underdetermines the normative interpretation in terms of scorekeeping, so that for any one interpretation of a set of behaviours proffered, it is possible to proffer (infinitely many) others that are consonant with the set of behaviours described in non-normative terms. The problem is (dis)solved, claims Brandom, once we recognize that we draw on our own conception of the norms in interpreting others, and, from within these implicitly grasped norms, the fear of gerrymandering does not arise.

This claim does not, however, provide the sought-after defence of the bold conjecture. That "interpretation begins at home" shows, at best, that in interpreting our gameplayers, not only must the interpreter have mastered the vocabulary required for making explicit implicit features of the gameplaying practice, but also that the interpreter must draw on her own norms in so doing in order to make interpretation possible. But this falls short of defending Brandom's bold conjecture, as not all norms are rational norms and not all vocabulary required to make norms explicit is logical vocabulary.[4] As such, even if "interpretation begins at home", it is still possible for the anthropologists to use their own norms in interpreting our gameplayers, and to master a vocabulary required to make explicit implicit features of this practice drawing on these norms, although this vocabulary is not identical with the interpreter's own logical vocabulary and the interpreter need not be able to converse with the interpreteds.[5]

This is not to deny that the claim that "interpretation begins at home" plays a significant role in our discussion of linguistic practice. In particular, it rules out the possibility that we might be able to interpret the performances of the gameplayers without drawing on our own norms.

Critics of Brandom's project in MIE often point to a tension between an apparently reductive story about norms that Brandom tells under the heading of a *phenomenalism about norms*, and a non-reductive story that he finally embraces under the heading of a *normative phenomenalism*.[6] The tension can be seen in comparing the following pair of claims made in MIE:

> (1) The notion of normative status . . . is in turn to be understood in terms of the practical deontic *attitude* of taking or treating as someone as committed or entitled . . . Looking at the practices a little more closely involves cashing out the talk of deontic *statuses* by translating it into talk of deontic *attitudes*.
>
> (MIE: 166)

> (2) The work done by talk of deontic statuses cannot be done by talk of deontic attitudes *actually* adopted . . . The . . . account incorporates a phenomenalist approach to norms, but it is a *normative* phenomenalism, explaining having a certain normative status in effect as being *properly* taken to have it.
>
> (*Ibid.*: 626, 627)

The difference between (1) and (2) is striking. According to phenomenalism about norms captured in (1), what it is for a performance to be appropriate is for it to be taken as appropriate (compare: what it is for something to be funny is for someone to laugh in response). According to normative phenomenalism captured in (2), what it is for a performance to be appropriate is for it to be appropriately taken as appropriate (compare: what it is for something to be funny is for it to be appropriate for someone to laugh in response).

Being taken in practice as appropriate is a practical normative attitude. In explaining normative statuses in terms of such attitudes, phenomenalism about norms provides a reductive account of the norms in terms of practical normative attitudes; that is, in terms of sanctioning performances. Being appropriately taken as appropriate is not something one does, a normative attitude; it is a normative status. In explaining normative statuses in terms of such statuses, normative phenomenalism provides a non-reductive account of the normative statuses. It is in offering a non-reductive account of the norms that Brandom can be seen to embrace the claim that "interpretation begins at home". We draw on our own norms in interpreting the gameplaying performances of others.

The central point here is that even if we are prepared to embrace normative phenomenalism and concede that interpretation must begin at home, this concession fails to provide a strong defence of the bold conjecture. Such a defence must demonstrate that any interpretation of the performances of rational and/or logical beings must draw not only from within this normative space, but also from within our own normative practices of giving and asking for reasons. The considerations advanced thus far fall short of such a demonstration.

The weaker defence: logical structure and the possibility of collapse

In comments made after the publication of MIE, Brandom seems to adopt a weaker defence of the bold conjecture. Conceding that there may be no outright proof of interpretability,[7] he maintains that it can be supported to the extent that its denial becomes “extremely implausible”.[8]

Here is how things look from the point of view of someone challenging the bold conjecture. Beginning with a set of abilities necessary and sufficient to deploy a ^{s}language^{s}, we have shown how to introduce, via algorithmic elaboration, another set of abilities sufficient to deploy a ^{s}logical^{s} vocabulary whose function it is to make explicit features implicit in the original set of abilities. The ^{s}logical^{s} vocabulary includes locutions that seem to play a role similar to our own logical locutions. For example, we have seen how to introduce into the practice ^{s}conditional^{s}, ^{s}“committed to . . .”^{s}, “^{s}says . . .^{s}” and ^{s}“knows that . . .”^{s} locutions, all of which function to make the structure of the ^{s}linguistic^{s} practice explicit. Indeed, it is possible to introduce ^{s}logical^{s} locutions, via elaboration and explication, that seem to mimic most of our own logical locutions. The weaker defence contends that once enough of our logical structure is reproduced in terms of the game’s ^{s}logical^{s} vocabulary, it becomes plausible to advocate dropping all these scare quotes, thereby treating the game as a linguistic practice, and the players as rational and logical beings (RPC: 239–40).

It is worth reminding ourselves that the challenge we are responding to is *not* a concern about projection; that is, that the only reason for treating the ^{s}rational^{s} practice described as rational practice (Brandom’s conjecture) stems from an unwarranted projecting of our own rationality onto our interpretation of others’ social practice. If this was the concern, then to respond that that projection is warranted since we are able to use our own logical vocabulary in explicating features of the ^{s}rational^{s} practice merely invites the subsequent rejoinder that this just involves more unwarranted projection, this time involving not only rational vocabulary but also logical vocabulary.[9] Our concern is not about projection, however, as this stems from a making/finding distinction that Brandom treats as inappropriate when it comes to rationality. According to [INT], *if any set of performances within a social practice is interpretable by us, in the sense that it can be mapped onto our own linguistic performances so as to make conversation possible, then the social practice interpreted is a rational practice.* Our concern is to justify the conjecture that the antecedent of the conditional [INT] obtains for Brandomian gameplayers. The weaker defence responds to this concern by claiming that it is plausible to treat the antecedent as obtaining in a case where we have been able to reproduce much of our own logical vocabulary in gameplaying terms.[10] In such a case, the game itself has sufficient structure to make the mapping possible, so that the issue of whether it is "merely mimesis or really real" ceases to be an interesting one.

This defence of the conjecture is weaker than the one described in the previous section in two ways. Not only is it mounted at the level of plausibility rather than proof, but it also allows for the possibility that one could achieve interpretive equilibrium without a collapse of levels between interpreter and interpreted. At best, the weaker defence shows that it is highly plausible that the anthropologists could converse with our gameplayers, not that they need do so in order to interpret them.[11]

Arguments aiming at plausibility rather than proof are unlikely to persuade the entrenched critic. Brandom compares someone who accepts that we can replicate much of this logical structure but refuses to accept that what is being introduced is logical vocabulary to a solipsist "who insists that whatever behaviour other humans might exhibit, it is nonetheless not accompanied by what he has: a mind" (RPC: 240). Arguing with the solipsist is exasperating. In invoking the parallel, Brandom implies that part of the source of the exasperation lies in the intellectual sterility of the encounter: the solipsist's constant nay-saying is not accompanied by any positive suggestion regarding how best to overcome the impasse, leaving an opponent with the impression that this is little more than an exercise in deliberate obtuseness. By analogy, asks Brandom, if showing the parallel structure between the game and linguistic practice does not make the bold conjecture plausible, what else would? "If something is missing here it is something magical" (*ibid.*).

To the reader who remains outside the grip of Brandom's broader philosophical project, the situations are unlikely to appear analogous. First, the defence of the conjecture under consideration depends on accepting a number of prior assumptions regarding the shape of the issues, such as [INT], that are the subject of genuine controversy. To deny that the ability to introduce logical locutions in a description of the practice provides sufficient reason for accepting the plausibility of the bold conjecture need not reflect a posture of deliberate obtuseness, but could stem from a legitimate intellectual difference with regard to this conception of the shape of the issues. Secondly, the exasperation involved in arguing with the solipsist stems from more than a sense of intellectual sterility. The close-to-unthinkable nature of the solipsistic position leaves the discussant with a feeling that her opponent does not take the position seriously herself, so that it seems to be little more than a "trumped up affair" and not worth engaging in real argument.[12] This has no parallel in our context. The boldness of the conjecture under consideration ensures that rejecting it remains a genuine, and very thinkable, alternative, and worth contesting even in the face of the structural considerations evinced above.

This last point does suggest a possible route towards eventual rapprochement between Brandom and his entrenched critic. The solipsist is not unaware of the behavioural evidence; he does not treat it as relevant, however, for he disagrees about the shape of the issues. In our case, by contrast, the evidence is far from obvious, and, as we have seen, a great deal of effort is required to show how to introduce various logical locutions in gameplaying terms. Engaging in the intricacies of the very tooling-up process begun here leaves the hope that the insights provided by such a process may persuade even the entrenched critic.[13]

From explanation to explication

Given the centrality of the bold conjecture to Brandom's account of sapience, it is disappointing to discover that the best defence of the conjecture available is, to appropriate a Brandomian turn of phrase, at best probative and not dispositive. In light of the boldness of the conjecture, this weak result is, perhaps, not surprising. Our discussion, however, does not end here. It is worth exploring ways to weaken the conjecture itself, so that it does become defensible without forfeiting too much of its elucidatory potential.

The problems encountered in trying to defend the conjecture stem from the need to bridge a gap between *explanans* and *explanandum*. The *explanandum* in this case is autonomous discursive practice; the *explanans* is the gameplaying model described. Brandom's conception of *reductive explanation* is such that the *explanans* is formulated in a vocabulary over which the explainer has full understanding, and the *explanandum* is explained using this already mastered vocabulary.

This differs from an *explication*, whereby one ends up "enriching" one's grasp of the set of concepts that one had already mastered in practice, so that by the end one explicitly grasps something that was already implicit at the outset.[14] On the reading of Brandom's project presented thus far, his goal is to explanatorily reduce the discursive practice to the gameplaying model.[15]

The problems encountered in demonstrating that such an explanatory reduction has been successfully achieved suggest a change of ambition: from aspiring to achieve a reductive explanation of discursive practice to aspiring to achieve an explication of this practice.

According to this suggestion, Brandom's work begins with us, rational beings, capable in practice of playing the game of giving and asking for reasons. In practice, we – you and I – are not *purely* rational beings, in the sense that we already do have mastery over some of the locutions required to make our rational doings explicit in the form of sayings. That is, we most probably have some logical abilities too. One goal of the work is to enrich and systematize this incomplete set of conceptual (logical) tools, to the extent that we can achieve *expressive completeness*. This is achieved when we are able to make explicit those implicit practical abilities that are constitutive of us as rational beings. In such a case, we have mastered the vocabulary required to state the theory itself.

For the theorist aspiring to give a reductive explanation of a puzzling phenomenon, both the start and end points are relatively clear. One begins with a theory capturing the relevant parts of the *explanans*, and uses it to reductively explain those puzzling aspects of the *explanandum*. Since the relevant aspects of *explanans* and *explanandum* are both in explicit form, it is in principle possible to place the two side by side, to see whether one can explanatorily reduce the latter to the former. Applied to our case, we get just the two-step process described by Brandom in his initial characterization of the goals of his system:

> The first step in the project is accordingly the elaboration of a pragmatics . . . that is couched in the practical scorekeeping *attitudes* of attributing and acknowledging deontic *statuses* of commitment and entitlement . . . The next step is to say what structure such a set of social practices must have in order to qualify as specifically *discursive* practice. (MIE: xiv)

Things are more complicated for the theorist aspiring to explicate linguistic practice. The goal of an explication is a practical movement from the implicit to the explicit, where a set of practical abilities is enhanced, so that the subject can finally express – bring into view – the practice itself. One could gloss this as a movement from practitioner to theorist, although the end point is not just theoretical mastery over practice, but also practical mastery over theory. Any philosophical attempt to provide an explication of linguistic practice, therefore, needs to operate both as a practical tooling-up manual and as a theoretical account of the process at the same time. Given this difficulty, it is useful for the explicator to have a stalking horse: a simplified, theoretical model of a practice that is loosely recognizable to the practitioner as sharing some of the structural features of his/her own practice. By getting the practitioner to view another practice from a theoretical stance, and then to explore the manner in which one can introduce into this model the vocabulary required to make explicit features implicit in such a simpler practice, the explicator facilitates the process of explication of the practitioner's own discursive practices.

It is possible to read the role of the gameplaying model outlined in Chapter 2 as just such a stalking horse. On this reading, its function is not to act as *explanans* in a reductive explanation of linguistic practice, but rather as a starting point in the complex process of explicating linguistic practice. We discursive beings are asked to consider a game described in basic normative terminology, and to consider what happens when, by elaborating upon the basic gameplaying abilities, gameplayers develop new abilities that are intimately related to the former ones. The game described is, on this reading, not a discursive one, and we have no conclusive reason available to us for thinking that we could converse with such gameplayers, although some similarities with our own practice may give us reason to consider that this may be possible. In viewing a gameplaying practice that has some affinities with our own game of giving and asking for reasons, we are able to begin the process of elucidating our own linguistic practice.

A stalking horse works, in part, by deception: attention is deflected from the real target by one that appears similar, which thereby allows the real target to get close enough to be brought into view. In our case, it is not so much deception as a stage-managed educational process. In the first stage, we are encouraged to consider, from a theoretical–interpretive stance, a practice similar to our own linguistic practice. Since our own linguistic practice is normally viewed from a practical–participatory stance, the first stage leads to a second, in which our own discursive practice comes into view from a stance that is at once theoretical–interpretive and practical–participatory.

The overall suggestion, therefore, is to treat Brandom as aiming at an explication of linguistic practice, and not at reductively explaining it. This is, without doubt, a more modest aspiration, and the proposal thus comes at a price. It does, however, seem to be one that Brandom can bear without altering his overall account too much. First, we suggested earlier that Brandom's motivation for attempting to domesticate intentional or semantic vocabulary was a kind of curiosity rather than a puzzlement regarding how such vocabulary coheres with a privileged vocabulary. While explication will not remove such puzzlement, which does require the independence of the *explanans* from the *explanandum* that is lacking here, it is not a principled problem for Brandom's motivating aspirations. Secondly, explication from within a discursive practice need not be accompanied by a kind of philosophical quietism to the effect that there is nothing systematic that we can say about our practices from within. Enriching one's explicit grasp of something already mastered in practice involves a kind of systematic approach. One can aim to systematically make explicit those very abilities that discursive beings find themselves implicitly exercising as they talk and think, even if one can only do so modestly from within the confines of a vocabulary described using intentional or semantic vocabulary.

How should this proposed move from explanation to explication be treated: as a sympathetic reading of Brandom's work ("his critics have misread his intentions as being reductive"); or in the spirit of a friendly amendment ("the project would be so much more plausible if only he would rescind his reductive aspirations")? The short answer is somewhere between these two. There is little doubt that Brandom's programmatic characterizations of his project made at the outset of MIE do suggest reductive explanatory ambitions. On the other hand, the dramatic denouement of MIE is explicitly pitched at the level of explication, so that by the end, we rational and logical beings "can not only make *it* explicit but we make *ourselves* explicit *as* making it explicit" (MIE: 650). The official reason for this transition from explanation to explication is the success of the bold conjecture that supposedly identifies the gameplaying model with our own discursive practice. Motivated by the concerns regarding the success of the conjecture marshalled here, and in light of the fact that the description of the gameplaying practice does not live up to the strictures required by such a reductive project, there is good reason to endorse the unofficial narrative advanced here.[16]

Summary

Part I has outlined a gameplaying practice that contains a distinctive kind of move involving a unique combination of intrapersonal and interpersonal authority and responsibility. It has also shown how to develop, via algorithmic elaboration, those abilities required to be treated as a gameplayer into the abilities required to deploy a vocabulary sufficient to make the gameplaying practices explicit and part of the game itself. The game and the vocabulary deployed bear a marked similarity to our own rational practices and logical vocabulary. Brandom's bold conjecture is not just that the game is interestingly similar to ours, but that it is ours, so that we should treat the gameplayers as rational and sapient beings and converse with them.

In this chapter, we have outlined two routes to defend this conjecture. The first is a weak defence of this bold conjecture, based on the following two assumptions: (a) it is possible to introduce, via elaboration, a wide variety of locutions that serve to make explicit the underlying structure of that gameplaying practice, and that seem to mimic the functions of our own logical locutions; (b) it is implausible that a practice with such a structure would not be interpretable by us. These assumptions, combined with [INT], the assumption that if any set of performances within a social practice is interpretable by us, in the sense that it can be mapped onto our own linguistic performances so as to make conversation possible, then the social practice interpreted is a rational practice, are offered as a reason in favour of the plausibility of the conjecture.

It was suggested that exploring in detail the way in which logical locutions are introduced into the gameplaying practice may play a role in persuading those who resist the plausibility of the conjecture. Although we have already explored the introduction of a number of relevant locutions in this manner, including the conditional, negation and assorted ascriptional locutions, the list is conspicuous in omitting a whole host of logical terms that bring out the representational dimension of discursive practice, terms such as "refers to . . .", "is true of . . .", and "is a fact . . .". Together these suggestions and omissions motivate an undertaking that forms a central component of Part II: an extended consideration of the introduction into the practice, via elaboration and explication, of a broad array of logical locutions that are normally seen introducing those representational aspects of discursive practice.

The second route begins by arguing for a reconception of Brandom's elucidatory goals from reductive explanation to explication. If Brandom aspires to the former, then a chasm opens up between the gameplaying model (*explanans*) and rational practices (*explanandum*) that requires closure. If Brandom aspires to the latter, then no such chasm opens up, and thus no argument is required by way of defence. A core principle of Brandom's account of mind and language, noted in Part I and to be developed in Part II, is the claim that what a person is actually committed to may both extend beyond that which he will explicitly endorse, and even conflict with that which he explicitly endorses. Although Brandom openly endorses a reductive conception as his elucidatory goal, an explicatory conception of his elucidatory aims may best capture both what he does and what he achieves.

Given the explanatory reliance of each stage on the achievements of the previous one, it is critical for the semantic representationalist that the account of truth and reference (R1) be provided in terms that do not invoke either other semantic concepts (R2) or the pragmatic dimension of discourse (R3). Brandom is motivated, for independent reasons, to accept a particular deflationary conception of the notion of truth that precludes it from playing the kind of reductive explanatory role in a theory of meaning that the truth-conditional theorist requires.[3] It is not possible to expand fully on this point until we have outlined Brandom's conception of truth, a task undertaken in Chapter 8. In broad strokes, however, the point is that the truth-conditional theorist requires the conceptual independence of the concept "truth" from the concept "meaning", so that one can use the former in an explanatory theory of the latter. Brandom's account of truth, however, relies on a prior account of meaning and therefore cannot be used as an explanatory primitive in delivering a theory of meaning.[4] Without the basic primitives of truth and reference available as semantic explanatory primitives, Brandom needs to find an alternative to semantic representationalism.

Brandom's inferentialist alternative can also be represented as a three-staged explanatory approach, with each subsequent stage building on the primitives provided by the previous ones. This alternative provides:

B1 An account of linguistic practice, incorporating the speech act of asserting.

B2 An account of the semantic content of linguistic items in terms of the inferential role of such linguistic items. The concept of inferential role is explained in terms of such linguistic items being caught up in the linguistic practice outlined in B1.

B3 An account of the representational dimension of semantic content, including the use of terms such as "true" and "refers", in terms of the notion of inferential role outlined in B2.

Such a three-staged approach rejects both of the assumptions that characterize semantic representationalism. First, the core primitive in the semantic theory in stages B2 and B3 is that of inference, and not those of truth and reference. Secondly, the explanatory dependence of this theory of meaning in stages B2 and B3 on the account of linguistic practice in stage B1 undermines the conceptual independence of semantics from pragmatics.

It is important that this talk of stages is understood to introduce claims about the order of understanding and not the order of being, of sense and not reference. We are not saying that each prior stage can exist independent of the latter. There can be no linguistic practice without inferentially articulated semantic content, nor can there be semantic content without there being a representational dimension to such content. We are saying that (a) one can develop a language to talk about each prior stage that does not yet mention the concepts definitive of each subsequent stage, (b) one can use this language as a metalanguage with which to make fully explicit the core features of the subsequent stage so that (c) each subsequent stage turns out to have been implicit in the prior stage all along. This is a claim about understanding: one understands representational content in terms of appropriate inferences, and appropriate inferences in terms of the role played by sentences in a linguistic practice.

Brandom is not the first to attempt to argue for the primacy of pragmatics over semantics. He is not the first to try to dislodge the concepts of truth and reference from playing the central role in a semantic theory. One thing that makes his theory particularly novel, and extremely ambitious, is just how much of semantic representationalism he is prepared to endorse, given this anti-representationalist starting point. Attempts to argue for the primacy of pragmatics over semantics are typically accompanied by a rejection of the need to engage in semantic theorizing at all, since the ever-changing and unsurveyable array of linguistic practices revealed by such a pragmatics purportedly precludes the possibility of systematic semantic theorizing. Attempts to dislodge truth and reference from the centre of semantic theory are typically accompanied by a total rejection of a representationalist approach to semantics, contending that this distorts our thinking about language, and is the source of many seemingly intractable philosophical debates about language can be simply cast aside once the representationalist grip on our thinking about language has been removed. Brandom, in contrast, thinks one can argue for the primacy of pragmatics over semantics, and for the rejection of truth and reference as the core semantic concepts, while still engaging in a systematic semantic theorizing that takes representational concepts to be indispensable to providing a complete account of language.

The aim of Part II of this book is to outline Brandom's inferentialist semantics with a view to understanding and evaluating this attempt at "having it all": incorporating representationalist insights from within a pragmatist perspective that asserts the explanatory primacy of pragmatics over semantics and replaces truth and reference with inferential proprieties as the core semantic concept. Chapters 5 and 6 aim to set out Brandom's inferentialist semantics (B2) above, and to relate it to the discussion of linguistic practice discussed thus far (B1). Chapters 7 and 8 explore the attempt to incorporate a representational dimension to language from within an inferentialist semantics (B3).

There is, of course, much more to discuss about an inferentialist semantics than will be considered here. We shall not, for example, explore in any detail vexed issues surrounding compositionality or holism, or the implications of inferentialism for philosophizing about logic. Approaching inferentialism by exploring its relationship to semantic representationalism is but one path, albeit a central one, through a rich and dense forest that demands further exploration.

Chapter 5

Sentential semantics

Introduction

Brandom's inferentialist semantic theory has three levels, which together comprise what he terms the "ISA approach". The first is the *inferential* level which invokes inferential relations among repeatable sentence types (such as the sentence type: "Mandela is a lawyer"). The second is the *substitutional* level, which invokes indirect inferential relations between subsentential repeatable expression types (such as the singular term type: "Mandela"). The third is the *anaphoric level*, which invokes indirect inferential relations between unrepeatable tokenings (such as the demonstrative tokening "that") and repeatable expression types.

The basic level is the inferential one. At this level, the semantic content of repeatable sentence types is identified with the appropriate role they play in reasoning, their inferential role. The substitutional level shows how to extend this to allow subsentential repeatable expression-types to have an indirect inferential role. The anaphoric level, in turn, shows how to extend this further to allow unrepeatable tokenings to have a similarly indirect inferential role. This chapter explores the core semantic primitive at the inferential level, while Chapter 6 considers its extension to the other two levels of the ISA approach.

It is worth being somewhat more precise about the notion of a sentence type at the outset, so as to avoid complications later on. In our context, a sentence token is any linguistic expression whose free-standing utterance is typically taken to have the status of an assertion. The act of putting forward a sentence token in this manner will be called a linguistic tokening. Actual and possible linguistic tokenings that are similar in a certain respect can be said to be tokening performances of the same semantic type. We shall assume (in this chapter) that what makes two different tokenings to be performances of the same type is what Brandom calls "lexical cotypicality".[1] Crudely, any two token utterances that sound the same or look the same (are "lexically similar") should be treated as being tokens of the same semantic type. For example, we shall consider two token utterances of "Mandela is a lawyer", asserted by two different people at two different times, as lexically cotypical, and therefore as being of the same sentence type. More formally, then, the bearer of semantic content at the sentential level is the equivalence class of actual and possible tokening performances that are lexically cotypical.[2]

Different tokenings of the same sentence type will have the same inferential role and thus mean the same thing, whilst different tokenings of different sentence types have different inferential roles and thus mean different things. To prevent the ensuing discussion from becoming any more cumbersome than it has already become, I shall just use the term "sentence" to refer to the semantic content-bearer for the inferentialist. The content-bearer at the subsentential level, to be discussed in detail in the next chapter, will here be referred to as an "expression" and that which it expresses, its indirect inferential role, will be called a "concept".

One more terminological caution at the outset: Brandom himself does not use the term "content-bearer", although he does use the term "content". One reason for this may lie in the fact that, whilst the idea of a sentence as a bearer with content is one often used in this area, it can be misleading from an inferentialist perspective. Inferential connections obtain between sentences. The inferentialist idea is, loosely, that such intersentence relations are constitutive of the content of each sentence: each sentence is contentful in virtue of standing in those intersentential inferential relations. The image of sentence as content-bearer is thus misleading for an inferentialist account as the content of a sentence is not a thing associated with each sentence on its own.[3] Even though we shall use the term "content-bearer" in this chapter, caution should be exercised in this regard.

As the introduction to Part II made clear, delivering an account of the semantic content of a sentence (and its extension to the subsentential) in terms of the inferential role associated with such items is only part of an inferentialist approach. "Part of what is distinctive about the present approach . . . is that what are here treated as *semantic* primitives are themselves explained in terms of a prior *pragmatics*, which in turn appeals to *normative* primitives . . ." (MIE: 681, fn. 6). The distinctive idea is that the explanation of the inferentialist semantic primitives, the inferential role associated with a sentence, lies in the pragmatics, the account of linguistic practice described in normative, gameplaying terms in Part I.

This chapter aims to explore both the idea of the inferential role of a sentence as inferentialist semantic primitive and the manner in which this semantic account is explained by a prior pragmatics. First we outline certain constraints on an inferentialist semantics that stem from its explanatory dependence on a prior pragmatics; secondly, we outline a version of an inferentialist semantics – strong inferentialism; and finally, we explore whether the strong inferentialist theory outlined lives up to the constraints.

Neo-pragmatic constraints on a semantic theory

Recent accounts of differing contemporary approaches to mind and language portray them as engaged in a kind of "Homeric struggle" between two warring camps, neo-Cartesian and neo-pragmatist.[4] One central battlefront concerns the potential autonomy of semantics from pragmatics. To say that semantics is potentially autonomous from pragmatics is to allow that there can be a semantic theory (an account of what is claimed in an act of claiming) that makes no potential contribution to pragmatic theory (an account of the act of claiming). Neo-Cartesians affirm, whilst neo-pragmatists deny, the potential autonomy of semantics from pragmatics.

A "Homeric struggle calls for heroes" and it is no surprise that Brandom is one for the neo-pragmatist camp. He is clear in his rejection of the autonomy of semantics from pragmatics:

> it is pointless to attribute semantic . . . content that does no pragmatic explanatory work. (MIE: 144)

> [P]ragmatic theory supplies the explanatory target of semantic theory – and hence is the ultimate source of the criteria of adequacy according to which the success of that theoretical enterprise is to be assessed. (PP: 42)

This, of course, is not to deny the need for a semantic theory, but involves a presupposition about the explanatory goal of such a theory. This neo-pragmatic presupposition yields the following constraint on semantic theory:

> [1] *Methodological pragmatism*: Any semantic theory must be able to make a potential explanatory contribution to pragmatic theory.[5]

What is at stake is not whether a semantic theory could make a contribution towards pragmatic theory, but just how central that contribution is to its being a semantic theory.[6] If, for example, a proponent of a particular semantic theory cannot, and resolutely rejects any need to, demonstrate the potential relevance of their favoured semantic theoretical posits associated with sentences to the use of those sentences, this provides strong indication that the theory is not a semantic one for the neo-pragmatist.

A second neo-pragmatic constraint that Brandom places on a potential semantic theory embellishes the kind of explanatory relationship that there must be between the theoretical posits of the semantic theory and those of the pragmatic one.

> Associating a meaning or content with a sentence . . . goes hand in hand with specifying in a systematic way how to derive from it various normative features of the use of that expression. (RPC: 229)

> If the semantic content and pragmatic context of [an assertion] are specified, a general theory of speech acts seeks to determine in a systematic way the pragmatic significance of that contentful performance in that context. (MIE: 133)

Let us formalize this second constraint as follows

> [2] *Derivability constraint*: It should be possible to systematically derive relevant aspects of the normative significance of a performance within the pragmatic theory from the postulated semantic primitive associated with that performance.[7]

Constraints [1] and [2] run from semantics to pragmatics. According to [1], the main point of associating a semantic "whatsis" with each sentence as part of the semantic theory is to contribute towards the explanation of pragmatic features of linguistic practice involving the use of that sentence. (A "whatsis" is a colloquial name for the more technical "thingamajig"). Since the pragmatic theory here is formulated in normative terms that are best seen from the viewpoint of the scorekeeper, one could say that, according to [1], the main point of associating a semantic whatsis with a sentence is to explain how it is appropriate to update the scores associated with each gameplayer in light of that sentence being asserted. [2] goes further, spelling out that the kind of explanation of pragmatics provided by semantics is that of systematic codification; it must be possible to use the semantic whatsis associated with a particular sentence to derive the appropriate score update following its assertion in a given context.

In addition to these two constraints running from semantics to pragmatics, Brandom can be seen to be adding a third neo-pragmatic constraint on a semantic theory that runs from pragmatics to semantics:

> [W]henever (the semantic theorist) associates with expressions some semantically relevant whatsis as its content or meaning, she undertakes an obligation to explain what it is about the use of that expression that establishes the connection between it and the semantically relevant whatsis. (PP: 43)

This third constraint is motivated by the plausible thought that since sounds or squiggles considered on their own do not have a meaning, it is something about the way in which the sentence is used that confers meaning on those sounds or squiggles. The constraint is that for any semantic whatsis associated by the theorist with a sentence, she is obliged to tell some explanatory story linking the use of the sentence (described, in our case, in terms of appropriate scorekeeping) to the establishment in practice of an association between a sentence and semantic whatsis. According to the third constraint:

> [3] *Semantic pragmatism*: The normatively described, functional role played by that sentence within a linguistic practice must be able to establish the connection between the theoretical posit of the semantic theory as semantic content and the sentence as content-bearer.[8]

Constraint [3] does not require the theorist to show how the use of a sentence as described in the pragmatic theory *determines* the specific semantic whatsis associated with the sentence in question. It does require the theorist to provide an account of how the link between sentence and semantic whatsis can be established in terms of the role that the sentence plays in the practice.

One quick route available to the semantic theorist who wishes to fulfil this third neo-pragmatic constraint is to take some aspect of the pragmatic theory itself as the semantically relevant whatsis. By way of illustration, suppose that our semanticist associates with each sentence in a language, as semantic posit, the norms of appropriate use of the sentence, those very norms that form an essential part of the pragmatic theory. In such a case, constraint [3] will be met "for free", as the "semantic features of a language are just a subset of the pragmatic ones".[9] Here, the pragmatic theory would automatically tell an explanatory story linking semantic whatsis to the pragmatic theory.

Brandom does not think that this easy route is mandatory for the neo-pragmatist.

> To insist on an account of what features of the use of an expression it is that confer on it the content associated with it . . . is not yet to say . . . that one ought to be restricted in one's choice of semantic interpretants features of the use of the expression so interpreted. (PP: 44)

> It is licit to postulate meanings, which need not themselves be thought of . . . as themselves aspects of use, in order to codify and explain how it is correct to use expressions. (RPC: 229)

Indeed, Brandom not only denies that the easy route is mandatory, but, as we shall see, he does not take it himself. That is, Brandom's inferentialist semantic theory does not *identify* meaning with an aspect of use nor claim that the meaning of an expression *consists* of just those norms governing proprieties of scorekeeping performances.[10] His conception of the relationship between pragmatic and semantic theory is fully captured by the three neo-pragmatic constraints outlined in this section, which do not demand the identification of meaning with an aspect of use.

In the following two sections we shall consider in detail the semantic whatsis associated with a sentence by the inferentialist semantic theorist. Following that, we shall consider the relationship between this semantic primitive and the pragmatic theory in light of the three constraints just outlined.

Strong inferentialism

The semantic primitive invoked by the inferentialist is the sentence's inferential role. The use of this semantic primitive points to the role that the sentence plays in reasoning, its role in the game of giving and asking for reasons, as key in an account of meaning, thereby forging a close tie between the notions of meaning and justification. The choice of the sentential level as basic in the semantic order of explanation is plausible in light of this tie, as it is the sentence which is the smallest linguistic unit with which one can make a move in such a game, and this is something for which reasons can be given and which can be given as reasons. The inferential role of the sentence, the correct inferences that that sentence enters into, captures that which is claim*ed* in an act of claim*ing*. Brandom sometimes talks of the inferential role of a sentence as "curled up" in that sentence, so that in making one claim explicitly, one is making claims involving others that, although not explicitly made, are implicitly contained in it.[11]

Most theorists would agree that inferential connections among sentences form a necessary part of the semantic content of an assertion, so that if, for example, the sentence were involved in (at least some) different inferential connections, it would mean something different.[12] What distinguishes the inferentialist from the rest lies in the addition of a sufficiency claim to this: the inferential connections among sentences *suffice* to determine its semantic content.

Among inferentialist approaches that share this starting point, it is possible to distinguish between hyperinferentialism and strong inferentialism.[13] The difference between them is best illustrated by considering attempts to define logical connectives, such as conjunction, expressed by "&", in terms of introduction and elimination rules that themselves do not contain the connective being defined. Introduction rules specify the set of premises that entail the sentences that contain the connective being defined, while elimination rules specify the set of consequential sentences that are entailed by sentences containing the connective being defined. For the connective &, an introduction rule would say that anyone committed to proposition p and proposition q is committed to p&q; the elimination rule would say that anyone who is committed to p&q is committed to p and committed to q. The connective is defined in terms of both the inferentially sufficient conditions for use of sentences containing the connective, and in terms of the inferentially necessary consequences of the use of sentences containing the connective.

The hyperinferentialist generalizes this beyond the case of the logical connectives to provide the meaning of all sentences, as well as subsentential semantic categories. In the sentential case, the idea is that its meaning is defined in terms of the rules for introduction; that is, those conditions that are inferentially sufficient for asserting the proposition, and the rules for elimination; that is, those conditions that are inferentially necessary consequents of asserting the proposition. Just as in the case of the logical connective, where these introduction and elimination rules suffice to determine the content of sentences containing the connective, the same is true for all sentences. Stating the appropriate circumstances under which one is committed to the claim, the appropriate consequences of such a commitment and the propriety of an inference from one to the other is sufficient for determining the semantic content of the sentence.

Whilst there may be some claims whose content is exhausted by its inferential role, it does seem less plausible for all claims. As Fodor and Lepore express the concern:

> If you find it prima facie not plausible that the semantics of, say, "bird", "oxidization", "xylophone", "zeugma" or "afternoon tea" is interestingly illuminated by the semantics of "and", you will be not be sanguine that this program will succeed.
>
> (Fodor & Lepore 2001: 466)

One may be more sanguine about the prospects of inferentialism if one considers a less extreme variety: strong inferentialism. Both hyperinferentialist and strong inferentialist agree that spelling out both inferentially sufficient conditions for, and inferentially necessary consequences of, asserting it, together with the propriety of an inference from one to the other, are sufficient for determining the claim's content. They differ in how they conceive the inferential articulation. The hyperinferentialist takes the introduction and elimination rules from the case of the logical connective as capturing all there is to such inferential articulation. The strong inferentialist allows a more relaxed conception of inferential articulation, thereby allowing for differences between logical connectives and other concepts while retaining the inferentialist insight.

Brandom advocates a form of strong inferentialism, allowing for four primary deviations from the case of logical connectives:

- The inferences involved are not just formally good inferences but also materially good ones.

- Whilst in the logical case, the circumstances and consequences are themselves claims with semantic content, in the non-logical case, the circumstances and/or consequences may be non-inferential.
- A variety of types of inferential relations are considered to be meaning-constitutive.
- Unlike the logical case, material inferences are, in general, non-monotonic.

We shall elucidate each in turn.

Material inferences

Consider the inference from:

> [a] this substance turns litmus paper red

to

> [b] this substance is an acid.

While this seems to be a good inference, in the lay sense that [b] follows on from [a], the standard view taught in introductory logic classes is that the inference is not valid as it stands, unless the premises are supplemented with the conditional:

> [a1] any substance that turns litmus paper red is an acid.

According to the standard view, once [a] has been supplemented with [a1], it becomes a formally good inference, as the argument from premises to conclusion instantiates a familiar formally valid schema (of conditional detachment).

The standard view thus treats the inference from [a] to [b] as enthymematic, requiring supplementation with the quantified conditional claim [a1]. Brandom terms this standard view "formalism", and resolutely rejects it (MIE: 97–105). This reflects Brandom's conception of the relationship between the rational and the logical explored earlier. In treating the inference as an enthymeme, the formalist treats someone who endorses the inferential move from [a] to [b] as endorsing a commitment to the quantified conditional claim [a1], and as having a logical capacity to detach from such a conditional. On this account, one could not have rational beings capable of endorsing inferences but lacking logical capacities. As we saw, a central Brandomian theme is to allow for rational beings capable of inferring but who do not yet have mastery over logical locutions, so that the role of these logical locutions is to make explicit what was already implicit in those rational capacities. Brandom thus rejects formalism and treats material inferences as good inferences without the need for supplementation.

How is one to understand the contrast between form and matter invoked in this contrast between formal and material inferences? Since the description of formalism mentioned the idea of a formally valid schema, one suggestion would be to use the notion of a scheme to distinguish between them. According to this suggestion, a good formal inference, but not a good material inference, is an instance of a general scheme of which every instance is a good one. In the case above, the general scheme could take the following form: p and (p $\rightarrow$ q), then q.

Invoking the notion of a general scheme *on its own* does not, however, provide the sought-after distinction between form and matter, as it is possible to generate a general scheme for which every instance is a valid one and yet the scheme generated is not formally valid. Take, for example, the inference from:

[p] x turns litmus paper red

to:

[q] x is an acid

This is a general scheme, of which the inference from [a] to [b] is an instance, and for which every instance is a good one. It is not, however, a formally good one in the sense we are after.[14] The problem is that we are not just looking for the idea of form, but the idea of specifically *logical* form. Invoking the notion of a scheme on its own yields an overly generalized notion of form.[15] To distinguish between form and matter in the sense we are after, therefore, requires both a way of generating a general form *and* the ability to distinguish between logical and non-logical form.

As we saw in Chapter 3, Brandom uses a pragmatic method of distinguishing logical from non-logical vocabulary, based on the function of the vocabulary. Logical vocabulary includes any universal LX (elaborating-explicating) vocabulary; that is, a vocabulary that can be elaborated from the capacity to deploy any vocabulary whatsoever, and that can be used to explicate constitutive features of any vocabulary whatsoever. Having identified logical vocabulary in this manner, we can use the notion of a scheme above to identify specifically logical form. An inference is good in virtue of its logical form when it is a materially good inference, and cannot be turned into a materially bad one by substituting non-logical vocabulary for non-logical vocabulary.[16]

Non-inferential circumstances and consequences of application

Another difference between the strong inferentialist and the hyperinferentialist lies in the possible inclusion of non-inferential circumstances and consequences as part of the claim's inferential articulation.

At the beginning of Chapter 1, when discussing the difference between the human reporter and the parrot, both of whom had a shared reliable differential responsive disposition to respond to instances of red swatches by producing the noise "the swatch is red", we focused on the inferentially necessary consequences of the claim. It was argued that the difference between human and parrot responders is that we attribute to the human reporter an understanding of (at least some of) the inferentially necessary consequences of making the claim. If we consider the inferential antecedents of the claim, these include the visible presence of a red-coloured swatch. Such circumstances are not linguistic, in the sense that they are not claimings. Brandom marks this by saying that they are non-inferential. The connection between such non-inferential circumstances of application and the inferential consequences is, according to the strong inferentialist but not the hyperinferentialist, an inferential connection in the relaxed sense under discussion.

Likewise, in certain conditions such as instances of acting, the consequences of a commitment to act include the production of a behavioural performance, which is itself non-linguistic and thus non-inferential. For example, a rational being can be trained to respond to an inferentially articulated claim (such as "the traffic light is red") by behaving in a particular manner (such as pressing the brakes sharply). The connection between such inferential circumstances of application and the non-inferential consequences is also, according to the strong inferentialist but not the hyperinferentialist, an inferential connection in the broader sense under discussion.[17]

One potential misunderstanding of strong inferentialism on this point would be to treat the inclusion of such non-inferential circumstances and consequences as a necessary feature of any linguistic practice. Although the inclusion of non-inferential circumstances and consequences is the case for our linguistic practice, Brandom controversially contends that this need not be the case for every linguistic practice (see Chapter 8). Both strong inferentialist and hyperinferentialist agree that it is possible for there to be a linguistic practice that does not include non-inferential language entries and exits. The hyperinferentialist contends, whilst the strong inferentialist denies, that this is always the case.

Suppose that elsewhere in the universe there is a planet ("twin earth") very similar to our own, on which there is an equivalent of every person and thing that there is on our earth.[18] The sole difference is that there is a liquid superficially identical, but chemically different, to water, composed of XYZ and not H_2O. Suppose further, that earthlings and twin earthlings have not yet developed the scientific expertise to discern the chemical composition of water. The performances of earthlings and twin earthlings regarding sentences containing the concept "water" would appear to them to be identical: they would each apply the term in what appears to be the same circumstances, and with the same consequences of application. Even though they may not be able to discern any difference, the inclusion of non-inferential circumstances and consequences as part of the claim's inferential articulation ensures that the content of claims involving the concept "water", such as the utterance of the sentence "water is my least favourite drink", have a different semantic content on earth and on twin earth, since they have different circumstances of application on the different planets.[19] While earthlings and twin earthlings would not be aware of this difference between water and twin water, we – you and I – are, and this story is told from our perspective.[20]

Three types of material inferences

Sentences can be said to enter into three types of material inferential relations to other sentences:

1. One sentence could deductively entail other sentences.[21] For example, the relationship between the sentences

    [c] the swatch is red all over

    and

    [d] the swatch is coloured all over.

2. One sentence could inductively entail another. For example, the relations between

   [e] the sky is red

   to

   [f] a storm is likely.

3. One sentence could be incompatible with another. For example, the relations between

   [c] the swatch is red all over

   and

   [g] the swatch is green all over.

According to Brandom's strong inferentialism, *all* of these are part of the inferential articulation of a claim.

Something special must be said about the relation between [c] and [g], which, after all, is not really an inferential relation. Brandom argues that it is possible to see such incompatibility relations as underwriting a particular kind of inferential relation, that of material incompatibility-entailment. The idea is that one claim, p, incompatibility-entails another claim, q, if everything incompatible with q is incompatible with p. His example of such an incompatibility-entailment is the inference from

[h] Pedro is a donkey

to

[i] Pedro is a mammal,

since everything incompatible with [i] is incompatible with [h]. Such an inference is a kind of strict implication that could be made explicit by saying: "Necessarily, anything that is a donkey is a mammal". Such relations are modally robust: if Pedro *were* a donkey then he *would* be a mammal.

Brandom argues, for reasons discussed below, that it is possible to rank these three by strength (MIE: 190–91; AR: 195). All incompatibility-entailments are commitment-preserving: if p incompatibility entails q then there is also a good commitment-preserving inference from p to q but not vice versa. Likewise, all commitment-preserving inferences are entitlement-preserving: if there is a commitment-preserving inference from p to q, there is also a (*prima facie*) entitlement-preserving inference from p to q. For the strong inferentialist, all three types of material inferences ranked thus are incorporated into that sentence's inferential role.

Auxiliary hypotheses and non-monotonicity

An inference is monotonic under the following condition: if sentence p gives a reason for q, it must be the case that for any other sentence (say r) in conjunction with p (p & r) will give a good reason for q. Not all inferences are monotonic, as Brandom illustrates with the following series of conditional claims (AR: 88):

- If I strike this dry, well-made match, then it will light ($p \rightarrow q$)
- If p and the match is in a strong electromagnetic field, then it will not light ($p \& r \rightarrow \sim q$)
- If p and r and the match is in a Faraday cage, then it will light ($p \& r \& s \rightarrow q$)
- If p and r and s and the room is evacuated of oxygen, then it will not light ($p \& r \& s \& t \rightarrow \sim q$).

Here we can clearly see that as we add additional premises to the original one, the set of conclusions drawn alters drastically. Brandom contends that the function of adding an "all things remaining equal" clause to the first claim ("If I strike this dry, well-made match, then it will light, *ceteris paribus* or *all else remaining equal*"), is to explicitly acknowledge this non-monotonicity and not to remove it. It is to acknowledge that the inference is a good one even though various defeasors of the inference are available.

The material inferences that comprise the inferential role associated with a sentence are generally non-monotonic. This has a number of important implications for strong inferentialism. One implication is that what follows from a particular claim will vary depending on what other claims one holds, so that holding different collateral or auxiliary premises ensures that the sentence will have different inferential significance. This raises a number of potentially devastating problems for communication between individuals who endorse different inferences; this is the subject of Chapter 7.[22]

For current purposes, the central point here is that in responding to the question "Which of the inferences that a sentence can enter into are meaning-constitutive?" the strong inferentialist plumps for the maximal response: "all of them".

The goodness of material inferences

Brandom appeals to the notion of a materially good inference as a primitive in delivering a semantic theory. What makes a material inference a *good* one?

It is tempting to use the notion of *truth* in answering this question: truth is what good inferences preserve. (One could, for example, think of the incompatibility of two sentences as the impossibility of both being true, or of truth being preserved in a good deductive inference.) This temptation should be resisted by the inferentialist, however, because it only becomes explanatorily informative if one has a prior semantic account of truth that is conceptually independent of the notion of inference. Rejection of such a prior semantic account of truth and reference is, as we noted in the introduction to Part II, precisely what motivates the inferentialist alternative.

Another suggestion that should be rejected by the inferentialist in explaining what it is that makes a material inference a good one points to the notion of one sentence providing a *reason* for another. Again, this should not be rejected because it is false, but because it is explanatorily uninformative until some insight is provided into these reason-giving relations. This is especially true for the inferentialist who also aspires to provide a reductive explanation of proprieties of inference in terms of a normative pragmatics, along the lines explored (though ultimately rejected) in Part I. For the explanation to be reductive, the vocabulary in which the *explanans* is formulated must not include intentional or semantic locutions such as "is a reason for . . ." or "justifies . . .". As a result, the notion of a reason cannot be used to account for the goodness of material inferences, unless it is further explained in gameplaying terms.

Instead, according to the inferentialist, correctness of material inferences depends on the *preservation of normative status* from premise to conclusion, those normative statuses of commitments and entitlements appropriately attributed by the implicit practical attitudes of scorekeepers in a linguistic practice.

- In the case of deductive inference, it is commitment that is preserved: if S is committed to p, then S is committed to q.
- In the case of inductive inference, it is entitlement that is preserved (*prima facie*): if S is committed and entitled to p, then S is *prima facie* entitled to q.
- Incompatibility is a kind of withholding of an entitlement: if S is committed to p, then S is not entitled to q.[23]

The idea of "preservation of status" can be captured by thinking of these relations from the point of view of one keeping score on performances. Consider a description of the game described in Chapter 2 from the perspective of Scorekeeper S, when Gampelayer G asserts sentence p. First, S adds p to G's commitment-box, as well as a group of related sentences. Suppose q is one such related sentence. We can now say that, according to S, there is a commitment-preserving inferential relation from p to q. Secondly, S adds p and a whole load of other sentences to G's entitlement-box. Suppose r is one such related sentence. We can now say that, according to S, there is an entitlement-preserving inference from p to r. Finally, S subtracts from G's entitlement-box all those sentences for which there is another sentence in G's commitment-box that S treats as incompatible with those. Suppose x is a sentence removed from G's entitlement-box. We can now say that p is incompatible with x.

According to a methodological phenomenalism, in asking the question what makes a material inference a good one, we should first ask what it is to *treat* a material inference as a good one. In our case, to treat a material inference as a good one is to update the score in the manner just indicated. According to a normative phenomenalism, we should say that to be a good material inference is for the inference to be *appropriately treated* as a good one. In our case, therefore, a good material inference is an inference that is appropriately treated as one.

The suggestion here is that we can make sense of the goodness of material inferences without using the notion of truth as a semantic explanatory primitive. This suggestion will only strike us as plausible if we are able to use the inferentialist semantic primitive to capture intuitive similarities and differences between the meaning of sentences at least as well as we could using truth-talk. A sceptical reader may think this unlikely, as there seem to be obvious counter-examples, that is, examples of sentences that intuitively mean different things, yet seem to have the same inferential role. Furthermore, this difference in meaning can be accounted for using the notion of truth as primitive.

Contrast the following two claims.

> [i] "This swatch is red".
> [ii] "The claim that the swatch is red is properly assertible by me now".

[ii] just makes explicit what is implicit in an act of asserting [i]. Indeed for any claim, it seems possible to generate another claim that

makes explicit what is implicit in asserting the former in this manner. For example:

[iii] "Spurs finished fifth yet again".
[iv] "The claim that Spurs finished fifth yet again is properly assertible by me now".

Let us call the former *the claim* and the latter its *e-claim*.

Intuitively, one wants to say that semantic content associated with a sentence expressing a claim differs from the semantic content associated with a sentence expressing its e-claim; [i] and [iii] mean something different from [ii] and [iv]. Furthermore, if we can help ourselves to truth-conditional talk, according to which the meaning of a sentence is given by the conditions in which the sentence is true, we can state why: the two claims have different truth conditions. For example, the claim, unlike its e-claim, could be true even if I have never existed. It does not seem possible, claims the sceptical reader, to capture this intuitive difference in meaning between a claim and its e-claim using the inferentialist semantic primitive, as there is no difference between S's keeping score on G following the assertion of a claim and its e-claim. If S treats G as committed to p as a result of uttering claim P, she will also be committed to p as a result of uttering e-claim P. There is, concludes the sceptic, more to meaning than inferential role.

This is the case, however, only if we concentrate just on the normative statuses of commitments and entitlements, without considering the interactions of these to introduce incompatibility relations (see AR: 196–204). Recall that two claims are incompatible just in case commitment to one precludes entitlement to the other. Taking incompatibility relations into account allows us to distinguish claim from e-claim. [i] and [ii] differ because there are things incompatible with [ii] but not [i], such as:

[iii] I do not exist.

Commitment to [ii] precludes entitlement to [iii], so [ii] is incompatible with [iii]; commitment to [i] does not preclude entitlement to [iii], so [i] is not incompatible with [iii]. It is thus possible to use the notions of normative status (commitments and entitlements) introduced in our gameplaying model to talk about the varieties of semantic content associated with a sentence in a manner that allows us to distinguish the semantic content associated with a claim from the semantic content associated with its e-claim.

In summary, Brandom's semantic theory provides a "rendering of [semantic] contentfulness in terms of material proprieties of inference" (MIE: 137). Associated with each sentence (content-bearer) as semantic content are the materially good inferences that the sentence enters into. Goodness of material inference is thought of in terms of preservation of normative status from premise to conclusion, where this is broadly conceived to include incompatibility relations based on interactions between commitments and entitlements. Meaning is not identified with those material inferences that anyone takes the sentence to enter into, but with propriety of inferential role associated with a sentence; that is, with those materially correct inferences that a sentence is appropriately taken to enter into.

Neo-pragmatic constraints on a semantic theory revisited

Introducing the notion of normative statuses at this point in our semantic theory points the way towards connecting the inferentialist semantic primitives and the scorekeeping practices required by neo-pragmatism.

Brandom provides the following summary of how this inferentialist semantic primitive fulfils the three neo-pragmatic constraints outlined earlier.

> The projects of semantic theory and of pragmatic theory are intricately interrelated. If the semantic content and pragmatic context of [an assertion] are specified, a general theory of speech acts seeks to determine in a systematic way the pragmatic significance of that contentful performance in that context. But besides the direction of explanation involved in the *local* determination of pragmatic significance by semantic content, there is also a converse direction of explanation involved in the *global* conferral of semantic content by pragmatic significance. It must be explained how expressions can be used so as to confer on them the contents they have . . . Once a *general* notion of content has been made sense of in this way, *particular* attributions of contentfulness can then be offered as . . . explicit specifications of the pragmatic significance of [an] . . . expression.
>
> (MIE: 133, italics added)

We are provided here with two different directions of explanations, each of which is offered at different levels. One direction of explanation, at the *global* level, runs from pragmatics to semantics, and makes sense of a *general* notion of content associated with a sentence. This explanation shows how the theory fulfils the constraint we termed *semantic pragmatism*. The second direction of explanation, at the *local* level, runs from semantics to pragmatics, and allows for the determination of pragmatic significance using the semantic content associated with a sentence. This explanation shows how the theory fulfils the constraints we termed *methodological pragmatism* and *the derivability constraint*.

We shall consider each level in turn, as well as the idea of a level of explanation, in the context of two problems that suggest these neo-pragmatic constraints cannot be fulfilled.

From pragmatics to semantics: the global level

Here is one difficulty facing the neo-pragmatic attempt to move from the use of a sentence to the meaning associated with it. Throughout our discussion we have assumed that there is a determinate semantic content associated with each sentence, a semantic content now thought of in terms of inferential role. In line with the semantic pragmatist constraint ([3] above), the neo-pragmatist contends that it is the role played by that sentence within a linguistic practice that establishes the connection between this determinate semantic content and the sentence as content-bearer. A version of what we earlier dubbed the gerrymandering problem, however, appears to undermine this neo-pragmatic contention.

According to the gerrymandering problem, for any finite set of performances, be they actual performances or dispositions to perform, it is possible to conjure up an infinity of mutually exclusive norms for which that set of performances would be an instantiation. As a result, it will always be possible to construct many intuitively different meanings that nonetheless agree with all actual and potential uses of the sentence. The actual and potential dispositions of the participants in a linguistic practice involving a sentence do not, therefore, determine a particular semantic content associated with a sentence in a language. How can the neo-pragmatist allow for the fact that the determinate semantic content associated with a sentence must, therefore, outrun the actual and potential use of that sentence by linguistic practitioners?

An important distinction that Brandom makes in this regard is between the grasping of a meaning and the meaning grasped.[24] One's grasping of a meaning, one's conception, consists of those linguistic moves involving a sentence that one is actually disposed to make. It captures what we would typically conceive of as our understanding of the meaning, what we think we are committing and entitling ourselves to when making an assertion. The meaning grasped, however, will differ from this conception. It involves what we are in fact committing and entitling ourselves to when asserting it.

Brandom prefers to use tactile imagery (e.g. "I can't quite *grasp* the basic concepts of Bayesianism") rather than visual imagery (e.g. "Ah, I finally *see* what Haack is saying") when talking about understanding.[25] The reason is that visual imagery tends to blur this distinction between concept and conception in a way that tactile imagery does not (MIE: 583, 632). When one grasps a large object, one has direct contact only with a part of the object, through which one may be able to gain some control over the remaining parts with which one is not in direct contact. Similarly, in grasping a concept, we bind ourselves by the concept grasped, even though what we are binding ourselves to inevitably outruns our conception of it.

> [O]ur practice puts us in touch with facts and the concepts that articulate them – we grasp them. But what we grasp by our practice extends beyond the part we have immediately grasped (its handles, as it were); that is why what we grasp is not transparent to us, why we can be wrong even about its individuation. (MIE: 632)

Our grip on a concept is such that it allows "the concept to get a grip on us" (MIE: 9, 636; AR: 80, 163–4). As a result, our cognitive reach extends far beyond that of which we are aware.

This distinction between concept and conception, between meaning grasped and grasp of meaning, is what Brandom calls *semantic externalism*. The semantic content a gameplayer has grasped is external to her, in that it extends beyond that which she takes herself to have grasped. The link between conception and concept for a gameplayer is provided by a scorekeeper interpreting the gameplayer's performances. Provided that the gameplayer has done enough for the scorekeeper to treat her as having grasped the concept, he treats her as bound by that which goes beyond her conception. Thinking of tokening sentences in terms of playing a counter in the game may make this idea more palatable; if a gameplayer has done enough for another player to treat her as playing that game, she is bound by the rules of the game whether she likes them or not.

It is also the scorekeeper interpreting the gameplayer's performances that overcomes the gerrymandering problem, and allows the inferentialist to fulfil the semantic pragmatist constraint.

> The general point is that while normative interpretation of a community as engaged in one set of practices rather than another is underdetermined by non-normatively specified actual behaviour, regularities of behaviour, and behavioural dispositions, *relative to such an interpretation*, concepts nevertheless are . . . unambiguously projectable. (MIE: 633, italics in original)

In treating G as a rational being, S interprets her linguistic performances as having determinate semantic content conferred on them by their role within the linguistic practice. According to S, the semantic content of a sentence used by G outruns her dispositions involving that sentence. Although these dispositions do not determine the semantic content of the expression, they allow her to grasp that content, provided that S treats her as having done enough to be bound by it. In interpreting G, S himself draws on his own semantic norms in determining the semantic content grasped by G. On this account, we specify the content grasped by G in terms of a potential interpretation of G's grasping performances by S, using his own conception of semantic content. If this seems circular, this is because it is. There is no non-circular way of stating what it is about G's performances that make her grasp one determinate semantic content as opposed to another.

What this means is that any attempt to specify the determinate semantic content associated with a sentence can take place only at the local level, the level involving the actual sorting out of what follows from what. This is to adopt the perspective of a scorekeeper on a linguistic practice, by engaging in the ongoing process of attributing and undertaking of commitments and entitlements. At the global level of semantic theory, we can do little more than state that it is the way in which sentences are caught up in such normatively described practices that establishes the connection between inferential proprieties and the sentence. This is a relatively trivial claim from a neo-pragmatic perspective: after all, what else could establish connection between content and content-bearer than the way in which the sentence is used in a practice?

From semantics to pragmatics: the local level

Here is one concern regarding the neo-pragmatic attempt to move from the meaning associated with a sentence to its appropriate use. The derivability constraint requires the possibility of the local determination of pragmatic significance from the postulated semantic primitive associated with that performance. The concern is that the required derivation is not available, since the inferentialist semantic primitive, proprieties of material inference, is not the same as pragmatic norms, scorekeeping proprieties. This difference between semantic and pragmatic norms raises a concern as to the availability of the required derivation.

One way of bringing out the difference between semantic and pragmatic norms is to consider what Brandom calls the "Harman point", which sharply distinguishes inferential *relations* from inferential *processes*.[26] The material inference from "this swatch is scarlet" to "this swatch is red" could be thought about in two ways. It could be seen as a description of a movement of thought running from premise to conclusion – as a description of a process (an "inferring"). Alternatively, it could be seen as spelling out relations between the claims that stand as premise and conclusion – as a description of a relation. The Harman point is that inferential relations do not determine inferential processes. To say that the conclusion of this material inference follows from the premises (a matter of inferential *relations*) is not to say that one ought to form the belief that this swatch is red in the circumstances that one believes the premises (a matter of inferential *processes*). One may, after all, have stronger evidence against the conclusion, and decide, therefore, to give up belief in the premise. The propriety of a material inference from p to q can be made explicit with the use of a conditional: if p then q. This does not say that the act of inferring q from p is permissible or obligatory. It says that q is a consequence of p. To make scorekeeping proprieties explicit one would have to use normative locutions such as permissions and obligations (e.g. S ought to add q to G's commitment-box whenever S treats G as having q in his commitment-box). Semantic norms are thus different from pragmatic ones.

By distinguishing inferential relations from inferential processes, it becomes clear that inferentialist semantic proprieties are not a subset of pragmatic scorekeeping ones. Distinguishing semantic from scorekeeping proprieties does not mean, however, that they are unrelated, and it is in spelling out this relationship that Brandom's inferentialism lives up to the neo-pragmatist constraints. Whilst the Harman point requires us to distinguish relations from processes, the former can be said to constrain the latter. If p entails q, it becomes rationally appropriate for S to add q to the score-box of someone committed to p. This scorekeeping performance has the normative status of being rationally appropriate because of the inferential relations between the sentences in question, even if these inferential relations do not determine that this is what the scorekeeper ought to do. In a sense, one could say that they dictate what the scorekeeper ought not to do: one should not treat someone as committed to p but not to q.[27] In playing their constraining function, inferential relations make certain practical doings rationally appropriate and others rationally inappropriate. The doings in question include scorekeeping performances.

The connection between the normative pragmatics and the inferentialist semantics lies, therefore, in the idea of updating the score. The core inferentialist semantic idea is that we, *qua* linguistic practitioners, associate with each sentence in a language a distinctive inferential role that determines how the score is to be updated once it has been asserted in a specific context, where the context itself is determined by the current score. If we associate such an inferential role with a sentence (semantic primitive), then it is possible to derive the significance that asserting the sentence has for the updating of the scores by the gameplayer (pragmatic primitive). In other words, if one can state (make explicit) the semantic content (inferential role) and pragmatic context (prior score) of a linguistic performance (asserting), then one can derive the pragmatic significance of that performance (in terms of the appropriate updating of the score). As we saw before, this determination of pragmatic significance of a tokening performance using semantic content is something that can only take place at the local level, drawing on the scorekeeper's own conception of those semantic norms and context on the course of his scorekeeping. "There is no bird's-eye view above the fray of competing claims from which those that deserve to prevail can be identified . . ." (MIE: 601). It is at this local level that the strong inferentialist can be seen as fulfilling the twin constraints of methodological pragmatism (1) and the derivability constraint (2).

Summary

Throughout this chapter, we have explored the relationship between three things.

1. The notion of semantic content, the primitive of our semantic theory. On the strong inferentialist theory outlined here, this is to be thought of as the materially correct inferences that a sentence is appropriately taken to enter into.
2. The notion of the normatively defined, functional role of performances within a linguistic practice, the primitive of our pragmatic theory. The relevant aspect focused on here has been the proprieties of updating the score in context following a significant performance within the practice.
3. The sentence, thought of as the equivalence class of actual and possible tokening performances that are similar in a certain respect. On the one hand, these are the bearers of semantic content. On the other hand, actual tokenings of such sentences are significant performances in the game that require the updating of scores.

The central point here is that we are able to use a normative vocabulary to describe proprieties of scorekeeping performances following the tokening of the sentence that are sufficient for treating an inference as a materially good one, and thereby confer semantic content on the sentence caught up in such a practice.

Is it possible for the Brandomian to allow for the possibility of pursuing an inferentialist semantic theory independent of a pragmatic theory? A neo-pragmatist orientation places constraints on the primitives used in the semantic theory, and stresses that such a theory, considered on its own, would be radically incomplete as an account of language and mind. This, on its own, does not rule out the pursuit of an independent semantic theory working within these constraints, and as part of a contribution to a broader pragmatic theory. That said, the dependence of semantic theorizing on a prior pragmatic theory in the manner explored here does diminish the attraction of such an independently pursued semantic theory.

Consider, for example, the claim noted above that all incompatibility-entailments are commitment-preserving but not vice versa. A Brandomian defence of the claim invokes issues in the normative pragmatics of scorekeeping by asking us to consider the twin dimensions of authority and responsibility associated with the speech act of asserting. Suppose that S treats G as committed to p because she treats G as having asserted that p. In so doing, she treats G as having issued a reassertion licence that authorizes others to assert that p on G's authority, and as having undertaken the responsibility of demonstrating entitlement to the claim if appropriately challenged. A challenge could involve the challenger asserting something that (according to S) is incompatible with p. Since, by definition, if p incompatibility entails q then everything incompatible with p is incompatible with q, every challenge to q will also be a challenge to p. This means that if S treats G as having successfully issued the reassertion licence to p, she assumes him to be capable of responding to any challenge to p and q. As a result, she treats G as having licensed others to assert p and q on his authority. In other words, if (according to S) p incompatibility entails q and if (according to S) G is committed to p, then G is (according to S) committed to q. According to this, incompatibility-commitments are thereby shown to be commitment-preserving by exploring the authority and responsibility associated with the speech act of asserting.

The question of whether all incompatibility-entailments are commitment-preserving would seem to fall firmly within the semantic domain of enquiry for the inferentialist. Yet answering the question involves straying into the pragmatic domain. As such, even if it may be possible to pursue, in a limited sense, a semantic theory without directly considering pragmatic matters, Brandom's inferentialism suggests that such an aspiration itself is unmotivated.

Chapter 6

Subsentential semantics

Introduction

In Chapter 5 we considered the first level in Brandom's three-tiered ISA inferentialist semantic structure, that of *inference*. In this chapter, this inferentialist semantics will be extended to incorporate the other two subsentential tiers, *substitution* and *anaphora*. The reason for extending an inferentialist semantics in this manner stems, in part, from the need to respond to two challenges facing the account developed thus far. We shall call these: *the challenge of token repeatability* and *the challenge of subsentential structure*.

The first challenge can be illustrated by comparing the counters used in the game as described in Part I with the counters used in an actual language, such as English. In introducing the game, the impression given was that the counter-types, the bearers of semantic content, should be thought of as equivalence classes of token counters that are similar in some physically specifiable respect, such as looking and sounding the same. In the case of English, this impression is erroneous, as lexical cotypicality is neither necessary nor sufficient for two tokenings to be occurrences of the same semantically significant counter-type. On the one hand, two tokening performances of the sentence "Mandela is a lawyer" may have different semantic content if, for example, the sentence is uttered in different contexts (e.g. a context involving Nelson Mandela, the former president of South Africa, and a context involving Mandla Mandela, his grandson and current chief of the Mvezo traditional council). On the other hand, one tokening of "Mandela is a lawyer" may have the same semantic content as another tokening (such as "he is a lawyer"), even when the two are not lexically cotypical. What is needed, therefore, is an account of the semantically relevant types of tokenings, the bearers of semantic content, without simply assuming that sameness of type is fully determined by lexical cotypicality. Providing such an account is responding to the first challenge facing inferentialism, "the challenge of token repeatability".

Further comparison with the case of actual languages leads to a second challenge for the inferentialist. In line with the inferentialist approach, the tokens that need to be repeatable, the bearers of semantic content, are those that can serve as premise and conclusion in an inference (such as the English-language sentence "Mandela is a lawyer"). In the case of normal languages, there is an additional level of semantic structure involving subsentential units, such as proper names (e.g. "Mandela") and predicates (e.g. "is a lawyer"). These subsentential units contribute to the inferential role of the sentence in which they occur, even though they are not able to serve as premise and conclusion in an inference on their own. Providing an account of the semantic role of subsentential units is a response to the second challenge facing inferentialism, "the challenge of subsentential structure".

These two challenges differ in an important way. It is simply not possible to play the kind of game described in Part I without some notion of token repeatability. In contrast, the very possibility of playing that game does not seem to require subsentential structure.[1] The demand that the second challenge be met stems, instead, from a striking feature of actual linguistic discourse: that competent speakers of a language are able to understand and express an indefinite number of novel sentences, including sentences never said before. The only known way of explaining this feature is via the discernment of semantically significant subsentential structure, so that understanding a novel sentence is somehow generated by operations on these already familiar subsentential parts.[2] Assuming that one wants to allow the game to permit such novelty, it is important to introduce semantically significant subsentential units into the practice.

Brandom's response to the challenge of subsentential structure is captured by the notion of substitution. His response to the challenge of token repeatability is captured by the notion of anaphora. We shall consider each in turn in this chapter, so as to complete the outline of the ISA approach to semantics.

Substitutional commitments and the challenge of subsentential structure

The "challenge of subsentential structure" is not the challenge of showing how to discern subsentential structure *per se*. It is, rather, the challenge of explaining how subsentential structure, however discerned, can be semantically significant.[3]

In answering this challenge, the inferentialist is faced with the following dilemma. On the one hand, she must maintain a commitment to the semantic primacy of sentences, for it is the freestanding utterance of a sentence that is the minimal unit that can be treated as making a move in the gameplaying practice. Uttering a subsentential unit, saying a word such as "slab", makes no such move, in the sense that it does not license alterations of the score by the scorekeeper. On the other hand, she must allow for subsentential units to play an indirect role in the gameplaying practice, or else it does not seem possible to account for the fact that competent speakers are able to understand an indefinite number of sentences that express novel contents. The inferentialist, of course, cannot overcome such a dilemma by simply attributing a non-inferential role, such as denotation, to such subsentential terms. Apart from anything else, this will not help explain how we are then to understand sentences that express novel contents conceived in terms of inferential role.

Brandom's solution to this dilemma is to take what he terms "the substitution scalpel" to the sentences that are taken as primary, in order to carve out semantically significant subsentential structure. Applying the substitutional scalpel is a two-staged strategy, involving decomposition and recomposition. The first stage begins with sentences and decomposes them, using the substitutional scalpel, in order to discern subsentential structural parts. Once decomposed, these subsentential parts are said to have an indirect semantic significance. In the second stage, these subsentential parts are recomposed into novel sentences, which can then be understood (in part) based on the indirect semantic role of the subsentential parts.

The central idea is that *two subsentential expressions have the same indirect inferential role when substitution of one for the other in sentences in which they occur preserves core features of the inferential role of those sentences.* The substitutional scalpel uses this central idea to chop up sentences into semantically significant subsentential parts.

Use of the substitution scalpel depends on sentences having certain core features that can be said to be invariant under such substitutions. It is possible to isolate two such features. The first is whether a freestanding uttering of the sentence can be said to make a move in the gameplaying practice or not. If it does, that is if uttering the sentence licenses any alterations in the score at all, it can be said to be a *well-formed sentence*. The second concerns the specific alterations in score licensed by uttering the sentence type, which we could call the *pragmatic potential* of the sentence. Two sentences have the same pragmatic potential if a freestanding utterance of either sentence, combined with the same auxiliary hypotheses, licenses the same alteration in score. With these two features, it is possible to use the substitutional scalpel to discern two types of subsentential structure: syntax and semantics. Two subsentential units share the same *syntactic* category if, in substituting one unit for the other in a sentence where one occurs, one does not turn the sentence from one that is well formed into one that is not.[4] Two subsentential units share the same *semantic* category if, in substituting one unit for the other of the same syntactic category in a sentence where one occurs, it does not alter the pragmatic potential of the sentence.

Much lies in the details of the proposal, a full account of which falls outside our scope. For present purposes, we will focus on the idea of *substitutional inferential significance*, since this is the key to responding to the challenge of subsentential structure.

By way of illustration, consider the inference from

> (1) The first democratically elected president of the Republic of South Africa spoke out against the current government's HIV-AIDS policy.

to

> (2) The author of *Long Walk to Freedom* spoke out against the current government's HIV-AIDS policy.

This is an example of what Brandom terms a *substitution inference*; the conclusion (2) is reached from the premise (1) in a single step, by substituting the definite description "The first democratically elected president of the Republic of South Africa" for the definite description "The author of *Long Walk to Freedom*". Sentences that are paired in this manner, in the sense that one can arrive at the second sentence by substituting one subsentential expression for another (of the same syntactic type), are said to be *substitutional variants* of each other.

Introducing some terminology to talk about such substitutional variation, one can say that sentence (1) is being *substituted in* and the definite description "the first democratically elected president of the Republic of South Africa" is being *substituted for*. In addition, one could also talk of the *substitutional frame*, which is what is common to the two substitutional variants. In this example, the substitutional frame is "α spoke out against the current government's HIV-AIDS policy". Strictly speaking, being a substitutional frame is not a role an expression can play; it is not really an expression or part of one at all, but more "a pattern discernible in . . . sets of [sentential] expressions" (AR: 132). As Brandom puts it, while being substituted for and being substituted in are the raw materials of the substitutional process, substitutional frames are its products.[5]

Substitution inferences relate two substituted-in sentences. In the previous example of a substitution inference, a definite description is substituted for as one moves inferentially from premise to conclusion. Substitution inferences relating two substituted-in sentences are not limited to such cases. Take the inference from

> (1) The first democratically elected president of the Republic of South Africa spoke out against the current government's HIV-AIDS policy.

to:

> (3) The first democratically elected president of the Republic of South Africa criticized the current government.

In this case, the substitutional frame "α spoke out against the current government's HIV-AIDS policy" is replaced by the substitutional frame "α criticized the current government". Here the conclusion is said to be a *frame variant* of the premise. Although the difference between substitutional and frame variants will occupy us later on, *both* are instances of substitution inferences.[6]

Consider someone who is committed to the appropriateness of the substitutional inference from (1) to (2). The appropriateness of such an inference is determined by a particular kind of commitment that one can attribute to that person regarding the subsentential expression that is substituted for. Brandom calls the commitment regarding the use of the subsentential term a "*simple material substitutional-inferential commitment*", or a SMSIC. The key to understanding SMSICs is to realize that anyone who treats the substitutional inference from (1) to (2) as appropriate is committed to the appropriateness of a number of substitutional inferences involving that expression that are instances of a general pattern. The general pattern is captured by the following formula:

> Any *X* such that
>
> (4) The first democratically elected president of the Republic of South Africa *X*
>
> is a sentence, the substitutional inference from (4) to
>
> (5) The author of *Long Walk to Freedom X*
>
> is a good one (where examples of *X* could be the expressions "is speaking", "is on TV yet again", and "is unsuccessfully trying to retire from public life", and so on . . .).

The same is true for frame variants. Anyone who treats the substitutional inference from (1) to (3) as appropriate is committed to the appropriateness of a number of substitutional inferences involving that sentence frame, that are instances of a general pattern. The general pattern is captured by the following formula:

> Any *Y* such that
>
> (6) *Y* spoke out against the current government's HIV-AIDS policy
>
> is a sentence, the substitutional inference from (4) to
>
> (7) *Y* criticized the current government
>
> is a good one (where examples of *Y* could be the expressions "Nelson Mandela", "The man affectionately known as Madiba" or "the most famous Robben Island inmate", and so on . . .).[7]

In calling such a substitutional-inferential commitment "material", Brandom is highlighting the fact that the appropriateness of the inference from (1) to (2), or from (1) to (3), does not stem from its formal validity. Logical beings, those possessing the relevant logical locutions needed to make such implicit commitments explicit, could turn such material inferences into ones that are formally valid. For example, if the beings have mastered the identity (=) locution, they could render the inference from (1) to (2) formally valid by adding the premise:

> (1′) The first democratically elected president of the Republic of South Africa is (=) the author of *Long Walk to Freedom*.

Likewise, the logical being who has mastered the use of quantified conditionals can render the inference from (1) to (3) formally valid by adding the premise:

> (1″) Anyone who speaks out against the current government's HIV-AIDS policy criticizes the current government.

On Brandom's understanding of the role of such logical locutions, they function to make explicit what is already implicit in the SMSICs from (1) to either (2) or (3).

In summary, the "challenge of subsentential structure" is to explain, from within an inferentialist framework, how subsentential structure can have an indirect inferential role. The Brandomian response outlined here involves applying a substitutional scalpel to sentences in order to carve out subsentential units that have an indirect semantic significance. The response to the "challenge of subsentential structure" is captured by the notion of an SMSIC: any subsentential expression so discerned will have indirect inferential content determined by the set of SMSICs relating that expression to others. Attributing such substitutional commitments to a game-player, in addition to inferential commitments, is the second tier of Brandom's inferentialist semantics.

Singular terms and objects; sentences and facts

In responding to the challenge of subsentential structure, we have used the substitutional scalpel to discern semantically significant subsentential units. In ordinary discourse, however, such subsentential units do not form a homogenous category, but come divided into various semantically significant types, such as singular terms (e.g. "Mandela") and predicates (e.g. "is a lawyer"). Here we shall focus primarily on Brandom's account of singular terms and their relationship to objects.[8]

Although we distinguished between substitutional and frame variants in our discussion of substitution, we treated both as instances of substitution inferences. The difference in the logical locutions required to make them explicit (the identity locution for substitutional variants and quantified conditionals for frame variants) reveals one reason why they were distinguished to start with. As the identity locution makes clear, substitutional inferences between substitutional variants is a two-way affair: anyone committed to the substitutional inference from (1) to (2) must also be committed to the inference from (2) to (1). This is not the case for substitutional inferences between frame variants: anyone committed to the substitutional inference from (1) to (3) need not be committed to the inference from (3) to (1). Claiming that Mandela criticized the current government does not entail commitment to the claim that he criticized the current government's HIV-AIDS policy.

It is possible, therefore, to group syntactically significant terms, depending upon whether or not the substitution inferences they enter into are reversible (or symmetric) inferences.[9] Those terms that do enter into such symmetric substitution inferences can be called "singular terms"; those terms that do not can be called "predicates".[10] Singular terms thus get grouped into equivalence classes that reflect the two-way substitutional inferences into which they enter. Predicates (or relations) thus get grouped into structures of substitutional inferences into which they enter. These are necessary conditions for a syntactically significant expression to be a singular term or predicate respectively.[11]

The impatient reader may wonder why Brandom does not simply say that singular terms are those that purport to pick out objects. In a sense, this is precisely what Brandom does say! Where he differs from the impatient reader, however, is that he does not assume an understanding of the notion of an object (and the activity of picking it out) prior to understanding what it is to use a singular term. As he provocatively states:

> What we are *saying* about the world when we talk about its objective structure including *objects* [and] *facts* about those objects . . . is not intelligible apart from an understanding of what we are doing when we use singular terms [and] make claims . . . [W]hat an object is is *essentially*, and not just accidentally, what can be picked out by a singular term . . . What a fact *is* is essentially what can be *stated* . . . (Brandom 2005b: 431)

This conceptual relation between facts and objects, on the one hand, and claimings and tokening of singular terms, on the other, is a relation that Brandom dubs *(reciprocal) sense-dependence.*

This suggestion may well have the effect of turning the impatient reader into a sceptical one, suspicious that this sense-dependence relation is a crazy form of idealism that slights the mind-independence of reality. To allay this fear, Brandom distinguishes this relation of sense-dependence from a relation of *reference-dependence*. The former is a claim about the order of understanding: one cannot make sense of concepts such as fact or object without understanding what it is to assert a sentence (purport to state a fact), and understanding what it is to use an expression as a singular term (purport to refer to an object).[12] The latter is a claim about the order of being; without the practice of making claims and using singular terms, there would be no facts and objects. Brandom rejects reference-dependence as a "crazy" view, and denies that it follows from the claim of sense-dependence.[13]

A helpful analogy Brandom invokes asks us to consider a scientist who, in order to support her theory that a particular kind of subatomic particle, dubbed a delta particle, could exist, develops a machine designed to produce and detect such particles. Having built the relevant machine, she is surprised to discover that delta particles already exist. It may be that, in the order of understanding, it is not possible to grasp the concept of a "delta particle" without grasping the concept of a "delta particle machine" (and vice versa). Having built the machine, one then discovers that, in the order of being, delta particles were there all along. In a similar manner, "our practices of claiming serve, inter alia, as fact detectors" (FNNF: 369). To understand the concept "fact", one must have at least implicit grasp of the concept "claim", but the practice of making claims allow us to state, and possibly know, facts that antedated the practice.

Although Brandom is surely right that commitment to the sense-dependence claim does not entail commitment to the crazy reference-dependence claim, the sceptical reader (still with us?) may suspect that it is only adherence to the latter that could motivate adherence to the former.[14] There is little doubt that the spectre of crazy idealism haunts Brandom's work, a theme to which we shall return at length in Chapter 8. Whatever the motivation for so doing, Brandom takes the claim of sense-dependence seriously, as demonstrated by the following example in which a claim in ontology (the privileging of a world of facts over a world of objects) is learned from a parallel claim regarding claim-making (the privileging of a top-down order of semantic explanation over a bottom-up one).

As we have seen in the previous section, the notion of subsentential semantic content for the inferentialist is derived from the notion of sentential semantic content. A sentence can be transformed into other variant sentences by substitutional inferences, so that the subsentential expressions that are substituted for each other to achieve the transformation are used to index the transformations between such variant sentences. For example, the transformation of the sentence: "*That rabbit* is injured" into the variant "*Jessie* is injured" is achieved by substituting the first italicized subsentential expression for the latter.[15] Since the very notion of a semantically significant subsentential expression is derived from the transformations between sentences, it cannot be available prior to a sentential semantics. For that reason, Brandom would reject a bottom-up order of semantic explanation that treats the semantic content expressed by subsentential expressions as prior, in the order of explanation, to the semantic content expressed by sentential expressions.

For the same reason, Brandom pursues an order of explanation in ontology that privileges a world of facts over a world of objects. "The world is understood in the first instance as a collection of *facts* and not *things*" (FNNF: 357). Just as one can make sense of the notion of a sentence without invoking the notion of semantically significant subsentential structure, but not the other way around, one can also make sense of the notion of a fact without invoking the notion of an object, but not the other way round.[16] This can be contrasted with an order of explanation in ontology that first conceives of reality as consisting of objects, and then tries to build an account of the facts involving them out of this.

For Brandom, facts are true claims, in the sense of what is claim*ed* and not the act of claim*ing*. Facts, that is, are (=) true claimable contents, where such contents are what would be express*ed* by possible acts of claim*ing*. According to the story about content that has been told here, claimable contents essentially stand in material inferential (and incompatibility) relations to one another. Facts, as true claimable contents, are thus inferentially structured. The notion of an object is to be understood in terms of the substitutional significance of terms that purport to refer to an object, that is, singular terms. What it is for a term to purport to pick out an object does not depend on a story invoking some kind of causal contact with an object, but on the distinctive kind of substitutional role that the term plays within discourse. One important feature of this account of objects is that this is not limited to objects with which one can be said to have causal commerce. Just as Brandom's account of facts recognizes a plethora of facts, including normative facts, conditional facts and negative facts, it also recognizes a plethora of objects, including, for example, mathematical objects and other abstract objects, as well as those that may be said to be causally efficacious.

This understanding of facts and objects, and the claim of the explanatory primacy of facts over objects, is learned from the inferentialist understanding of sentential and subsentential categories, and the claim of the explanatory primacy of sentential tokenings over subsentential tokenings. That such lessons can be learned clearly reflects the relationship of (reciprocal) sense-dependence between ontology and the practice of claiming that Brandom advocates.

Anaphoric commitments and the challenge of token repeatability

Let us turn from issues arising from Brandom's response to the challenge of subsentential structure, to his response to the challenge of token repeatability.

The response to the challenge of subsentential structure just considered was captured by the notion of a substitution commitment, such as commitment to the inference from (1) to (2). A logical being who has mastered the identity locution is able to make the SMSIC governing this substitution inference explicit by claiming that "The first democratically elected president of the Republic of South Africa is (=) the author of *Long Walk to Freedom*". What stands on either side of the identity sign are not tokens (or tokenings), but types. That is, the substitution inference from (1) to (2) involves a commitment to the substitution of tokens of the type "The first democratically elected president of the Republic of South Africa" with tokens of the type "The author of *Long Walk to Freedom*". Brandom's response to the challenge of subsentential structure, therefore, presupposes a response to the challenge of token repeatability, the challenge of spelling out when a particular tokening of a subsentential expression is a recurrence of the same subsentential counter-type.

Brandom's solution to the challenge of token repeatability invokes the notion of anaphora. This is generally seen as a technical notion in linguistics, involving the relationship between a pronoun and its antecedent, such as the role of the pronoun "he" in the following sentence:

> (10) Jeremy is desperate to finish the chapter tonight, but he is bound to be disappointed.

The simplest way of expressing this role is to say that a pronoun is a linguistic token (in this case "he") that stands in for another token that we could call its antecedent (in this case "Jeremy"), so that the pronoun inherits its meaning from its antecedent ("he" refers to whatever "Jeremy" does).[17] The term "he" is an anaphoric dependent, since it depends on a prior term for its meaning. In this example, an anaphoric relationship exists between two subsentential tokenings, so that as a result of this relationship, the tokenings can be said to form a single anaphoric chain.

Brandom's account moves discussion of anaphora from being of peripheral semantic concern to the very centre of our ability to think and talk. Focus on the narrowly linguistic uses, such as pronouns, can, however, provide a sense of the proposal, provided that one bears in mind that the proposal is not limited to such cases. The case of pronouns shows how distinct tokenings can be linked together to form an anaphoric chain.[18] Each subsentential tokening can be linked to other tokenings via anaphora. An anaphoric chain is thereby formed that constitutes the subsentential type, which can then feature in substitution inferences. The response to the challenge of token repeatability thus involves an appeal to yet another kind of normative commitment that can be attributed by scorekeeper to gameplayer: an anaphoric or recurrence commitment.[19] Such a commitment involves treating one tokening as dependent on another tokening seen as its antecedent.

First let us introduce some terminological conventions designed to overcome any type-token ambiguities, by following Brandom in distinguishing between terms surrounded by angle brackets <term> and terms surrounded by subscripted backslashes /term/$_I$. The former designates the type while the latter designates a tokening. Considering the word "designates" in the previous sentence, therefore, one can say there are two tokenings (/designates/$_i$, /designates/$_j$) of the same lexical type <designates>. If we were interested in using the notion of lexical cotypicality as a way of spelling out token recurrence, we could capture this by saying *Recur(/designates/$_i$, /designates/$_j$)*. This states that the two tokens are of the same semantically relevant type, since the second token is a recurrence of the first.

As noted above, lexical cotypicality is neither necessary nor sufficient for capturing the notion of a subsentential semantic type that features in substitutional inferences. In (10) above, a scorekeeper attributes an anaphoric commitment regarding two tokens /Jeremy/$_i$, /he/$_i$ to a gameplayer, a commitment that can be captured by saying *Recur(/Jeremy/$_i$, /he/$_i$)*, even though the two /tokens/ are not lexically cotypical. The italicized phrase makes a recurrence commitment explicit.

Note that this recurrence commitment is nothing more than a commitment that the two tokenings form part of a single anaphoric chain, so that they have the same meaning, *whatever that is.* Anaphoric commitments, therefore, do not provide the meaning of subsentential /tokenings/; meaning is provided by the SMSIC governing the term <types>. Loeffler captures the interplay between substitution and anaphoric commitments well when he notes that

> [a]naphoric and substitutional commitments . . . give discourse a dense two dimensional structure. Anaphoric commitments tie the term tokens making up different linguistic performances into tight, concrete anaphoric chains, thus . . . giving discourse, so to speak, spatiotemporal depth. And substitutional commitments . . . constitute paths between anaphoric chains, thus linking different linguistic performances, in which members of the two chains occur, together and giving discourse, so to speak, breadth. (Loeffler 2005: 44)

The "spatiotemporal depth" provided by such chains should not be thought of in terms of a causal model, with each link in the chain being caused by the previous one. Brandom is clear about this:

> Anaphoric chains running through bits of discourse are not naturalistic features of them like which audience produces the tokening, or when or where it is produced. They are *normative* features attributed to the discourse by deontic scorekeepers . . . – of the obligation that the significance assigned to, or score kept on, one part of the discourse answer in systematic ways to the significance assigned to, or the score kept on, another. (MIE: 460)

The issue is not how we go about determining the recurrence class in practice, a complex matter best left, thankfully, to psycholinguists. The relevant issue here is a normative matter, best seen from the point of view of the scorekeeper attributing such anaphoric commitments to the gameplayer. From this perspective, the question is: what is it to treat two tokenings of the gameplayer as forming the same recurrence class for the purposes of keeping score? The solution here is that the scorekeeper treats the gameplayer as committed to certain tokens being part of the same anaphoric chain as other tokens, in much the same way that the scorekeeper attributes substitutional commitments to the gameplayer regarding the interrelation between these recurrence structures.

If the SMSIC governing a subsentential term captures its indirect inferential role, anaphoric commitments allow this role to be inherited from subsentential token to subsentential token within an anaphoric chain. There is, however, an important difference between the attribution of substitutional and anaphoric commitments that will play a key role in Brandom's account of communication (discussed in Chapter 7). Substitutional commitments vary from perspective to perspective, so that in attributing a substitutional commitment to a gameplayer, a scorekeeper allows for these commitments to differ from those of other gameplayers, including the scorekeeper herself. This is not the case when attributing anaphoric commitments, where there is a default assumption that recurrence relations are the same across perspectives, so that all participants in a conversation agree, and are assumed to agree, in their anaphoric commitments.[20]

In order to appreciate the pivotal role that Brandom gives to such anaphoric commitments, it is important to move beyond the case of pronouns, such as in (10). A number of limiting features are involved in that case that are not shared by all examples of anaphoric chains.

First, in (10), /Jeremy/$_i$, is an anaphoric initiator and /he/$_i$ is an anaphoric dependent, and this is a case in which the chain has only one dependent. It is, however, possible for one chain to have any number of such dependents (or, at least, limitations on the number of dependents that there may be are dictated by the practical difficulties in keeping track).

Secondly, in (10), there is a single chain operating within one sentence. It is possible to have cases in which there are a number of differing chains operating within and across sentences, as in:

> (11) # Jeremy is desperate to finish the chapter tonight but he is bound to be disappointed. It requires much more work, and he is extremely tired. #[21]

Here one can discern at least two anaphoric chains running across the sentences, captured by the following two anaphoric commitments: Recur(/Jeremy/$_i$, /he/$_i$,/he/$_j$) and Recur(/the chapter/$_i$, /it/$_i$).

Thirdly, as in the following example, such anaphoric chains are not confined to the token utterances of one speaker.

> (12) # *Jeremy*: I finished the chapter last night. *Yoni*: It is about time you finished it as you have been working on it far too long already. #

While (10) and (11) are examples of intrapersonal anaphoric chains,

(12) is an example of an interpersonal chain. It involves a relationship of anaphoric dependence between discursive partners.

Fourthly, the pronoun <he> in (10) wears its anaphoric status on it sleeve as it were, in the sense that /tokens/ of this same lexical <type> cannot but function as anaphoric dependents. Brandom extends this potential category of both anaphoric antecedents and dependents widely to incorporate term types that are not obviously functioning within anaphoric chains. Indeed, on Brandom's account, most proper-name and predicate tokenings (including natural-kind terms) function like pronouns, as anaphoric dependents in complex and long interpersonal anaphoric chains.[22] For example, not only is the token /he/ in (10) an anaphoric dependent, but so too is the token /Jeremy/: it should be treated as a token in an anaphoric chain that is "anchored in some name-introducing token" (MIE: 470). This is why different tokenings of the type <Jeremy> may be names of different people. The token /Jeremy/ used in the introduction to this book, and the token /Jeremy/ used in this chapter, pick out different people. (I am no Benthamite.) Just as many people can be referred to as <he>, many people can be referred to as <Jeremy>. Such potentially confusing cases are the result of a failure to treat such terms as tokenings in separate anaphoric chains.

Given this extremely broad extension of the usage of anaphora, to the extent that almost every recurrence structure is anaphoric, does Brandom recognize any distinction between anaphoric cases of token recurrence and cases where recurrence class of a tokening is determined by reference to its lexical type? Both yes and no. As in the case of substitutional commitments, Brandom recognizes a distinction between symmetric and asymmetric recurrence structures (MIE: 457). In the former, where the recurrence class is determined by lexical type, there is a class of tokenings which all share a feature – their lexical similarity – that makes them a member of that class. In such a case, all tokenings are related to each other in the same way. In the latter case, however, where the recurrence class of a tokening is determined anaphorically by reference to another tokening, the roles of anaphoric antecedent and dependent are different, and it is this very difference that allows them to form part of the same recurrence class. Even in the symmetric case, however, Brandom contends that the anaphoric mechanism still plays an important role.

> Apparently type-recurrent expressions . . . should in fact be understood as having their tokenings linked by relations of

> anaphoric dependence. The relations between these tokenings in these structures can be symmetric, by contrast to the asymmetry of paradigmatic pronoun-antecedent links, because and insofar as those tokenings owe allegiance to a common antecedent.
>
> (MIE: 471)

In summary, the "challenge of token repeatability" was to give an account of the semantically relevant types of tokenings, the bearers of semantic content, for our gameplaying practice, without simply assuming that sameness of type is fully determined by lexical cotypicality. Brandom's response is to invoke yet another commitment, an anaphoric commitment. This commitment could be made explicit by stating $Recur(/tokening/_i, /tokening/_j)$ for any tokening. Attributing an anaphoric commitment to a gameplayer generates repeatable expressions, even in situations in which the tokenings in question do not seem to be repeatable expressions, since the tokenings look and sound different. While substitutional commitments govern the semantic use of repeatable expressions, anaphora generates such repeatable expressions. Attributing such anaphoric commitments, in addition to inferential and substitutional commitments, is the third and final tier of Brandom's ISA approach to semantics.

Anaphoric initiators

Our account of anaphoric commitments has focused on anaphoric dependents. The meaning of a dependent is derived, first, from being part of an anaphoric chain, and secondly from the substitutional commitments taken to govern that chain. Nothing explicit has yet been said about anaphoric initiators, or how they get their meaning. A variety of term types could function as anaphoric initiators. Let us concentrate on one pointed example: deictic vocabulary, including demonstrative terms such as <this> and <that>.

Here is a line of thought that provides a sketch of an account of anaphoric initiators, albeit a heretical one for a Brandomian. Anaphora is a word–word (horizontal) relation; tokenings are linked to other tokenings in a chain. According to this account, each tokening inherits its meaning from the previous tokening. A potentially vicious regress looms if the initiator itself also derives its meaning from another token. It must, therefore, derive its meaning from a word–world (vertical) link. A tokening of the term /this/$_i$ gets linked to what it is about without describing that thing in any way. It does so via a demonstration. Subsequently, one can pick up that tokening in an anaphoric chain, so that all subsequent tokenings of the chain inherit their meaning from the meaning of the anaphoric initiator. On this account, anaphoric chains link all the anaphorically dependent tokening, via the initiating tokening, out to the world. The meaning of the initiator is simply the worldly object demonstrated.

The problems with this sketch for the Brandomian begin with the idea that the meaning of an anaphoric dependent is inherited from a previous link in an anaphoric chain. If we are considering anaphoric commitments alone, however, no issue of meaning is yet in play. Meaning of subsentential tokenings is captured by substitutional commitments between whole anaphoric chains, and not from one tokening to another within one anaphoric chain. On this account, therefore, the meaning of the anaphoric initiator itself, even /this/ and /that/, is thus derived from the substitutional role of the whole chain that it initiates. To say that an elicited response has a meaning on its own goes against the holism that has been central to an inferentialist semantics from the very outset.

Deictic expressions are unrepeatable tokenings: one is rarely in the same position to utter /this/$_i$, again, and even if one can, there will always be a question as to whether the second /this/$_j$ is a repetition of the first, or another unrepeatable tokening. In order for it to function within a conversation, it has to be able to enter into substitution inferences. These, however, govern repeatable expressions, and seem to preclude such unrepeatable demonstratives. It is the possibility that these deictic expressions can be picked up anaphorically that allows what are otherwise unrepeatable tokenings to become repeatable, and feature in discursive practice. A rabbit runs in front of you, and you, in response, utter "gleeb". Now, the rabbit is no longer present to be demonstrated. You can nonetheless continue talking about *it*, even when the rabbit is no longer present to be demonstrated. "*That* was so cool". "*It* was just here". Others, even those not having seen the rabbit, can talk about it. "Was *that* a rabbit?" "I didn't see *it*". Here we have a group of pronouns linked anaphorically to an initial tokening. As a result, we can continue to talk about what was demonstrated at the start of the anaphoric chain, and bring it into meaningful conversation.

If this is correct, then one cannot have deictic uses of language (such as demonstratives) without anaphora. Brandom formulates this as a slogan: *deixis presupposes anaphora*.

> [A]naphora is more basic than deixis, for there can be languages that have anaphoric mechanisms but no deictic ones, while there cannot in principle be languages with deictic mechanisms but no anaphoric ones. (MIE: 621)

> No semantically significant occurrence of a subsentential expression can be discerned unless it is governed by substitution inferences, which requires token recurrence: no (semantically significant) *occurrence* without (the possibility of) *recurrence*. (*Ibid*.: 465)

Notice that this parallels the claim at the sentential level that one cannot have a discursive practice consisting of just non-inferential observational reports, such as the parrot's tokening of "This is red". The reason is that for such reports to be claims, and to have cognitive significance, they need to be able to be used in reasoning, as the premises and conclusions of inferences. Just as deictic mechanisms presuppose anaphoric ones, non-inferential reporting mechanisms presuppose inferential ones.

At the subsentential level, our heretical thought is that if someone has reliable differential responsive dispositions (RDRDs) to apply the term <gleeb> only in the presence of a particular object, say that rabbit, why not treat the tokening as an anaphoric initiator whose meaning is captured by the object to which it is applied? /Gleeb/ refers to that rabbit. Why not treat such sorting abilities as the practical mastery required for generating meaningful anaphoric initiators?[23]

In response, Brandom asks us to imagine someone who is presented with a machine that he is told is a gleeb tester; it lights up only in the presence of gleeb things (MIE: 122). Imagine, further, that having learned from the machine over time, he is now able to reliably respond differentially to gleebness, and to claim that "this is gleeb". In other words, he has developed RDRD abilities regarding gleebness. Furthermore, the machine establishes a kind of projectible standard, according to which things can be mislabelled as gleeb. Brandom's claim is that while the reliable sorter may be able to "know" what things are gleeb, unless he has mastery over some of the inferential involvements of the claim, he does not understand the claim, and is not treated by others as having such understanding. Having sorting abilities with regards the term "gleeb" allows one to label "gleeb" instances without having any mastery over what follows from applying such a label. In part, it is mastery over some of the circumstances and consequences of application of the term that turns "gleeb" from being a mere label that is applied to being a concept that is applied.[24] The point is not merely that we have been focusing on the wrong RDRDs, sorting abilities as opposed to inferring abilities. The point is, rather, that thinking should be thought of in terms of making a move within a linguistic practice that is recognized as such by other rational beings, and that a condition for being so recognized is having practical mastery over some of the inferential involvements of the claims made for that tokening to be the application of a concept and not just a label.[25]

Summary

We finally have in front of us all three tiers of Brandom's ISA approach to semantics, which fill in some of the details implicit in the inferentialist mantra that: "[semantic] contentfulness should be understood in terms of inferential articulation" (MIE: xiv).

In the top tier, described in Chapter 5, sentences are treated as having meaning in virtue of their inferential role, broadly conceived. In the second tier, subsentential expressions, such as singular terms and predicates, are treated as having meaning indirectly, in virtue of the significance that their occurrence has for the inferential role of the sentences in the top tier. The difference between these different subsentential types is captured by the difference in the substitutional commitments they are involved in. A necessary condition for a subsentential expression to be a singular term is that it is involved in at least some symmetric substitution inferences, whilst a necessary condition for a subsentential expression to be a predicate is that it is involved in at least some asymmetric substitution inferences.

In the bottom tier, actual tokenings, type-recurrent expressions (such as proper names) or unrepeatable tokenings (such as deictic expressions) are treated as forming parts of anaphoric chains, which can then be treated as having an indirect meaning in virtue of the substitutional inferences they enter into in the second tier. The difference between such repeatable and unrepeatable tokenings is captured by the different types of recurrence chains they are involved in. The former enter into substitutional inferences as a result of forming (lexically cotypical) repeatable tokenings, whilst the latter enter into substitutional inferences as a result of anaphoric chains of unrepeatable tokenings.

In the introduction to Part II, Brandom's inferentialism was portrayed as involving a three-staged explanatory strategy. The first stage (B1) delivers an account of a linguistic practice. The second stage (B2) uses this account to explain the semantic content of linguistic items caught up in this practice. The third stage (B3) uses this inferentialist account of semantic content to explain the representational dimension of semantic content. Our discussion in Chapters 5 and 6 has attempted to outline stage (B2), against the background of (B1) discussed in Chapters 1–4. In Chapters 7 and 8, we shall consider Brandom's attempt to explain the representational dimension of semantic content (B3) in light of the discussion thus far. A central Brandomian thesis regarding (B3) is "that the representational dimension of thought is conferred on talk by the social dimension of the practice of giving and asking for reason" (MIE: 496). We begin the discussion of (B3) in Chapter 7, therefore, by considering this social aspect, concentrating on a puzzle facing an inferentialist account of communication.

Chapter 7

Communication

Introduction

A common challenge facing the family of views that think of semantic content in terms of inferential role stems from their seeming failure to allow for the possibility of communication between conversational partners.[1] The challenge is particularly strong for Brandom's version, since he openly endorses those features of inferentialism that are taken to lead to the problem, and he eschews most of the moves that have been suggested as ways of solving it.

Here is a preliminary statement of the problem, using only commitments explicitly undertaken by Brandom. On the one hand, understanding the claim of another involves "tracing out" the inferential significance of the claim made.[2] As a result, a claim made by one may become available to be used by another as a premise in her own reasoning. On the other hand, the inferential significance of a claim depends on those auxiliary hypotheses that are available to serve as collateral premises. Different speakers will have different sets of collateral commitments. Therefore,

> [a]s long as there are differences in the collateral set of commitments with respect to which the content of the claim expressed by a sentence needs to be assessed, the sentence in one mouth means something different from what that same sentence means in another mouth. (MIE: 510)

Together, these claims give rise to a problem of communication;

participants in a linguistic practice cannot communicate with or understand each other, as they each associate a different inferential role with the sentences tokened. The thrust of the problem is that the relativity of inferential significance to auxiliary hypotheses, and the fact that such hypotheses will differ among participants in a practice, seems to preclude any interaction between the alteration of scores associated with different players.

This chapter considers Brandom's attempt to solve this problem of communication by looking more closely at the idea of interperspectival navigation that forms the centrepiece of the approach to sapience pursued here. First, we note some alternative responses to the problem. Next, we outline Brandom's response, and compare this with the alternative responses noted. Finally, we consider two challenges to Brandom's response: that it undermines the practice of holding claims to objective assessments of correctness, and that it invokes an untenable, objectivist conception of communication.

Roads not taken

Before considering his solution to the problem of communication, it is worth travelling briefly down some of the more commonly trodden roads not taken by Brandom.[3] An obvious reason for this excursus is that it provides some points of comparison that motivate treating the Brandomian route as having perhaps the better claim. A less obvious reason is that the alternative route taken by Brandom runs pretty close by these more familiar ones, thereby allowing glimpses of familiar terrain from unfamiliar angles.

Similarity of meaning

Road not taken number one involves a retreat from identical meaning to *similarity of meaning*. The idea here is that whilst the inferential significance of the claim may differ between participants, there is sufficient overlap of meaning to facilitate communication and understanding between them. To adopt one of Brandom's examples, although Rutherford's use of the term "electron" is very different from mine, I can nonetheless understand his remarks, as there are enough collateral commitments that we share to facilitate communication, understanding and disagreement (MIE: 480–81). We share, for example, some of the inferential consequences of application of the term (perhaps those that can be made explicit by conditionals such as: "if this is an electron then this is negatively charged and a subatomic particle and . . ."), and some of the language entry and exit moves. Just how much overlap is sufficient to facilitate communication is not at issue. The point of the response is to claim that some level of similarity suffices to facilitate communication between interlocutors, despite the relativity of inferential significance to auxiliary hypotheses which differ between participants in a practice.

The problem with this rejoinder is not only that it is question-begging: to assume that Rutherford and I share the commitment that electrons are subatomic particles, for example, despite other differences, presupposes the very notion of a shared commitment that it is supposed to explain.[4] More critically, it ignores the point that concepts such as "subatomic" and "particle" themselves have a different inferential role coming from my mouth than they do coming from Rutherford's.[5] The problem of communication is not merely that the relativity of inferential significance to auxiliary hypotheses leads to non-identical meanings between interlocutors, but that there seems to be no shared semantic content whatsoever.

Retreat to extension

Road not taken number two involves a *retreat to extension*. The basic idea is that while Rutherford and I may differ in our collateral commitments when we claim that the electron is a subatomic particle, we are still both speaking about the same thing: electrons. In retreating to the extensional, we focus solely on what it is that what we are talking *about* – in the case of a singular term, the object we are referring to (assuming it so refers). It is the fact that we are both referring to the same thing that secures understanding and communication. Inferential significance of a claim may differ from interlocutor to interlocutor for the holistic reasons noted above, but this is irrelevant to communication, since the ^s^semantic^s^ feature relevant to communication and understanding is extension.

Reference and extension are normally seen to invoke "vertical" relations between mind and world that are the hallmark of the representational approach to semantic matters. For the inferentialist to turn to an extensional semantics for central contexts such as communication and understanding may seem closer to surrender than retreat. An inferentialist who wishes to adopt the "retreat to extension" strategy in response to the problem of communication has to show both how to incorporate a referential dimension to semantics within an inferentialist framework, and to demonstrate that the holistic nature of that framework still permits referent-sharing. Merely invoking a retreat to reference alone cannot suffice as an inferentialist response to the problem.

Content as function

Road not taken number three involves treating *inferential content as a function* that takes collateral commitments as arguments, and yields inferential significance as value (MIE: 482). (The idea of a function is simply illustrated by appeal to garden-variety mathematical manoeuvres, such as the multiplication function that takes certain integers as input, and yields an integer which is the product as output.) The idea is that this function is shared by interlocutors, and this facilitates communication between them despite different collateral commitments.

This solution of course implies that interlocutors in successful instances of communication do indeed share such a function. As Brandom points out, this implication seems implausible in certain cases. In comparing use of the concepts "electron", "mass" and "particle" by Rutherford, on the one hand, and contemporary physicists, on the other, Brandom plausibly contends that

> [i]t would require considerable argument to show that they had nonetheless used their expressions according to [functions] that left room for all our radical rethinkings, which could accordingly be represented just by differences in the context of assertional commitments with which each claim is conjoined. (MIE: 483)

Given the intuitive implausibility of such a claim, it is not possible for the inferentialist to simply assume that they all share the same function in such cases, in advance of substantive theorizing to explain how, appearances to the contrary, this is the case.

Inegalitarianism

Road not taken number four distinguishes between those inferences that are somehow meaning-constitutive (analytic), and those that are not (synthetic).[6] Once such an "inegalitarian attitude towards the different inferences a concept is involved in" (MIE: 634) is adopted, it is hoped that one can use the privileged inferences to secure the possibility of communication despite some differences in auxiliary hypotheses.

It has been suggested that such an inegalitarian path is not open to the inferentialist, since the very definition of analytic is "valid in virtue of meaning", and it would be circular to appeal to analyticity in giving an explanation of meaning.[7] This concern should not worry Brandom: he could deny that inferentialism is an attempt to give a reductive explanation of meaning, or distinguish those analytic inferences in terms that do not invoke meaning.

Brandom, however, does not opt for such an inegalitarian route. One reason for this is that linguistic practice fails to display the sharp boundaries between changes of meaning and changes of belief that such an analytic–synthetic distinction would predict.[8] Here is an example that will occupy us later (in Chapter 8): suppose one assumes that if something tastes sour it is an acid, and if something is an acid it turns litmus paper red. If one then comes across something that tastes sour and turns litmus paper blue, one has a problem and something needs to give. The relevant point for the moment is that whether the result is best thought of as a change of beliefs about acids or a change in what "acid" means is unclear. Here we have an example of the neo-pragmatist constraint on a theory of meaning doing some work: since the main point of semantic theory is to explain pragmatics, and the latter does not reveal the difference between performances that invoking an analytic–synthetic distinction as part of the semantic theory would lead us to expect, we should reject the analytic–synthetic distinction.

Even if one could somehow adopt such an inegalitarian attitude, Brandom provides reasons for thinking that this will not help solve the communication problem (MIE: 635). First, if it is to help with the problem of communication, even those inferences that are accorded preferential treatment for whatever reason have to be shared between interlocutors, and there is no reason to think that this will be the case. Secondly, even if we are able to privilege certain inferences, and are able to assume that these privileged inferences are shared between interlocutors, we still need to be able to account for the effect that non-privileged auxiliary hypotheses would have on the inferential significance of the privileged ones. This is because the semantic content associated with these privileged inferences will not suffice to determine when it is correct to make such claims, as this may depend on the inferential role of collateral commitments that stand as auxiliary hypotheses. In order to ensure that the privileged inferences play a role here, we have to assume that they are accompanied by formal inferences capturing, in the form of conditionals, all other material inferences. Brandom's inferentialism cannot tolerate such a possibility, as it would turn all materially good inferences into formally good ones (cf. Shapiro 2004: 152).

As a result, even if we could (a) stipulate some criterion that singles out certain inferences that an expression is involved in as central to the meaning of the term, this will only help facilitate communication if we also (b) assume that endorsement of these privileged inferences will not vary between perspectives, and (c) assume that these invariant inferences are supplemented with claims corresponding to all other materially good inferences. None of these options is straightforwardly open to Brandom without abandoning core aspects of his inferentialism.

Navigating between perspectives

Our presentation of Brandom's preferred route towards solving the problem of communication proceeds in two stages. In this section, we rethink what it means for interlocutors to share meaning in a conversation, moving from a Lockean conception implicit in the way that the challenge has been set up to a conception of communication as navigation between perspectives. In the next section, we consider in fine detail the scorekeeping required to navigate between perspectives.

On a Lockean conception, communication is thought of as the transmission of something, "meaning", from speaker to hearer, so that they both end up sharing it. The speaker's utterance should, in a successful instance of communication, produce in the hearer the same idea that the speaker had. The statement of the problem of communication at the outset of this chapter rests tacitly on just such a Lockean conception; it assumes that communication requires the sharing of something. The difficulty of the holism associated with inferential significance is that it undermines the possibility of ending up with something common and shared.

In contrast, Brandom thinks of understanding as the ability of the scorekeeper to navigate between the perspective of the interlocutor and her own. In a successful instance of communication, interlocutors are able to make use of each other's remarks in their own reasoning, both about what the other has reason to do and say, and what they themselves have reason to do and say. On this conception, understanding and communicating involve navigation and coordination between these two perspectives, and not sharing one meaning between interlocutors.

The difference between these two models of communication and understanding arises not from the idea of sharing something *per se*, but from the idea, accepted by the former and rejected by the latter, that each participant has something complete on their own, which, after a successful instance of communication, is repeated by others, so that they too have something complete on their own. Brandom illustrates the different conceptions of sharing with the following comparison:

> Conversational partners should not be pictured as marching in step, like soldiers on parade, but more as ballroom dancers, each making different movements (at any moment, one leads and the other follows, one moves forward and the other back, one sways left, the other right, and so on) and *thereby* sharing a dance that is constituted precisely by the coordination of their individually different movements. (FNNF: 363)

In the case of the soldiers, each individually is doing something which is then repeated by all of them. In the case of the ballroom dancers, nothing is repeated by each of them in this manner. What is shared is the dance, which *requires* each of them to do something *different*. The Lockean picture conceives of communication and understanding as sharing something in the former manner. On the Brandomian picture, in contrast, communication is more like a shared dance that requires participants to do different things in coordination with each other (cf. MIE: 479).

Conceptual or semantic content is "essentially perspectival" (MIE: 58); expressing semantic content is something that can only be done against a background of collateral commitments that form a point of view. These collateral commitments will differ between interlocutors. Conceptual content can, however, be shared in the non-Lockean sense, albeit specified in a different manner according to each perspective. Understanding the significance of a remark requires the practical skill to grasp such essentially perspectival contents. To do this the scorekeeper must be able to navigate between the perspectives.

Two styles of belief ascription

In the course of keeping score on gameplayer G, scorekeeper S attributes various normative statuses to G. In this section, we shall explore in detail some of the mechanisms used in such scorekeeping by looking at the ascriptional locutions required to make this explicit.

More specifically, we shall focus on the ascription of commitments, instances of what philosophers more commonly call "belief ascription". This gloss is somewhat awkward, as Brandom does "not officially believe in beliefs" (AR: 174), and tries to avoid using the term in setting out his system. One reason for this reluctance stems from the fact that talk of belief tends to equivocate between two different senses: an *empirical* sense in which one only believes what one would be sincerely disposed to avow; and a *normative* sense in which one believes the consequences of one's acknowledged beliefs, whether one is prepared to avow these or not.[9] To overcome such ambiguity, Brandom replaces talk of belief with talk of commitment; the difference between the empirical and the normative then depends on whether the commitments are acknowledged or not.[10] Whilst this may be his [s]official[s] position, he frequently strays into common parlance and uses the term "belief", resorting to the regimented terminology when there could be possible confusion. We shall follow him in this.

The act of ascribing a belief involves both attributing something and undertaking something. When S ascribes the belief that p to G (for example, by S saying explicitly that G believes that p), S both attributes a commitment to G, and undertakes a commitment herself. The commitment undertaken is not the same as the commitment that S would undertake were she to utter p herself. It is an expressive commitment. In ascribing a belief, the scorekeeper makes an ascription explicit by choosing a particular form of words, and so commits herself to a particular way of making such an ascription explicit.

There are three parts to an explicit formulation of a belief ascription: the first indicates the target of the ascription; the second indicates the type of commitment attributed; and the third indicates the content of the commitment attributed. If, for example, S states that "G claims that a is F", the target of the ascription is identified as G, the type of commitment is identified as that of claiming and the content of the commitment is identified, in this case that "a is F". In light of the dependence of inferential significance on those auxiliary hypotheses that are available to serve as collateral premises, there are two ways of specifying the content of the claim ascribed, depending on whether one considers the collateral commitments of the ascriber S, or the target of the ascription G. If the former, we have a *de re specification* of the content of the commitment; if the latter, we have a *de dicto specification* of the content of the commitment.[11]

It may seem strange to use the collateral commitments of S in specifying the content of the belief, as it is, after all, G's belief that the ascription is trying to capture. This concern ignores the distinction just drawn between the normative and empirical senses of belief. Assume, for example, that G believes that a is F. If S believes that a = b (i.e. S is committed to the substitutional inference made explicit by this identity claim), then in the normative sense of belief S can ascribe to G the belief that b is F, even if G explicitly denies this. If we are considering the ascription of beliefs in the normative sense, then we should draw on those collateral beliefs of S and not of G. If, however, we are considering the ascription of beliefs in the empirical sense, we should draw on G's, and not S's, collateral commitments. If G is disposed to disavow that a = b, then S should not ascribe to G the belief that b is F, irrespective of what S himself believes. Brandom is emphatic that these are not two different beliefs that are ascribed or two different belief contents, but two styles in which the content of a single belief can be ascribed by S (MIE: 503, 584).

An example will help clarify this. The secretary (G) calls the chair of the selection committee (S) to inform her that the first interviewee for the post has arrived. The words G utters into the telephone receiver are:

> U1 "Candidate number one is here."

S puts down the receiver and informs the other members of the committee that G says that the first interviewee has arrived. The words S utters in making that ascription are:

> U2 "G says that the first interviewee has arrived."

Here we have two token utterances (U1 and U2) made by two different interlocutors (G and S) at two different times (t1 and t2). The utterances stand in a relationship that Davidson calls "samesaying".[12] On Brandom's analysis of this relation, S's utterance U2 at t2 ascribes to G a commitment that she assumes G would acknowledge as an expression of his own commitment undertaken by the uttering of U1 at t1. A way of thinking about this samesaying relationship uses the notion of deferential potential. One of the things that a scorekeeper is able to do with the ability to make belief ascriptions is to make explicit deferrals of justificatory responsibility. In uttering U2, S is making explicit (to other members of the appointment committee, for example) that it is G who shoulders the epistemic responsibility for the claim that the first interviewee is here. When two claims are standing in a samesaying relationship, the scorekeeper takes it that if U2 were uttered, deferral to U1 would be appropriate.

U2 is an example of a *de dicto* style of belief ascription. The relationship of samesaying ensures that G would, according to S, be disposed to avow the belief ascribed in U2 herself. Let us continue the example to show how the same commitment can be attributed in the *de re* style.

The first interviewee is the committee's front-runner for the post. For once, confidentiality in the appointment process has been taken seriously, and G, who is not a member of the appointment committee, is unaware of this. While S is committed to the substitutional-inferential commitment that the first interviewee for the post is (=) the front-runner for the post, G would not endorse such a substitution. From S's perspective, G is committed to the claim that the front-runner for the post has arrived, even though he may not be disposed to assent to this. Suppose that following G's call, S tells the other committee members:

> U3 "G says that the front-runner for the post has arrived."

In this case, the relationship between the content ascribed in U3 at t2, and U1 at t1 is not that of samesaying, as G would not acknowledge the content ascribed in U3 as an expression of his own commitment undertaken by the uttering of U1 at t1. This ascription depends on S's own undertaking of a collateral commitment to the propriety of substituting "first interviewee for the post" with the "front-runner for the post".

Since the ascription of the belief to G made explicit in U3 draws on S's, and not G's, collateral commitments, it is a *de re* ascription. Its form does not, however, reveal it to be such. That is, unless one had knowledge of the beliefs of the various individuals involved in the conversation, one would not be able to distinguish a *de dicto* style ascription, such as U2, from a *de re* style attribution, such as U3. Brandom provides a three-step recipe for reformulating such a *de re* claim so that it wears its *de re* style on its sleeve. The raw ingredient is the *de dicto* style ascription

U2 "G says THAT *the first interviewee has arrived*"

where the content ascribed (*italicized*) falls completely within the scope of the THAT-operator. According to the recipe, one transforms this *de dicto* style ascription into a *de re* one by (i) exporting a singular term (or what is, according to S, a substitutional equivalent) from within the scope of the THAT-operator, (ii) prefacing it with "OF" and (iii) placing a pronoun in the original position of the singular term exported. The result of this transformation is:

U3 "G says OF **the front-runner** THAT *he has arrived*."

The result is a *de re* style ascription of the same belief, expressed in a manner that it is clearly a *de re* style ascription.

Clunky though such a reformulation may be, it makes clear who is responsible for what in the content ascribed. The italicized section, which falls within the scope of the THAT-operator, is the part of the content for which S treats G as responsible, in the sense of what he (G) would acknowledge being committed to. The bold section, which falls within the scope of the OF-operator, consists of the substitutional commitments undertaken by S. This is what S treats G as committed to, even though he (G) may not acknowledge such a commitment.

The case just considered is one in which a commitment is attributed to G by S, whilst responsibility for the way in which the content of the commitment is expressed is undertaken by S. The reverse is also possible: one can undertake a commitment while at the same time ascribing responsibility for the way in which the content is expressed to someone else. Continuing our example, suppose that R is a member of the interview committee who vehemently disagrees with S's assessment of the potential of the first interviewee for the post. When S announces that the front-runner for the post has arrived, R makes her disagreement public by saying:

U4 "^{s}the front runner for the post^{s} is a misogynist pig, and a deceitful one at that."

The ^{s}scare quotes^{s} allow R to make reference to the person for the purposes of joint conversation (and to add ironic effect) in a manner that overtly disavows responsibility for the expression used. U4 is clearly a claim that R is undertaking, although responsibility for the way part of it is expressed (the section within the scare quotes) is attributed to S.

It is worth making explicit the central role that anaphoric links are playing in this example. Suppose that, following S's utterance of U2, R wanted to make a *de dicto* belief ascription and say that

> U5 "S claims that the front-runner for the post has arrived."

This is awkward for R, as she does not take the person who has arrived to be the front-runner. R can nonetheless use scare quotes to express the claim in a *de dicto* style by saying

> U6 "S claims that ^{s}the front-runner for the post^{s} has arrived."

Here she is picking up the expression anaphorically (it refers to whoever S refers to as ^{s}the front-runner for the post^{s}), while at the same time refusing to undertake responsibility for this way of picking out the person referred to.

In one last extension of this example, suppose that in addition to disagreeing with S's assessment of the candidate, R also has information that G, the departmental secretary, has mistaken a passer-by who happened to enter his office for the first interviewee for the post who had been delayed in traffic on the way to the interview. In response to the chair's announcement that the front-runner for the post has arrived, R demurs by uttering

> U7 "He has not arrived, and he is not the front-runner for the post."

Despite the fact that R explicitly disagrees with everything S says about the candidate, she manages, through the use of the pronoun "he", to stipulate coreference with the anaphoric antecedent of S's expressions, whoever that antecedent is. Such anaphoric chains do not give the meaning of the expression in question. The meaning is given by the substitutional inferences entered into by the terms, which in this case are not shared by S and R. Nonetheless, the anaphoric relations between the terms mean that a scorekeeper will treat both claims as being *about* a common topic of conversation.

Alternative paths revisited

The previous section was a detailed detour through some of the technicalities involved in ascribing belief. Its aim was to formalize some of the expressive resources, especially the distinction between *de re* and *de dicto* styles of belief ascription, needed to bring Brandom's alternative path into view.

One important lesson learnt on the detour is that whenever conceptual content is made explicit in the form of an ascription, there will always be the possibility of two different styles in which such content can be expressed: *de dicto* and *de re*. This means that *any* contentful commitment can have its content specified differently, depending on whether the ascriber draws on those auxiliary commitments attributed to the speaker, or those undertaken herself. This can be thought of as a kind of double-book scorekeeping. An interlocutor maintains two scorebooks when ascribing a belief to another: one book that keeps score on the commitments undertaken by a speaker in light of the collateral commitments of the speaker, and one book that keeps score on the commitments undertaken by the speaker in light of the collateral commitments of the scorekeeper. Keeping track of the different inferential significances of the claim made relative to the different sets of collateral commitments, in a way that provides a kind of mapping from one to the other, is the practical recognition of the essentially perspectival character of conceptual content.

Understanding the significance of a remark requires the practical skill to grasp such essentially perspectival contents. When this skill is made explicit, it will make use of the kinds of locutions introduced in the preceding section, such as the difference between *de re* and *de dicto* ascriptions, the role of anaphoric and ascriptional indirect descriptions, and the use of scare quotes. This ability to express the contents of claims from these two points of view in the manner detailed in the previous section is the explicit version of the interlocutor's implicit ability to navigate between the two perspectives.

Brandom's account of communication as navigation between perspectives is a "three levelled approach", which moves from (i) inferential significance to (ii) extension to (iii) conceptual contents (MIE: 484–7, 635–6). The *inferential significance* of a claim varies from perspective to perspective. Using substitutional and anaphoric commitments, it is possible for a scorekeeper to move from the claim to what the claim is about, to the *extensional*. Following this, one can then introduce the notion of *conceptual content* as a way of systematically relating the different perspectives. These two moves, from inferential significance to extension and from extension to content, capture Brandom's solution to the communication problem in a manner that affords a helpful comparison with the alternative paths traversed above.

In keeping score, substitutional and anaphoric commitments can be used to group expressions into equivalence classes within and across perspectives. In our extended example, S takes it that the expressions "the front-runner for the post" and "the first interviewee" are intersubstitutable expressions. One could make this point by saying that these terms *co-refer*. There is, therefore, something correct about road not taken number three, as this is a kind of retreat to *extension*. In viewing this path from an inferentialist perspective, however, this retreat looks quite different. In particular, the notion of extension here is something that emerges *from* the social-perspectival dimension of scorekeeping, and is not available *prior to* such a dimension. One should not, for example, begin thinking about the extensional as an array of unlabelled objects waiting to be labelled by co-referring singular terms, so that the retreat to the extensional is a retreat to that antecedently grasped array of unlabelled objects. Rather, "[t]o be an object is to be something that can be referred to in different ways" (MIE: 424), as captured by the substitutional inferential significance of a term.

The account of communication does not stop with this retreat to the extensional. We also need to introduce the notion of *conceptual content* as a way of systematically relating the different perspectives.[13] As we have seen, such contents are essentially perspectival, and can be thought of as a kind of function from perspective to inferential significance. So there is something correct about road not taken number two: *content as function*. Conceptual content as a function from perspective to significance, however, is only shared between participants in the non-Lockean sense that both do something different that is grasping the essentially perspectival function. There is no shared content beyond this.

The upshot of our discussion of road not taken number one was to deny that interlocutors share anything whatsoever, if we limit this to the Lockean sense of sharing. It should be apparent by now that even if one accepts the relativity of inferential significance to auxiliary hypotheses, there are nevertheless things relevant to communication that are shared by interlocutors even in this Lockean sense. First, they are able to share non-semantic matters via anaphoric chains. By using a term as an interpersonal anaphoric dependent, the scorekeeper treats the token uttered as forming part of the same anaphoric chain as a token of the scorekeeper, whatever that is. This of course is not a shared meaning, but a rather shared recurrence structure; meaning will be given by the substitutional inferences the chain enters into, many of which will differ between interlocutors. What is shared via anaphoric commitments is, nonetheless, central to achieving communicative success. Secondly, and more importantly, what is shared by participants is the practice, which as Brandom notes "can retain its identity even though the functions implicit in it are different (at different times and from different doxastic points of view)" (MIE: 485). This involves sharing, in a non-Lockean sense, the ability to participate in the dance of discourse.

In sum, three of the four more commonly trodden paths for resolving the problem of communication – the retreat to extension, the notion of content as function and the idea of something be shared – all feature in Brandom's account, albeit in the unfamiliar context provided by double-book scorekeeping. The one path not taken by Brandom at all is probably the most popular: adopting an inegalitarian approach that treats some, but not all, appropriate inferences as meaning-constitutive.

Perspectives all the way down?

Does the essentially perspectival character of semantic content mean that it is a matter of perspectives all the way down? If it does, does this undermine our everyday practices involving claims that express such contents, according to which we subject these claims to objective assessments of correctness, in which "the correctness of an application of a concept answers to the facts about the object to which it is applied, in such a way that anyone (indeed *everyone*) in the linguistic community may be wrong about it" (MIE: xvii)?

The manner in which dual-book scorekeeping has been presented until now may have given the impression that we should answer both these questions in the affirmative. The account has made it seem as if there is some arbitrary choice to be made by the scorekeeper when ascribing a belief, in terms of which set of collateral commitments to draw on. A *de dicto* style attribution is the scorekeeper taking the gameplayer's perspective on the gameplayer's perspective, whilst a *de re* style ascription is the ascriber's perspective on the gameplayer's perspective. If it is perspectives all the way down, then the everyday practice of objective assessments of correctness of claims appears to be ill founded. Everybody has won, and all must have prizes.

One way of reconciling the account of dual-book scorekeeping with the everyday practice of objective assessment of claims is to postulate some privileged perspective, be it the perspective of the community or some idealized member of the community, possibly in idealized circumstances. Either way, the objective correctness of certain claims is seen as what is, or would be, endorsed by such an idealized perspective. In this manner, the tension between the essentially perspectival character of conceptual contents and the objective assessment of applications of conceptual contents is reconciled. It *is* perspectives all the way down, but one perspective is just better than all others. Conformity with this privileged perspective determines the winner who gets the prize.

This is *not* Brandom's path towards reconciling the everyday practices of objective assessment of claims with the essentially perspectival character of conceptual content. He wants to allow for the possibility that any and every perspective could be mistaken, and therefore will not endorse this idea of a global privileged perspective (cf. Brandom 1994). The Brandomian alternative

> is to reconstrue objectivity as consisting in a kind of perspectival *form*, rather than in a non-perspectival or cross-perspectival *content*. What is shared by all discursive perspectives is *that* there is a difference between what is objectively correct in the way of concept application and what is merely taken to be so, not *what* it is – the structure, not the content. (MIE: 600)

This is a *structural* construal of objectivity: objectivity is a structural feature of the essentially perspectival form of conceptual contents, as recognized in practice by each scorekeeping perspective. The remainder of this section aims to clarify this difficult idea.

As the normative notion of belief makes clear, there is always the possibility of a disparity between someone's actual normative status, including the commitments that one actually has, and the normative status that the person is prepared to avow. This disparity between self-attribution of normative status and actual normative status (the one "undertaken" whether or not it is self-attributed) stems from the fact that there are ways of being committed to p without actually avowing it. For example, the commitment may be undertaken consequentially, as a consequence of a commitment that one has avowed.[14] Indeed, one can be so committed consequentially even if one is prepared to disavow such a consequence.

In the first-personal case, whilst one can acknowledge the structural possibility of such a disparity between actual normative status and self-attributed normative status, one cannot go beyond that in articulating the content of such a disparity. That is, I can acknowledge that my actual commitments may differ from those commitments I attribute to myself, but I cannot say what this difference is. In the third-personal case, the scorekeeper can not only acknowledge the structural possibility of a disparity between what the gameplayer is disposed to avow and what he is actually committed to; the scorekeeper can also make the content of this disparity explicit in the way in which beliefs are attributed.

That there are always two styles of belief attribution available to the scorekeeper is a reflection of this structural possibility. A particular attribution in the *de re* style articulates the content of this disparity. According to the scorekeeper, a *de dicto* style belief attribution reflects the content that the gameplayer treats himself to be undertaking in performing certain speech acts. For this reason, the scorekeeper will draw on the gameplayer's collateral commitments in ascribing the belief in the *de dicto* style. In contrast, a *de re* style attribution is the scorekeeper's articulation of what (she thinks) are the commitments that the gameplayer has actually undertaken. For this reason, the scorekeeper will draw on what (she thinks) actually does follow on from what, i.e. her own collateral commitments. Here, in the third-personal case, not only is the possibility of a disparity between self-attributed normative status and actual normative status acknowledged; the attribution specifies the content of this disparity (from the scorekeeper's point of view).

The phrases in parentheses in the previous three sentences, relativizing the *de re* claims made to the perspective of the scorekeeper, are critical. Although the scorekeeper will accede that these parenthetical qualifications could be added, this is not how matters actually look to her. In making a *de re* attribution, she does not take herself to be merely reflecting one possible perspective out of many, but is expressing what she takes to be the case. The choice between a *de re* and a *de dicto* attribution may seem to us, reading these sentences, as an arbitrary choice between two perspectives. This, however, is not how matters seem to the scorekeeper.

The formal possibility that such parentheses could always be added is the scorekeeper's acknowledgement that no perspective, including her own, is *globally* privileged. That this is not how she treats this specific attribution is an acknowledgement of a *local* privilege with regard to acts of scorekeeping. Since there is no global privilege,

> [s]orting out who should be counted as correct, whose claims and applications of concepts should be treated as authoritative, is a messy retail business of assessing the comparative authority of competing evidential and inferential claims. Such authority as precipitates out of this process derives from what various interlocutors say rather than from who says it; no perspective is authoritative as such. There is only the actual practice of sorting out who has the better reasons in particular cases. (MIE: 601)

This is just what is meant by I–Thou scorekeeping: every perspective is privileged locally, but none is privileged globally.[15]

Objectivity and autonomy

One may, with a good deal of justification, harbour various worries regarding this construal of objectivity as "a structural aspect of the social-perspectival form of conceptual contents" (MIE: 597). There are three broad areas of concern. The first is whether this construal yields anything like a recognizable notion of objectivity. The second is whether this construal can accommodate commitment to what Brandom calls the autonomy thesis, the claim that "one is bound only to what one acknowledges that one is bound" (TOMD: 219). The third is whether there is more to objectivity than Brandom's account, even if successful, delivers. This last concern is a question best left to Chapter 8, considered in the context of an extended discussion of the threat of linguistic idealism. We shall briefly consider the first two here.

> *Does this structural construal capture an aspect of what we normally mean by the objective assessment of claims?*

One reason that such a worry is hard to assess stems from the notorious ambiguity of this "recognizable" notion of objectivity, reflection upon which has led some to contend that there is no overall concept in play but rather various different conceptions that do not fit neatly together.[16] As a result, rather than answer the question directly, let us highlight a common approach to questions of ontology, rejected by Brandom, which may underpin worries of this kind.

This common approach treats ontological questions as conceptually independent of, and to be addressed prior to, any consideration of the social practices of making claims. When addressing the notion of objectivity, this approach begins with an attempt to delineate the kinds of things that are objectively real (possibly in different grades of reality). As a result, a social practice of making claims is objective when the claims made in the practice are about such objective kinds of things. Brandom's approach to ontology reverses such an order of consideration. For him, all questions of ontology are questions about the authority structure implicit in the social practice of claiming. For example, the ontological category of the social can be identified with the category of things that members of the community are indefeasibly authoritative about in their claimings. In our case, the category of the objective is identified with those matters regarding which the pronouncements of no individual member of the linguistic community is indefeasibly authoritative.

Brandom's commitment to this social approach to ontology stems from an assumption that he takes as a (the?) lesson of the Enlightenment, to the effect that any matter of "authority or privilege – even the sort of authority exercised on what we say by what we talk about – is ultimately intelligible only in terms of social practices that involve implicitly recognizing or acknowledging such authority" (VP: 159). In this spirit, he endorses the slogan, due to John Haugeland, that "all transcendental constitution is social institution".[17] This, as Brandom himself describes it, is a pregnant remark, requiring much interpretation (TOMD: 370). For our purposes, one needs only to read this as a reciprocal sense-dependence, and not reference-dependence, claim. In other words, it is a claim that our grasp on the ontological category of the social or the objective cannot be separated from our grasp of the normative structure of social practice. It need not be read here as a claim to the effect that all transcendental institution is brought into being by an act of social institution.[18]

Given this social approach to questions of ontology, Brandom thinks that he will have succeeded in delivering an adequate account of objectivity when he is able to describe the structural features of a very peculiar social practice in which each member of the practice, at the local level, recognizes the possibility that each and every member of that practice, including themselves, could be wrong. That is, the practice is such that each member of the practice withholds authority from those they recognize as fellow participants, including themselves, on at least some topics, topics in which no pronouncement within the practice is indefeasibly authoritative. In so doing, participants grant authority over certain topics to what, in virtue of that very authority structure, counts as what they are talking about. Brandom claims to have proven that his model of linguistic practice has this structure and thus incorporates the category of the objective.[19]

> *Does this structural construal of objectivity stand in tension with the Enlightenment ideal of autonomy that Brandom endorses?*

The classic example of this Enlightenment ideal is the case of political authority; genuine (read: legitimate) political authority over an individual is derived from its acknowledgement by a subject over whom it is exercised. Generalizing from this, the ideal is that any legitimate normative authority, even the rational constraint exercised by what thoughts are about over acts of thinking, is only so by the authority that is acknowledged by a subject over whom that authority is exercised.[20] Once again, the acknowledgement of the subject need not be understood in a constitutive vein; it is enough, for our purposes here, if such self-endorsement is treated as a necessary, though not sufficient, condition for the legitimate imposition of the relevant norms. If, following this ideal, one is legitimately bound only to what one acknowledges as being bound to, this does seem to stand in some tension with the account of objectivity just provided. As our discussion of *de re* attributions of commitments made clear, an individual gameplayer can be committed to claims even if he were to explicitly disavow this.

Brandom attempts to resolve this tension by drawing on the model of mutual recognition in the context of his I–Thou sociality. The idea behind the solution is a social division of labour: it is up to me whether I am committed to the norm, but the content of the norm to which I am thereby committed is not up to me. The content of the norm to which I am bound is administered by others that I recognize to so administer. It is these others, via their scorekeeping performances, who hold me to my commitments and thereby administer such norms. For example,

> I get to decide which piece in the game I will play – say, the one labelled "That metal is molybdenum" . . . – but I do not then get

> to decide *what* I have committed myself to thereby, what further moves are appropriate or obligatory for one who has played that piece. My authority is real, but it is partial. And the same can be said of the others who play the game with me and simultaneously referee it. For they have no authority over my acknowledging of commitments. (TOMD: 221)

An individual is able to bind herself by linguistic norms because she enters into an up-and-running linguistic practice that is maintained and administered by the attitudes of others she recognizes to so administer, perhaps metallurgical experts in this case. These others treat her as bound by those norms in virtue of her decision to play that linguistic counter.

According to this social division of labour, the content of a norm does not swing free from the recognizing performances of those bound by the norm, where the performers include *both* gameplayer and scorekeeper bound together in a relationship of reciprocal recognition. It does, however, swing free from the recognizing performances of the individual bound. Whether this retains the main insight of the autonomy thesis is a difficult question. A motivation for the thesis is the removal of the threat of coercion by, and alienation from, the rational norms to which one is bound in any instance of legitimate normative authority. The standard model of individual autonomy, whose basic unit of account is the individual, tries to achieve this by highlighting the free act of undertaking a commitment by that individual. The model of mutual recognition, whose basic unit of account is the I–Thou pairing of scorekeeper and gameplayer, cannot follow the standard model in this, as the undertaking of a commitment is not something that an individual can achieve on her own. The gameplayer's contribution to the division of labour is her autonomous decision which piece to play in the game. This cannot be glossed by saying that this is her autonomous decision to undertake a commitment. To undertake a commitment for Brandom is to do something that makes it appropriate for others to attribute that commitment to the individual. This is something that an individual cannot do alone, however much she wills it, or however elaborate her own performances. If so, the model of mutual recognition cannot point to an individual's free decision to make a move in the game as a way of overcoming fears of coercion by, and alienation from, rational norms.

Any account of normative authority based on the notion of a social practice is susceptible to the charge that individual autonomy is sacrificed on the altar of the social group. It is by stressing the mutuality of recognition involved in an I–Thou conception of the social that Brandom hopes to appease the Enlightenment gods. Brandom sometimes attempts to bolster this strategy of appeasement by pointing to the positive freedom gained from being constrained by linguistic norms.

> Subjecting oneself to linguistic norms . . . is undeniably a form of constraint. It involves the surrender of what Isaiah Berlin calls negative freedom – that is, freedom *from* constraint . . . But since it also enables one to make and understand an indefinite number of novel claims, formulate an indefinite number of novel concepts, frame an indefinite number of novel purposes, and so on, subjecting oneself to constraint by the norms implicit in a vocabulary at the same time confers unparalleled positive freedom – that is, freedom *to* do things one could not only not do before, but could not even want to do. As Sellars says: "Clearly human beings could dispense with all discourse, though only at the expense of having nothing to say". (VP: 177–8)[21]

This is a form of a cost–benefit analysis: the cost of being bound (reduction in negative freedom) is vastly outweighed by its benefits (increase in positive freedom), the freedom to entertain an infinite number of new thoughts and ideas. (As the Sellarsian quotation highlights, this is not a cost–benefit analysis that one could be in a position to undertake prior to constraint by linguistic norms; this is a retrospective justification for accepting the costs of being bound by rational norms, made at a later time from within an up-and-running discursive practice.) Even if one concurs with this analysis, it will only appease if it can be shown that the reduction in negative freedom does not come at the expense of coercion and alienation of the individual involved. Whether the model of mutual recognition achieves this is far from settled.[22]

Given the centrality of this issue to Brandom's project, such an open-ended conclusion is frustrating. The twin demands of objectivity and autonomy require him to perform an extremely tricky juggling act, ensuring that the individual is at once genuinely bound beyond that which she endorses, while, at the same time, leaving room for the recognition of the authority of such a bind. Adjudicating his success in so doing requires a clear statement and defence of the autonomy thesis and its relationship with the model of mutual recognition. This is something that Brandom has not provided thus far with anything approaching the rigour characterizing other areas of his work.[23]

An objectivist conception of communication?

Let us turn from concerns arising from matters pertaining to objectivity to a concern regarding the account of communication as a double-book scorekeeping process. It is not too hard to motivate the suspicion that this account omits something central to the communicative process. Whilst the scorekeeper does not stand outside the practice upon which she is keeping score, there is a sense that she remains a voyeur on a process rather than an active participant in a two-way conversation. This suspicion is not ameliorated by noting that the scorekeeper is herself a gameplayer: two one-way ˢconversationsˢ between the same pair of interlocutors is not the same as one two-way conversation between them.

In the course of an extended discussion of Brandom's work, Jürgen Habermas criticizes Brandom's account along these lines. He argues that Brandom's scorekeeping conception of communication involves an overly "objectivist conception of communication" (Habermas 2000: 332) that ignores the second-personal relation central to such communicative interactions. In this final section of the chapter, we distinguish between two versions of this "objectivist" challenge that differ in the notion of the second-person utilized: the first draws on the notion of a second-personal act as *targeted*; the second as *addressed*. It will emerge that, although Habermas's challenge focuses upon the notion of targeting, it is the notion of address that raises the more interesting challenge to Brandom's account of communication.

Habermas frames his critique around a distinction between the relation that obtains between speaker and *listener* (a third-personal relation), and the relation that obtains between speaker and *hearer* (a second-personal relation). He illustrates this distinction by referring to an example in MIE that involves a courtroom exchange between prosecutor and defence attorney. Habermas comments:

> [c]ertainly, in the courtroom the judges hearing the case and the jurors listening to it are the ones who in a sense are keeping

> account of the progress of the discussion and forming a judgement as to who is scoring what points in order to be able to say in the end, for example, how the statement of the controversial witness is to be assessed. During the dispute, however, a reaction is required not from the listeners but from the parties directly involved who address utterances to one another and who expect each other to take positions. (Habermas 2000: 345)

Three distinct aspects combine to form Habermas's conception of the second-personal relation of hearing between interlocutors. First, he makes this distinction between listening (of judge and jury) and hearing (of prosecutor and defence attorneys) in terms of the expectations of the participants in the communicative interchange. Secondly, as a result of these expectations, the speech act targets a specific audience, the hearer(s), in a way that is different from anyone else overhearing ("listening to") the performance. Thirdly, the expectation draws the hearers into a critical, interactive dialogue with the speaker, which provides the joint social integration between communicants that according to Habermas is the main aim of communicative interaction.

As Habermas sees matters, Brandom's account of communication fails because the scorekeeper in a Brandomian communicative exchange is cast in the role of listener, and not hearer. The account, complains Habermas,

> identifies the interpreter with a public that assesses the utterance of a speaker – and not with an addressee who is expected to give *the speaker an answer*. Every round of new discourse opens with an ascription that the interpreter undertakes from the observer's perspective of a *third* person.
> (Habermas 2000: 345, italics in original)

Such a third-personal conception misses the very purpose of communication: to achieve mutual understanding between first- and second-personal interlocutors (*ibid.*: 346). Brandom, in response, accepts this objectivist reading as a "fair characterization" of his account of communication, but rejects the implication that such an omission is problematic in the way Habermas implies. The challenge is based on a claim about the point of linguistic practice; Brandom, in turn, simply denies that linguistic practice can be said to have a point at all: "It does not as a whole have an aim or a goal", even though "it may fulfil various functions". The reason is that one of the functions of discursive practice is to "transform the very concept of an end or a goal" so that nothing can "intelligibly be taken to be its point, aim or end" (FNNF: 365–6).

Brandom's dismissal of Habermas's challenge is too quick here, moving straight from a rejection of Habermas's way of making the distinction between listener and hearer to a rejection of the distinction as relevant *per se*. As noted above, the claim that the distinction between listener and hearer has relevance for an account of communication such as Brandom's is one with strong intuitive appeal. Whilst there are features of Habermas's way of making the distinction that preclude Brandom's straight acceptance, there are other ways of making the distinction that could be incorporated into Brandom's account.

Two aspects of Habermas's way of making the distinction already highlighted mandate Brandom's perfunctory dismissal. The first is Habermas's reliance on the expectations of the participants to ground the distinction between hearer and listener. Brandom makes nothing of the role of such attitudes in accounting for speech acts, preferring to root matters in a structural account of the speech act that specifies the idealized function of that speech act as it would feature in a linguistic practice. This is done by describing, in structural terms (i.e. in terms of its authority and responsibility structure), the ideal outcome of a successful instance of the act in the context of its performance in an up-and-running instance of such a practice. Lesson one: if talk of the second-personal relation is to speak to Brandom, it must be made in terms of the structural role of a second-personal speech act.

The second aspect that mandates dismissal is Habermas's reliance on the notion of targeting in formulating the idea of the second-personal. Put in structural terms, to say that a speech act is second-personally *targeted* is to say that the ideal structural outcome of a performance of the act is limited to altering the normative statuses associated with one (or a particular group of) gameplayer(s). This is not to say that others outside of the target audience cannot learn from, or keep score upon, the speech act. There is, however, a difference between the ideal effect of the act on the target group and any effect on those overhearing the speech act. Any act for which an account of the act leads to this hearer–overhearer distinction is a targeted act in this sense.[24] The primary speech act in a Brandomian linguistic practice is the speech act of asserting. He is clear that asserting is not a targeted speech act: it gives rise to no distinction between hearer and overhearer of the act (cf. MIE: 186). Lesson two: the centrality of asserting ensures that for talk of the second-personal relation to speak to Brandom, it must be developed in a way that does not require the speech act in question to be targeted.

Let us contrast this notion of targeting with the notion of address. To say a speech act is second-personally *addressed* is to say that the reciprocal act of acknowledgement of the address by the audience is an essential part of the act that it is. This act of acknowledgement need not take the form of a conscious thought or judgement by the addressee, to the effect that "I have been addressed by you in this manner and hereby respond appropriately". It can, for example, take the form of the addressee undertaking performances appropriate to her new normative status on the authority of the original addresser, to whom she will defer if challenged about its appropriateness.

An act can be targeted but not addressed, and addressed but not targeted. (It could, of course, be both or neither as well.) Some may find it peculiar to talk of an untargeted though addressed act as involved in a second-personal relation between addresser and addressee, since it makes nothing of relations of intimacy, or acquaintance, or awareness, or face-to-face interaction that are often taken as essential to this relation. Whether this is a peculiar usage or not, the normative nexus forged between addresser and addressee as the result of a successful instance of the act is significant. By performing the act I address you, calling on you, among other things, to recognize the address in your subsequent doings. Your recognition of the address in your subsequent doings is an intrinsic part of the act that it is, binding us together in this instance in a normatively significant I–Thou relation. As a result, the addressee, once bound, cannot *ignore* the address; she can only *reject* it.[25] That is, if she has recognized the address, but fails to respond appropriately, she is not passively ignoring the address, but is actively refusing it. The hallmark of a second-personally addressed speech act is that once it is recognized as the act that it is, it cannot be ignored.[26]

Brandom is clear that asserting is not a targeted act. He is not explicit as to whether asserting is an addressed act. There does not seem to be any principled problem for Brandom to incorporate such a second-personal address into his account of asserting, thereby delivering a positive account of the I–Thou terminology used to describe the relationship between gameplayer and scorekeeper in MIE.[27] Furthermore, so doing would provide much of that intuitive sense of reciprocal interaction, of hearing and not just listening, that seems missing in an account of communication that excludes the notion of address. Brandom, nonetheless, says nothing explicit about the role of second-personal address in his account of asserting. More than that, the language used in talking about asserting tends to invoke terms more suited to a non-addressed act. For example, asserting is described as placing a claim in "public arena . . . available for others to use in making further assertions" (MIE: 170), or that "assertions are fundamentally fodder for inferences" (*ibid.*: 168). This is a shame, as it is not difficult to incorporate the feature of address into an account of Brandomian speech acts including asserting, and because so doing would help allay the intuitive suspicion that Brandom's conception of communication is overly objective.[28]

Nowhere does Brandom promise to provide a full account of communication between interlocutors, let alone one that captures those features central to our own linguistic interactions. A proper challenge to Brandom's objectivist account of communication would have to demonstrate that his model of linguistic practice requires that at least some speech acts in the practice are second-personally addressed. Our discussion here, based on intuitive suspicions grounded in our communicative interactions, falls short of that. The suggestion here is best treated as a kind of pre-emptive defence, by showing that Brandom need not endorse all aspects of the objectivist account of communication that Habermas depicts.

Summary

Communication between interlocutors is typically taken as a challenge to Brandom's inferentialism, since the holism of the latter seems to preclude the possibility of achieving the former. By looking at the ascriptional locutions required to make double-book scorekeeping explicit, we have outlined a model of communication that overcomes this challenge. The key is to stop thinking of communication as the transmission of something ("meaning") that is shared by interlocutors. Communication for Brandom is rather thought of as the practical ability to navigate between perspectives. Such navigation involves a kind of double-book scorekeeping, whereby a scorekeeper is able to substitute the claim found in an interlocutor's scorebook for a claim in her own, even though the inferential significance of the claim will differ as it features in each of these scorebooks. In navigating between perspectives, a scorekeeper can, by attributing and undertaking various anaphoric and substitutional commitments, move from the inferential significance of a claim relative to a gameplayer's collateral commitments to a kind of extensional content that eventually allows the claim to enter her own scorebook.

At the heart of this account of communication is the I–Thou relationship between gameplayer and scorekeeper that occupies pride of place in Brandom's system. We raised two challenges regarding this relationship. The first can be thought of as worrying about the I side of the relation: does the Brandomian contention that an individual can be bound beyond that which she endorses undermine the autonomy of that individual? The second can be thought of as worrying about the Thou side of the relation: does the untargeted nature of the speech act of asserting condemn the scorekeeper to playing the third-personal role of hearer rather than second-personal role of listener? We have tentatively considered ways in which Brandom could return a negative response to both these questions.

Our interest in detailing Brandom's response to the challenge that communication poses to an inferentialist semantics is derived from the broader task set for Part II of this book: exploring the way in which Brandom's inferential role semantics can incorporate the representational dimension of discourse. Brandom tells us that the representational dimension (B3) emerges from considering semantic content (B2) in the context of the social dimension of the practice of giving and asking for reasons (B1). The discussion of communication in this chapter has brought this social dimension to the fore. Chapter 8 considers whether Brandom is successful in explaining the representational dimension of discourse from the explanatory raw materials assembled here.

Chapter 8

ˢLosing the worldˢ?

Introduction

The headline "Card-Carrying Pragmatist Rejects Representationalist Totalitarianism"[1] is unlikely to generate much surprise in a philosophically aware audience. Ever since Dewey, the rejection of a representationalist conception of the function of language, and its influence into other areas (including the conception of philosophy itself), has been taken to be the hallmark of the pragmatist tradition.[2]

It should come as no surprise, therefore, that Brandom portrays his inferentialist approach to semantics in contrast "to the representationalist idiom for thinking and talking about thinking that has been so well worked out over the last three centuries" (MIE: xxii). His first published paper opens by contrasting two opposing schools within the philosophy of language. The first school assumes that "the central feature of language is its capacity to represent the way things are"; the second assumes that "language is best thought of as a set of social practices", so that "to understand how language works, we must attend to the uses to which sentences are put and the circumstances in which they are used" (Brandom 1976: 137). Brandom locates himself "squarely within the language-as-social-practice tradition" (*ibid.*: 146), in contrast to the representationalist orthodoxy.

What is surprising about Brandom's approach in this regard is not this rejection of representationalism, but rather how much of what are normally taken to be core features of the representationalist orthodoxy he is prepared to embrace. For example, he explicitly places accounting for the representational dimension of linguistic discourse as a key criterion that must be satisfied by his inferentialism. "The major explanatory challenge for inferentialists is . . . to explain the representational dimension of semantic content – to construe *referential* relations in terms of *inferential* ones" (MIE: xvi). The reason for such an explanatory challenge stems, we are told, from the centrality of a representational dimension to our thought and talk:

> [W]hatever is propositionally contentful does necessarily have such a representational aspect; nothing that did not would be recognizable as expressing a proposition . . . [T]here is no propositional (and hence no conceptual) content without this representational dimension. (MIE: 496, 497)

Brandom's project aspires to "turn the explanatory tables on the representationalist tradition" (*ibid.*: 136), by reconstructing the representational aspect of language from an approach that remains firmly within the language-as-social-practice tradition.

An attempt to "have it all" in this manner, to say "yes" to both the representationalist and language-as-social-practice camps, inevitably draws objections from both: one accuses Brandom of compromising too much; the other accuses him of conceding too little. Rorty, from the language-as-social-practice camp, worries that Brandom is "abandoning hard-won ground by making the notions of 'representation', 'fact' and 'making true' respectable . . . [M]y hunch is that Brandom . . . is trying too hard to find a compromise in an uncompromisable dispute, and so falls between two stools" (Rorty 1998: 132, 134).[3]

Fodor and Lepore, bad guys from the opposing camp, conclude their attempt to delineate "Brandom's Burdens" by stating that his inferentialist approach simply fails to take the referential dimension of discourse seriously:

> Brandom says of some of his main conclusions that they are "odd and marvelous." And indeed they would be if only they were true. As things stand, the relevant points against "inferentialism" are banal and obvious: You . . . can't abstract the notion of truth from the notion of inference . . . and truth is a symbol–world relation . . . Will anybody who finds any of this in the least surprising please raise his/her hand? (Fodor & Lepore 2001: 480)

In this final chapter, we consider whether a viable compromise position is possible, and explore the relationship between this question and the widely held suspicion, voiced in the title of this chapter, that Brandom's language-as-social-practice approach remains too firmly on "the word side of a word–world divide" (BSD VI: 3). We first argue that an important Brandomian claim mandates a strict cleavage between these issues, requiring us to explore questions surrounding the role of representations in the social practice tradition separately from suspicions of linguistic idealism. We then consider the expressive role played by the terms "is true" and "refers" as a way of evaluating his response to the former, and his account of empirical content as a way of evaluating his response to the latter.

Separating the questions

Considering whether there is a compromise position available between the language-as-social-practice and representationalist traditions requires, as a first stage, answering the following interpretive question regarding Brandom's aspirations.[4] In aligning himself with the language-as-social-practice tradition, Brandom is explicit in rejecting representationalist totalitarianism. But just what is he rejecting: the representational dimension or its totalitarian aspirations? If the former, then Brandom's inferentialist alternative should be seen as rejecting the claim that the notion of representation plays any non-trivial role in our thinking about thinking *in toto*. On this reading, Brandom's attempt to turn the tables on representationalism is best seen as an attempt to explain away representational locutions. If the latter, however, then Brandom's inferentialist alternative can countenance the explanatory value of positing representational relations, but they are not permitted to provide the overarching theoretical framework within which to consider language and thought. On this reading, Brandom's attempt to turn the tables on representationalism should be treated as aspiring to reconstruct representational relations from within an inferentialist framework.

In order to clarify this exegetical question, let us first ask why resolving it matters. This is no mere delaying tactic; it is required to rule out a common line of thinking that leads to a basic misunderstanding of the options between which the exegetical question requires us to choose.

According to this erroneous line of thought, answering this exegetical question matters in order to be able to rescue the social practice tradition from the contention that it "must inevitably [s]lose the world[s] – trading its solidity for a froth of words" (MIE: 331). This line of thought begins by distinguishing between horizontal relations between thoughts and thoughts, and vertical relations between thoughts and things. Inferential relations are horizontal, whilst representational relations are vertical. Unless Brandom can permit genuine representational relations from within his language-as-social-practice approach, there is no vertical connection between thought and thing, and the practice becomes little more than a "frictionless spinning in the void".[5] Brandom himself raises this very suspicion, conceding that inferentialism

> can make it look as though *all* that is in play is words and their use. If the *world* is left out of the story, what justification can there be for saying that *meaning* has not been? . . . Doesn't the story I have been telling remain too resolutely on the "word" side of the word/world divide? (BSD VI: 2)

According to this line of thought, the choice between treating inferentialism as rejecting representationalism *in toto*, or just its totalitarian aspirations, is portrayed as the choice between either accepting or rejecting the claim that the world somehow constrains our linguistic practice.

This, however, is resolutely *not* how the interpretive question is to be understood. This line of thought construes linguistic practices as standing on one side of a divide, with the world of facts and objects standing on the other, and representational relations crossing this chasm between word and world. We presented the inferentialist order of explanation in semantics as following three stages, beginning with an account of a discursive practice (B1), which is then extended to provide an account of the semantic content of linguistic items (B2) and which, in turn, is extended to provide an account of the representational dimension of semantic content (B3). In this order of explanation, and contrary to the line of thought just pursued, the first stage (B1) includes a model of an up-and-running discursive practice which is *already world-involving*.[6]

> Discursive practices incorporate actual things. They are solid [(even lumpy – MIE: 632)] – as one might say *corporeal*: they involve actual bodies, including both our own and others (an mate and inanimate) we have practical and empirical dealings with. They must not be thought of as hollow, waiting to be filled up by things. (MIE: 332)

Representational relations, introduced in (B3), are not required to bridge the chasm between linguistic practice and world. This is because (B1) is already world-involving, and therefore there is no gap to be bridged.

One question that will occupy us here is what (non-representational) resources are available for Brandom to explain the supposed solidity of linguistic practices in the first stage (B1). Let us call this "the solidity question". Once answered, one may begin to wonder why a third stage in our inferentialist account is needed at all. If the function of representational talk is not to draw the world into our linguistic practice, why should the language-as-social-practice tradition concern itself with incorporating such locutions?

Answering this is "the interpretive question" raised above. One suggestion is that the third stage tries to explain why, despite appearances to the contrary, our everyday use of representational locutions does not provide any explanatory insight into the link between claimings and what those claimings are about. That is, it aims to explain representational locutions away. Another suggestion is that such locutions do afford explanatory insight into the relation between claimings and what those claimings are about, even after we have rejected the picture whereby representational relations establish the link between practice and world. The interpretive question, therefore, concerns the third stage (B3) of the inferentialist account, and asks us to adjudicate between these two readings.

Having separated the interpretive question from the solidity question, we can now sketch the plan for this chapter in greater detail. In the next two sections, we shall consider the interpretive question. In the first, we outline Brandom's account of those locutions used to make the representational dimension of semantic content explicit, and draw on this account, in the second section, to complete stage (B3) of the inferentialist account. In the final two sections, we will consider the solidity question. In the first, we outline Brandom's account of empirical content as an optional extra to his account of linguistic practice in (B1), and in the final section we consider an influential critique of this account of empirical content.

Explanatory versus expressive deflationism

In line with the methodology pursued throughout Brandom's work, a good place to begin the discussion of the interpretive question is with the expressions used to make the representational dimension of linguistic discourse explicit. Brandom divides them into two groups.

The first are relatively technical expressions, such as "true" and "refers", that are used by the representationalist as the core semantic primitive. The second are relatively colloquial expressions, such as "of" and "about" (as used in sentences such as "She was talking of – or about – a misogynist pig and a deceitful one at that"), that are used in everyday discourse to say what or whom is being talked about or represented. Having discussed the latter group in Chapter 7, let us focus on the former, especially the "is true" locution.

A *proform* is a category of expressions that stands in for other expressions, where the relation between a proform and the antecedent it stands in for is the anaphoric link already introduced. Included in this category are *pronouns* that inherit their content from an expression that is their anaphoric antecedent, and *prosentences* that inherit their content from a sentence that is their anaphoric antecedent. Brandom treats "is true" as a *prosentence-forming operator*: one places a noun phrase specifying an anaphoric antecedent in the open space (. . .), to form a prosentence that is anaphorically dependent on that specified antecedent tokening. He similarly treats "refers" as a *pronoun-forming operator* that applies to an expression picking out a term tokening and produces a pronoun anaphorically dependent upon it. In both cases, the locutions allow a speaker to both *mention* another sentence tokening, and to *use* it.[7] Some examples will help to clarify this.

Imagine an irritating game played by a group of young schoolchildren obsessed with the term "ditto". A teacher going round the class with a question would receive one answer, followed by the word "ditto" repeated nineteen times by twenty highly amused students. Saying "ditto" in this case is not ascribing a property to something, but is a way of picking out another sentence as anaphoric antecedent (the sentence kicking off the chain), and using it (claiming it oneself). "Ditto", as used by these children, is a relatively limited term. One can pick up only an anaphoric antecedent that immediately preceded its utterance in time (along a chain), and the relationship between the antecedent and dependent tokening is little more than "cutting" a tokening from one context and "pasting" it on to another. Even in this simple case, however, saying "ditto" is more than just another way of making the same claim that the previous child made. The dependence relation has the effect of the second child expressing agreement with the first, thereby avoiding a form of "assertional plagiarism" (Beebe 2003: 3), although so doing is hardly their concern.

This "is true" locution functions in a similar manner to "ditto", although in a far less limited manner. Unlike "ditto", the antecedent of the prosentence formed using the "is true" locution can be picked out in a variety of ways, the content can be inherited in a variety of ways and the determination of meaning may require certain modifications that move beyond a cut-and-paste model.

Consider, for example, the role of the italicized expression containing the truth predicate in the following sentence.

> [1] David says that the student lied, and I believe that *it is true.*

Brandom treats the role of the italicized clause as functioning in the same manner as the italicized expression in the following sentence:

> [2] # A: Have you seen Borat yet? B: No, I have not seen *it*, and doubt I will. #

In [2], the italicized, anaphorically dependent tokening inherits its content from another tokening that is its anaphoric antecedent, in this case the name of a movie. In working out what sentence [2] means, one first needs to compute its anaphoric antecedent, and then determine the meaning of the sentence in light of this. In the same way, the italicized clause in [1] picks out a sentence that operates as its anaphoric antecedent, so that one can work out the sense of the anaphorically dependent statement in light of the meaning of its anaphoric antecedent.

Other cases are more complicated. Take the philosopher's standard example of a true sentence:

> [3] "Snow is white" is true.

Here, the truth operator is applied to a quoted sentence "Snow is white" to yield [3]. Brandom treats "'Snow is white'" as a quote-name for the sentence "Snow is white". In other words, [3] picks out its anaphoric antecedent by naming it. Once the anaphoric antecedent is worked out and the meaning of the resulting sentence is determined, it becomes obvious that [3] is equivalent to:

> [4] Snow is white.

Quoting is not the only way of picking out the anaphoric antecedent. Consider:

> [5] The standard example of a true sentence used within contemporary analytic philosophical discussions of truth is true.

Here the antecedent is picked out by describing it, rather than by quoting it. Either way, it is equivalent to [4].

The way in which the antecedent tokening has been picked out in these last two cases is more complex than the "ditto" case, as these cases use a range of linguistic resources (such as describing or quoting) to work out the relevant antecedent. Once the anaphoric antecedent has been identified, the semantic content of the prosentence needs to be computed. In the "ditto" case, this was easy: it is a simple matter of repetition, "cutting and pasting" the antecedent. There are many cases, however, in which this is not the case. Consider, for example,

> [6] # D: I have thoroughly defended that claim in the second chapter. J: That is true. #

Even once one has identified D's remark as the anaphoric antecedent of the prosentence, one cannot simply cut and paste the remark to give the prosentence's meaning, for J is not saying "I have thoroughly defended that claim in the second chapter". It is not hard to understand what kind of transformation is required to yield the meaning of the prosentence, especially in light of the discussion of indirect discourse in Chapter 7. The point here is that the second stage requires modifications and transformations easily overlooked in the "ditto" case.

Although in one sense the anaphoric mechanisms discussed in these examples (much as the "ditto" tokenings) are redundant, there is an important sense in which they are not. They are redundant in the sense that they fundamentally involve a form of repeatability: they make the content of one tokening dependent on its antecedent, so they permit a kind of repetition of the former. They are not redundant in the sense that adding these locutions to a language allows us to say things that we could not say without using these terms. In Brandomese, these locutions afford those who have mastered them significant additional expressive abilities.

Here is one of Brandom's examples that combines the discussion of truth locutions with belief ascription (the two groups of representational locutions), in a manner that demonstrates just how important the expressive role of such locutions are. Suppose A says:

> [7] Senator McCarthy believed OF **the first sentence of the Communist Manifesto** THAT *it was true*.

(Uttering a sentence in this regimented form in actual conversation is only likely among hard-core Brandom-philes. Other, less regimented

– though still representational – locutions that achieve a similar effect are available for ordinary folk.) If asked, Senator McCarthy would most probably have vehemently denied that he believed any sentence of the Communist Manifesto. Yet the first sentence of the Manifesto claims that "the spectre of communism is haunting Europe", undoubtedly something that McCarthy believed. In a *de dicto* style ascription one could say that:

> [8] Senator McCarthy believed that the spectre of communism is haunting Europe.

The *de re* style in [7] ascribes the same belief to the senator, but places the entire content within the scope of the OF operator, placing a sentence formed from "true" in the remainder. [7] and [8] ascribe the same belief to McCarthy, although the former does so in a manner that makes clear that this way of putting the belief ascribed is something that the person to whom it is ascribed would not endorse. Representational locutions, of both the technical and the colloquial varieties, are used here to move from *de dicto* to *de re* attributions. These attributions specify the content of a single belief from two different perspectives. The *de re* ascription made possible by representational locutions is A's expression of what it is that should be consulted to determine the truth or falsity of McCarthy's belief, and is essential if A is to use McCarthy's claim as a premise in her own reasoning.

A theorist who takes an attitude of *expressive deflationism* towards the "is true" and "refers" locutions contends that there is nothing we can say using these terms that we cannot say without them. Brandom rejects expressive deflationism with regard to these locutions.[8] Anaphoric and substitutional mechanisms are essential in facilitating interpersonal communication between interlocutors despite different collateral commitments that each holds, in allowing the introduction of unrepeatable tokenings into thought and talk and in allowing the transfer or deferral of justificatory responsibility essential to cases of direct and indirect discourse, as well as the transmission of knowledge. "True" and "refers", together with the terminology needed for *de re* and *de dicto* style belief ascriptions, make these complex double-book scorekeeping performances explicit in ways that further facilitate such aims.

A theorist who takes an attitude of *explanatory deflationism* towards the "is true" and "refers" locutions denies that these locutions can be appealed to in a semantic theory that aspires to explain what semantic contentfulness consists in. Explanatory deflationism comes in two varieties. A *local explanatory deflationist* denies that we can use the terms "true" or "refers" in explanations of the meaning of particular sentences or expressions. A *global explanatory deflationist* denies that a semantic theorist can appeal to an antecedently understood notion of truth or reference in an explanatory theory of the semantic contentfulness of sentences or expressions. Brandom endorses a global, but not a local, version of such explanatory deflationism.

Here is an example of a local explanation of meaning: I explain to someone the meaning of the concept "gleeb" by telling them that "an object is gleeb if only if it is red". Provided my interlocutor has mastery over the meaning of the claim on the right-hand side of this biconditional ("it is red"), she will have grasped something about the meaning of the claim on the left hand side ("an object is gleeb"). In more familiar philosophical parlance, one would say that I have explained the meaning of the term "gleeb" by providing the truth conditions of its application; that is, those conditions under which applying the concept in a claim is true. In other words, I could have explained the concept to her by saying something like: " 'that is gleeb' is true whenever 'that is red' is true". Our anaphoric account of truth has told us how to understand a statement of the form "is true", so that we can make sense of explanations of the meanings of terms in this manner. Brandom's prosentential account of truth and pronominal account of reference, therefore, give no reason for embracing local explanatory deflationism about such locutions: *we can use "true" and "refers" in local explanations of meaning.*

On the other hand, this account of truth and reference does motivate a global explanatory deflationary attitude towards truth and reference. One may be able to explain meaning by using truth conditions in the local sense just illustrated, but one cannot explain semantic content in general in terms of truth conditions and reference. To be able to explain semantic contentfulness using truth and reference as primitives requires the things doing the explaining (truth, reference) to be available prior to the thing being explained (semantic contentfulness). The account of truth and reference outlined here, however, is reliant on the account of anaphora which, in turn, is parasitic upon a prior conception of semantic contentfulness. Truth and reference cannot, therefore, be used in a global explanation of semantic contentfulness. In other words, Brandom's prosentential account of truth, and pronominal account of reference, mandates a global explanatory deflationism about such locutions.

The interpretive question

The interpretive question concerns stage (B3) of the inferentialist explanatory strategy, and asks whether Brandom aspires to explain representational locutions away or to accord representational locutions a non-trivial explanatory role in semantic theorizing. The discussion of the "is true" and "refers" locutions makes it clear that Brandom opts for the second of these. He contends that the language-as-social-practice theorist can make explanatory and expressive use of an array of representational locutions, provided they are treated as operating at the local level. In other words, Brandom rejects representationalist totalitarianism, the claim that we should accord explanatory primacy in semantics to the notion of representation at the global level, but he does not reject representationalism *tout court*.

Even claims that are standard representationalist fare, such as talk of "a claim representing how things are" or "facts making claims true", can have explanatory value at the local level. Introducing such talk at the local level "comes cheaply", as "it is not meant to have any explanatory value except what can be cashed out in terms of the social-perspectival articulation of our discursive practices" (FNNF: 361). The key to cashing out representational locutions in this manner is to focus on the speech act of asserting, because "we derive our practical grip on the notion of 'representing how things are' from our practical mastery of assertion: representing how things are is what we are doing when we make claims" (VP: 168).

In making an assertion to which one is entitled, the asserter licenses a scorekeeper to attribute further commitments with different contents to the asserter, as well as commitments with the same content to other interlocutors. A practice incorporating moves that have this structure of authority and responsibility is one in which there is an "implicit norm of commonality": a default assumption, operative in practice, that whatever is a good reason for one interlocutor to undertake a commitment is a good reason for another as well. This "presumption of heritability" of normative status ensures that participants in the practice implicitly share the assumption that "[W]henever two believers disagree, a diagnosis of error or ignorance is appropriate for at least one of them" (MIE: 240). In such a practice, "talk about belief as involving an implicit commitment to the Truth as One, the same for all believers, is a colourful way of talking about the role of testimony and challenge in the authority structure of doxastic commitment" (*ibid.*). On Brandom's account, representational talk, even talk of "a claim representing how things are", can be incorporated cheaply into a local explanation of linguistic practice, for it too is a colourful way of talking about the authority and responsibility structure implicit in the speech act of asserting.

It is not surprising that Brandom here makes claims that, as Rorty puts it, will make the non-representationalist's "hair stand on end" (Rorty 1998: 132). One of Rorty's examples is taken from MIE (331), where Brandom "cheerfully" says "[t]he non-linguistic facts could be largely what they are, even if our discursive practice were quite different (or absent entirely), for what claims are true does not depend on anyone's claiming of them". According to Rorty, the only reason for allowing representational vocabulary *any* explanatory role is bewitchment by a philosophical picture in which beliefs aspire to cut reality at nature's own joints, joints that are not relative to human needs and interests. If the language-as-social-practice tradition aspires to provide any alternative to the representationalist orthodoxy, claims Rorty, it lies in the rejection of that philosophical picture.

Brandom disagrees. As we saw in Chapter 6, Brandom contends that facts are true claimable contents, where such contents are what would be express*ed* by possible acts of claim*ing*. To say that what is claimed is true is to endorse the claimable content, not to ascribe a property of truth to anything. The relationship between facts and acts of claiming is one of (reciprocal) sense-, and not reference-, dependence. To understand the concept "fact", one must have at least an implicit grasp of the concept "claim", but the practice of making claims allow us to state, and possibly know, facts that antedated the practice. These conceptually structured facts, that potentially antedate our practice of claiming in the order of being but not in the order of understanding, are truth-makers. Brandom reassures us that "[t]his sense of 'makes' should not be puzzling: it is inferential. 'John's remark that [*p*] is true because it is a fact that *p*,' just tells us that the first clause follows from the second" (VP: 162). According representational vocabulary an expressive and local explanatory role in this manner does not, therefore, stem from tacit acceptance of the representationalist metaphysical picture.

Rorty's response to this suggestion is to complain that this inferential sense of a fact as truth-maker is as "useless for explanatory purposes" as the explanation provided by Molière's doctor that opium makes people sleep because it has a dormitive power. Here too, Rorty points out, the first clause too follows inferentially from the second.[9] Both Molière's and Brandom's purported explanations are useless, until they provide "independent tests for the maker and the made" (Rorty 2000: 186).

This is one instance where the distinction between global and local explanatory role is important. Treated as a general remark purporting to provide some explanatory insight into the nature of semantic contentfulness, Rorty is correct that using representational locutions is explanatorily useless. The anaphoric account of truth and reference explicitly rules out the possibility of an independent test for maker and made offered at the global level. Brandom, however, countenances the explanatory role of such remarks at the local level, understood in terms of the difference in social perspective between the one doing the assessing, the scorekeeper, and the one assessed, the gameplayer. In this social (I–Thou) context, correspondence is, according to the scorekeeper, between the claim undertaken by the scorekeeper and as attributed to the gameplayer. For a scorekeeper to say that a claim is true, or corresponds to a fact, is for the scorekeeper to endorse the claim. Even at this local level, the expressive role played by a claim such as "John's remark that [*p*] is true because it is a fact that *p*" is hardly enlightening. There may, however, be situations in which expressing oneself in this manner is useful. (Perhaps it is made in the context of an acrimonious debate, where the speaker wants emphatically to endorse the claim that p herself, in a manner that expresses her agreement with John.) Enlightening or not, we can nonetheless understand the expressive function of such talk at the local level without succumbing to the representationalist temptations.

In response to the interpretive question, we have argued that Brandom rejects the totalitarian aspirations of representationalism, but not the expressive and local explanatory use of representationalism in some cases. The phrase "totalitarianism" is particularly apt for what is rejected. It marks not just the contention that we should treat representation as the basic explanatory tool for theorizing about language *in toto*, but also that, like many a heavy-handed regime, it tries to impose a forced sense of unity in place of an unwieldy and potentially subversive plurality. In other words, one effect of the single-minded focus on representation is the implication that language has some kind of overarching and unified purpose, which can be used to assess the utility of any application of a vocabulary.[10] Rejecting representationalist totalitarianism has the effect of bringing diversity of use into view: in place of a one-size-fits-all approach, it allows an appreciation of the array of wildly differing and ever-changing uses of applications of expressions.

One may question whether Brandom's according a primacy to the speech act of asserting is itself guilty of ignoring such plurality of purpose (cf. Kukla & Lance 2004). Such a suggestion need not, however, lead to the tyranny of the assertoric, so that anything not able to be assessed according to its purpose is treated as a secondary phenomenon, one parasitic on the *real* goal of language captured in asserting. The notion of language having an assertoric centre was captured earlier in the formal idea of an autonomous discursive practice: "a language game that one could play though one can play no other". Asserting is central, since its inclusion in a social practice is both necessary and sufficient for that practice to be a linguistic one. Non-autonomous language games, including a plethora of diverse uses of expressions, are at the periphery in this sense only. Brandom himself spends much time exploring the roles of such non-autonomous vocabularies and their interrelations, belying any suggestion that they are to be accorded a lesser role. Recognizing that language has an assertoric core thus ensures that representational locutions could be usefully applied at the local level to any linguistic practice. Numerous other speech acts are not helpfully thought of in such representational terms. As Price insightfully points out, it is only someone in the grip of representationalism itself who would conclude that this somehow downgrades the importance of non-assertoric uses of expressions (Price 2004).

The solidity question

It is common to claim that intentionality is the mark of the mental. Brandom distinguishes between two types of intentionality: *that-intentionality* and *of-intentionality* (e.g. Brandom 2007b). It is the difference between what is said or thought, and what we are thereby talking or thinking about. By considering the interpersonal dimension of inferential articulation, Brandom has charted an explanatory course beginning with an account of that-intentionality and ending up, as we have just seen, with an account of of-intentionality. On this explanation of of-intentionality, representational relations are not treated as reaching out of linguistic practice to something outside of it, thereby linking up the otherwise disparate realms of word and world.

The solidity question asks in virtue of what, if not representational relations, is the linguistic practice described world-involving.

How, it worries, does Brandom manage to circumvent the palpable suspicion that the game so elaborately described is more than mere word-play?

One way of unpacking this suspicion returns us to the pessimism regarding the intuitive plausibility of the inferentialist programme voiced by Fodor and Lepore earlier: can an approach that has roots in addressing the meaning of mathematical or logical concepts plausibly be extended to concepts with empirical content such as "'bird', 'oxidization', 'xylophone', 'zeugma' or 'afternoon tea'" (Fodor & Lepore 2001: 463)? We have already made some moves towards ameliorating such pessimism, notably the introduction of material inferences, so that the focus on inferential relations is not to be dismissed as empty formalism, in the sense of excluding talk of semantic content. Until we can provide a satisfactory account of specifically *empirical* content within this strong inferentialist approach, however, these manoeuvres are unlikely to remove this suspicion. This section explores the manner in which Brandom attempts to incorporate empirical content into his account of linguistic practice; the next considers an influential critique of this attempt.

In the preface to MIE, Brandom tells us:

> Chapters 3 and 4 present the core theory . . . It is here that sufficient conditions are put forward for the practices a community is interpreted as engaging in to count as according performances the pragmatic significance of *assertions* – and hence for those practices to count as conferring specifically propositional contents. Everything else in the book either leads up to the presentation of this model or elaborates and extracts consequences from it.
>
> (MIE: xxii–xxiii)

This is not quite right. It is chapter 3 of MIE alone (rehearsed in Chapter 2 of this book) that presents the core theory. By the end of it, we already have a description of a linguistic practice with the features described: it incorporates the speech act of assertion in a manner that confers propositional content on performances within the practice. Chapter 4 is an add-on to this core theory, an optional extra as it were, extending the practice to incorporate the phenomena of perception and action. This add-on allows, among other things, for such practices to have empirical content.

Brandom is clear that a practice that does not incorporate such phenomena (in the sense discussed below) can nonetheless include propositionally contentful claimings.

> Discourse recognizable as mathematical can be like this: reasons are given and demanded, claims communicated, challenged and justified; and regresses of entitlement inheritance halted by appeal to axioms, free moves that anyone is treated as entitled to at any point in the conversation. (MIE: 221)

A self-standing practice like this one, completely lacking empirical content, may be far removed from anything that we recognize. It is, nonetheless, a conceptually contentful practice. Inferentialism is, therefore, a claim about conceptual content, irrespective of whether the content involved is empirical or not. The entire discussion thus far in Part II, including issues of both objectivity and representation, applies in full to such a non-empirical practice.

The issue at hand is to extend this discussion to incorporate empirical content as an optional extra to a Brandomian linguistic practice, in order to help allay fears of linguistic idealism. In Chapter 1, we outlined Brandom's two-ply account of observation, according to which the making of an observation report involves an exercise of two distinct practical capacities: the ability to respond differentially to some stimulus, and the ability to make a move in the game of giving and asking for reasons. There we focused on how *not* to understand the relation between these two plies; that is, anything that falls prey to the Myth of the Given. It is high time to say something positive about the relation between them, and thereby incorporate specifically empirical content into a Brandomian linguistic practice.

It is possible to describe the first of the two plies in the physicalist vocabulary that we would use to describe the performances of other non-discursive reactive systems, such as talking of these systems reading and writing stimuli. In these terms, an observation report such as uttering "the swatch is red" following perceptual exposure to a red swatch, is an exercise of a practical capacity to respond differentially to red stimuli. In describing this first ply, when we say that the response is the product of the exercise of such a capacity, we are not justifying the response. We are explaining its occurrence by positing a causal process that occasions such responses.

It is possible, however, to incorporate such causal processes into the context of keeping score on such a claim, so that the postulated mechanism itself is invoked in the context of justifying the claim made. Suppose that S keeps score on G, in such a way that whenever S takes G to be committed to the claim "the swatch is red" as a result of having produced an observation report by such a causal mechanism,

S treats herself and everyone else as *prima facie* entitled to the same claim.[11] In endorsing such a scorekeeping inference from commitments that S attributes to G to *prima facie* entitlements acknowledged by S and attributed to others, S is treating G as a reliable reporter in this case. Keeping score in this way, endorsing what could be called a *reliability inference*, is what one has to do to take someone else to be a reliable differential responder.

Brandom describes the first ply as a reliable differential responsive disposition (RDRD). It should now be clear that the first *R* of these *R*DRDs, *R*eliability, is something introduced from the perspective of the scorekeeper. It is S who treats the differential responsive dispositions of another person as a *prima facie* reason for endorsing a claim. This is reflected in what Brandom terms "the intensionality of assessments of reliability" (AR: 121), i.e. the sensitivity of attributions of reliability to the manner in which the processes are described. This was deliberately glossed over in the previous paragraph, where it was claimed that in endorsing a reliability inference, S treats G as a reliable reporter *in this case*. What is *this case*? A reliable reporter of red swatches? Of red things? Of colours? Of red swatches in good lighting conditions? These will depend on the collateral commitments used by S in order to use the claim as a premise in S's own inferences. Reliability does not, therefore, reside in the process itself, but in the assessor's taking that process as reliable in the course of keeping score.

In introducing reliability into the description of the first ply from this scorekeeping perspective in this way, it becomes possible to incorporate differential responsive dispositions into the game of giving and asking for reasons, thereby providing a link between the two plies. We are not just provided, therefore, with two independent plies that coincide in making an empirical claim; via reliability inferences, the scorekeeper is able to incorporate reliable responsiveness into the inferential articulation of conceptual contents. It has been suggested that, in light of the inclusion of non-inferential circumstances (and consequences) as part of the semantic content of a claim in this manner, inferentialism is an incorrect label.[12] The norms governing the use of observational reports, however, are inferential, based on the goodness of such reliability inferences. As a result, even if the circumstances or consequences are not "inferential", and the observation reports have been elicited causally, their status as significant moves in a practice stems from such inferences.

Discursive practices that incorporate the authority and responsibility structures through participants endorsing-in-practice the goodness of reliability inferences, are "empirically and practically *constrained*" (MIE: 331). One oft-repeated example that Brandom gives of such constraint is:

> if I perceive a liquid as tasting sour, infer that it is an acid, infer further that it will therefore turn litmus paper red, and, intending to match a red pigment sample, accordingly dip litmus paper in the liquid, I may nonetheless subsequently acquire perceptually a commitment to the result being a blue, rather than a red, piece of paper . . . (*Ibid*.: 332)[13]

In such a case, I have non-culpably acquired incompatible beliefs. I have good reason for being committed to both the claim that this liquid turns litmus paper blue (justified inferentially from other beliefs I am entitled to), and to the claim that this liquid turns litmus paper red (justified via a reliability inference from my non-inferential reporting abilities). Commitment to one precludes entitlement to the other. I can, of course, be committed to both despite the incompatibility. I frequently am so committed without realizing it, and sometimes even when I do. I cannot, however, be entitled to either. This is a point about the semantic content of the two sentences: I cannot be entitled to both, and I ought not to be committed to both. As we have noted in Chapter 5, semantics here does not tell me what I ought to do in such a situation. I could, for example, relinquish commitment to the goodness of the inference from a liquid being sour to it being an acid. I could, instead, reject my reliability as a non-inferential reporter on one of these occasions, either of colour or of taste.[14] Either way, the incorporation into the practice of the goodness of reliability inferences makes it possible for there to be some kind of collision, some kind of "friction" (BSD VI: 13) between those commitments a participant in the practice finds herself with non-inferentially and those that are the result of inferences.

This two-ply account of observation reports captures the sense of experience that is "one of Brandom's words", experience as a transactional learning process. This process is constrained by how things are, since anyone involved in the process may find themselves with incompatible commitments deriving from a clash between those that have the authority of non-inferentially acquired commitments, and those that have the authority of inferentially acquired commitments.

In such a situation, the subject is responsive to how things are in the way she responds by somehow removing the incompatibility. We are not just provided with two plies that act as two separate orders specified in different vocabularies.[15] We can make sense of the contribution of each ply to the other from within the other vocabulary, as well.

The practitioners of *any* linguistic practice, empirical or otherwise, must be able to respond differentially to the utterances of others, and must be able to produce utterances of their own. That is, they must be able to read and write in the strict sense of those terms invoked in Chapter 1. In claiming that a linguistic practice need not incorporate the phenomena of perception and action, Brandom is not denying this.[16] The point is that there can be a linguistic practice in which participants do not keep score in the manner captured by reliability inferences. In such a practice, participants do not accord any special authority to non-inferential reportings. As a result, such a practice lacks empirical content, although the claims made in such a practice still have conceptual content.

Empirical content and rational constraint

The account of empirical content just outlined has been subject to a protracted and influential critique in the writings of John McDowell.[17] Although, for reasons discussed below, McDowell eschews this way of construing the issue, for our purposes his argument can be reconstructed in the following way.[18] McDowell contends that thought is not intelligible as having semantic content, as being *about* something, unless the thought can be rationally constrained by how things are with the objects those thoughts are about (henceforth "the *constraint"). It is not enough for those thoughts to be causally influenced by the way things are with those objects (henceforth Option 1). Nor is it enough for those thoughts to be rationally constrained by other thoughts (henceforth Option 2). What is needed, at minimum, to fulfil the *constraint, is for thoughts to be rationally constrained by experience, on a conception according to which "experience enables the layout of reality itself to exert a rational influence on what a subject thinks" (McDowell 1994: 26) (henceforth Option 3). McDowell treats Brandom's account as "the most-worked out" (McDowell 1998a: 491) version of Option 2, and dismisses it as falling short of what he sees as the sole option that can live up to the *constraint, i.e. Option 3.

The *constraint stems from the "sheer commonsense" (McDowell 2002b: 98) assumption that "the very idea of conceptual activity . . . must have objective purport in order to be recognizable as conceptual activity at all" (McDowell 1998b: 407). The *constraint is a straightforward way of unpacking this notion of objective purport: it requires that how things are with the objects a given thought purports to be about can exercise a rational constraint on that thought. If the fact that the swatch is red can have no rational bearing on my belief that the swatch is red, then it is hard to see in what sense my thoughts are about the red swatch at all.

Options 1 and 2 fall short of fulfilling this *constraint, according to McDowell. Option 1 can only be thought of as fulfilling the *constraint if one treats causal relations as providing justificatory relations. To think this is to fall prey to one manifestation of what was called, in Chapter 1, the Myth of the Given. On such a picture, our thinking is constrained by something alien, in the sense that it is outside the domain of what is thinkable. As McDowell puts this, an appeal to such an alien impact can, at best, provide an exculpation for our thought by rendering the thought inevitable, and thereby exonerating the thinker.[19] It does not provide the rational justification that the *constraint requires.

Option 2, in effect, just gives up on the *constraint, conceding that it is not facts that can exercise a rational constraint on my beliefs, but my beliefs about the facts that so do. The only relation between my thoughts and the way things are with the objects those thoughts purport to be about is a causal, and not a justificatory, one. But, complains McDowell, if the only rational constraint on beliefs is other beliefs, then thinking threatens to be a "frictionless spinning in a void" (McDowell 1994: 5) in which judging and reasoning are little more than "moves in a self-contained game" (*ibid*.: 5). The fear here is not just narrowly epistemological; that is, the fear that we would never be able to adequately justify our beliefs. It is transcendental, in that one cannot make sense of the very notion of a semantically contentful belief without fulfilling the *constraint.

According to Option 3, unless thoughts can be rationally constrained by experience, they cannot fulfil the *constraint. As McDowell develops this idea, in order for our acts of thinking to have conceptual content, it must be possible for those very same conceptual capacities exercised actively in having a thought to be capable of being passively exercised in sensory experience. More precisely, the idea is that we can only understand both thinking *and* experiencing in terms of both being structured by the same conceptual capacities that are passively exercised in experiencing and actively exercised in thinking. McDowell combines this with a conception of experience as a transparent openness to the facts. As I understand it, this means that an experience is an occurrence in which a fact is made manifest to a person, so that there is no gap between an experience and the fact experienced. As a result of this openness, the transcendental question of how an experience is about the world, akin to the question of how thought is about the world, simply does not arise.

Fortunately, we do not need to really understand this conception of experience in any detail in order to consider the challenge that these McDowellian reflections pose to Brandom. According to Brandom's two-ply account of observation, an observation report is an exercise of two distinct practical capacities: the ability to respond differentially to some stimulus, and the ability to make a move in the game of giving and asking for reasons, whose joint exercise suffices for the observation report to have empirical content. As McDowell reads this, it is the second ply that is supposed to play the role of providing rational constraint on our thoughts. This, however, just involves confronting observational beliefs with other beliefs. It is, therefore, a version of Option 2, and falls short of fulfilling the *constraint for such reports are not rationally constrained by how things are with the objects those thoughts are about; that is, by the facts themselves. If so, claims McDowell, what Brandom thinks of as beliefs are not really beliefs as they lack objective purport – they are not *about* anything.

In what follows, I distinguish between Brandom's response to McDowell's challenge, and what it should be. Brandom's response, it is argued, is far too conciliatory toward McDowell's claim, and a bellicose alternative would cohere better with the rest of Brandom's system.

The conciliatory response

Brandom's actual response to McDowell is to a large degree conciliatory. He accepts the *constraint and agrees that Options 1 and 2 do not fulfil it. He even claims that he is in "deep agreement" (FNNF: 373) with a core implication of Option 3, that there is no outer boundary around the sphere of the conceptual, beyond which is located the reality on which thought aims to bear. As Brandom expresses this:

> the boundary . . . between practices of concept use and the non-concept-using world in which that practice is conducted is not construed as a boundary between the conceptual and the non-conceptual tout court. In an important sense there is no such boundary, and so nothing outside the realm of the conceptual.
> (*Ibid*.: 357)[20]

According to Brandom, the main disagreement lies with the question of whether the only way of living up to the *constraint is Option 3. He points to a gap between the *constraint and Option 3: whilst the former requires that beliefs must be rationally constrained by the facts, it does not follow that the beliefs must be rationally constrained by *experience*. Brandom contends that his minimalist account of empirical content fulfils the *constraint, while not conforming to this aspect of Option 3. "Experience", says Brandom, "is not one of my words" (AR: 205).

On Brandom's account of empirical content rehearsed in the previous section, a scorekeeper can rationally assess another gameplayer's observational reports

> by comparing it with the facts that responsively elicited those reports, according to the norm that one ought to say of what perceptibly is that it is . . . From the point of view of the interpreter . . . the relation between the facts and the reports . . . is not merely a causal one. But also one rationally assessable in terms of the truth of those reports . . . relative to the independent facts.
> (1996: 252)

Brandom claims that binging in the possibility of this social perspective, where the assessor is a different person from the person having the belief, allows for the *constraint to be fulfilled, since a belief can be rationally assessed in light of the facts, and not just in light of other beliefs.

> If a suitable story is told about how [beliefs] are rationally criticizable by those who key their correctness to their correspondence to the facts reported, and about their entitlement to the reliability of the noninferential process that elicits them, then rational constraint by how things actually are is secured.
> (1998: 372)

The reason that McDowell ignores the availability of this suitable story, suggests Brandom, is because he fails to appreciate the social articulation of the space of reason, captured here in the interplay between scorekeeper and gameplayer (KSOR: 908). Once recognized, the *constraint can be fulfilled without resorting to experiences.

In response, McDowell complains that the manner in which the debate has been portrayed by Brandom does not reflect the kinds of concerns he is addressing. One way of bringing this out invokes a distinction McDowell makes, between reasons for believing something that are available "from the standpoint of rationality", and "the subject's reason for believing something" (McDowell 1994: 163). His example of the former is the relation that obtains between the movements of a cyclist and the curves in the road to which he responds. The curves explain why those movements are rationally appropriate but, in normal circumstances, they are not the cyclist's reasons for those movements. Facts can thus be said to offer two kinds of rational constraints on beliefs: those that are, and those that are not, available from the believer's own first-personal point of view. McDowell claims that the notion of rational constraint that features in the *constraint are the subject's reasons for believing something. Let us, therefore, reformulate the *constraint to reflect this distinction. According to this reformulation (henceforth the **constraint), thought is not intelligible as having semantic content, as being about something, unless the thought can be rationally constrained *from the first-personal point of view* by how things are with the objects those thoughts are about. McDowell's critique is that Brandom's account cannot live up to the **constraint.

By way of illustration, contrast the case of the chicken sexers much discussed by epistemologists in recent years, with what we will call human sexers. As the story gets told,[21] chicken sexers are able to reliably distinguish male from female chicks, even though they have no conscious experience in any sensory modality of what it is that they are responding to. Human sexers are able to reliably distinguish male from female human beings through conscious visual experience of anatomical differences. Suppose a chicken sexer comes to know that a particular chicken is male because she has become aware, via testimony, of her reliability in these cases. Whilst we could say that her inclinations to endorse the claim that the chicken is male are intelligible to her, this sense of intelligibility is no different from that available from a third-personal perspective; that is, available to a scorekeeper who is also aware of the facts of her reliability. In contrast, in the case of the human sexer, there is an additional sense in which his inclination to say that this human being is male is intelligible to him, that is not available to a third-personal scorekeeper with knowledge of his reliability as a human sexer. In this additional sense, what makes his inclination to say that this human being is male is that the fact that this human being is male is sensibly present to him (McDowell forthcoming).

For Brandom, there is nothing outré from a semantic or epistemic perspective about the case of the chicken sexer: it captures all the rational constraint by the facts that is required for empirical thoughts to have empirical content. It is clear, therefore, that Brandom's account of empirical content does not fulfil the **constraint, for the rational constraint by the facts that his account permits is not available from the first-personal point of view.

A bellicose alternative

Brandom's conciliatory response to McDowell contends that his version of inferentialism is immune to the problems that McDowell rightly raises. We have just seen, however, that this is not the case, as Brandom's account of semantic content is not responsive to McDowell's concerns as expressed in **constraint. The bellicose alternative is for Brandom to discard the assumption that they share common concerns, and reject the **constraint. This proposal is not for *ad hoc* reasons, fuelled solely by fears raised in the discussion in the previous section. Rather, there are independent reasons for the Brandomian inferentialist to accept the *constraint but reject the **constraint.

The *constraint aims to articulate a minimal requirement for it to be intelligible that a thought has semantic content, to be *about* something. Consider this requirement in the context of the strong inferentialist programme. According to this, for thoughts to have semantic content is for those thoughts to be inferentially articulated. The inferential significance of a claim depends on auxiliary hypotheses that will differ between interlocutors. In communicating with others, a scorekeeper needs to keep clear who is committed to what, sorting out those commitments and entitlements undertaken from those commitments and entitlements attributed, in light of these differences in auxiliary hypotheses between interlocutors. The expressive function of representational locutions is to make such sorting out explicit. According to the *constraint, the minimal requirement for it to be intelligible that thought is about something is that it can be rationally constrained by the facts and objects it is about. This *constraint is fulfilled on the inferentialist account by incorporating the social structure of the inferential articulation of semantic content.

We have stressed in this chapter how general this notion of semantic content is. In particular, it is not limited to the case of empirical content. On Brandom's account, any kind of contentful thought, even mathematical thought, can be seen as rationally constrained by the facts and objects it is about. The *constraint made no mention of specifically empirical content. Nor, according to a plausible line of thinking motivating its imposition, should it. What motivates the *constraint is the thought that in order for a belief that p to be about the fact that p, it must be possible for the fact that p to exercise rational constraint on the belief that p. This should apply to non-empirical facts too.

According to the *constraint, if there are thoughts with non-empirical content, it must be the case that such thoughts are rationally constrained by the facts, or else they are not intelligible as being about something, and thus not intelligible as thoughts at all. According to the **constraint, these facts must be able to feature as the subject's reasons for believing something. Imposing the **constraint on thoughts with non-empirical content requires that either the facts that rationally constrain the thought are available in sensory consciousness, or that there is some other non-sensory way for such facts to play a rational constraint from the subject's first-personal point of view. Neither option is easy to sustain (cf. MacFarlane 2004). The first seems to require positing a special kind of non-empirical sensory experience, while the second seems to require the possibility of a special kind of non-sensory, though first-personal, acquaintance with non-empirical facts. Whilst these options should not be ruled out, neither is straight-forward. A less complicated option is to accept the *constraint and reject the **constraint.

All this is not to adjudicate between McDowell and Brandom, but to offer a broad reading of the debate in which basic differences between them are not artificially blurred in a manner that all but precludes adjudication. On this reading, Brandom provides an account of what he sees as the intertwined components of intentionality (that-intentionality and of-intentionality) as emerging out of a general account of semantic content as inferential role, broadly construed to include the interpersonal dimension of inferential articulation. Separating out specifically empirical content is an optional extra to this account of intentionality, and is itself achieved via an account of the role played by reliability inferences in a practice. McDowell too thinks one needs an intertwined account of of-intentionality and that-intentionality, but thinks that the account must allow for there to be some rational relation between semantic content and actual or possible sensory experience. Specifically empirical content cannot, as a result, be an optional extra. McDowell treats Brandom's inferentialist account of content as empty or mere play since it does not allow for the answerability to the world in sensory experience. Brandom, at least on this bellicose approach, should treat McDowell's approach as falling short of providing an overarching conception of semantic content, whether empirical or otherwise.[22]

Summary

Brandom's inferentialism was introduced as a three-staged explanatory approach, with each subsequent stage building on the previous ones. (B1) is an account of linguistic practice, incorporating the speech act of asserting. (B2) is an account of the semantic content of linguistic items in terms of the inferential role of such linguistic items. (B3) is an account of the representational dimension of semantic content. In this chapter, we have distinguished between two different questions regarding Brandom's account that are often run together. The first, the solidity question, challenges the inferentialist to substantiate the claim that the linguistic practice described in (B1) is already world-involving, without recourse to any representational relations. The second, the interpretive question, asks the inferentialist to clarify the explanatory role of the representational relations introduced in (B3). More specifically, does it aim to explain away representational locutions or to reconstruct these in inferential terms?

The answer to both questions lies in recognizing the interpersonal dimension of inferential articulation. The key to answering the solidity question is the recognition of a reliability inference that permits a scorekeeper to recognize the authority of non-inferential reportings, and thereby introduce specifically empirical content into linguistic practice. The key to answering the interpretive question is to take seriously the social structure of the inferential articulation of semantic content. By showing how to reconstruct representational relations from within an inferentialist framework in this manner, Brandom reveals that his version of the language-as-social-practice approach rejects the totalitarian aspirations of representationalism, but not the importance of representational locutions *per se*.

Brandom's inferentialist account of semantic content does not accord any special pride of place to a practice involving claims with specifically empirical content. We concluded by suggesting an advantage of this conjecture, namely that it allows for a clear sense in which thoughts can be constrained by the facts that those thoughts are about. To avail himself of this advantage, Brandom needs to adopt what was termed a bellicose strategy that highlights, rather than blurs, differences with another approach, that of John McDowell. Many critics of Brandom's writings complain of his tendency to strive towards agreement with the opinions of admired others, where this is only achieved through a highly selective and/or misleading reading of alternative positions that allows them to be artificially recreated in his own image.[23] Our discussion of Brandom's conciliatory attitude towards McDowell's challenge suggests that this is an instance of this broader tendency. In this sense, I endorse McDowell's complaint of being unfairly co-opted by Brandom into a joint project. (His image is that of being portrayed as the hind legs of a Pittsburgh neo-Hegelian pantomime horse – (McDowell 2002a: 97).) The positive suggestion motivated here is that Brandom's own position in this case would appear stronger if he acknowledged its distinctiveness, as this provides additional resources for overcoming the kinds of suspicions voiced in the title of this chapter.

Conclusion

Towards a historical conception of rationality

In the introduction to TOMD, Brandom lays out five different conceptions of rationality in a progressive sequence, so that each subsequent conception incorporates the insights of the previous one, while amending or advancing it in some way (TOMD: 1–17). Since one of the five conceptions is Brandom's own inferentialist one, one would expect it to be the fifth and final in the sequence, thereby portraying it as the most complete conception of rationality available. Surprisingly, inferentialism is the fourth of the conceptions presented, and is incorporated into and improved upon by a fifth, a historical conception of rationality.

What does Brandom consider wrong with, or missing from, the inferentialist conception? How does the historical conception overcome this deficiency? Does the historical conception require an emendation of inferentialism or merely mandate a supplementation of it? It is not possible to provide complete answers to these questions, as the historical conception is only beginning to emerge in Brandom's writings and there is no full or definitive account available to date.[1] What follows is a brief attempt to discern some relevant themes in this emerging literature, so as to suggest an agenda for future research.

What does Brandom consider to be missing from the inferentialist conception?

According to the historicist, the inferentialist conception relies on certain assumptions that it neglects to submit to theoretical interrogation.

> The historicist about rationality . . . points out that the inferentialist takes for granted a set of inferentially articulated norms

> as an already up-and-running enterprise. But under what conditions are determinate conceptual norms possible? What do we have to *do* to establish or connect with, subject ourselves to, such determinate norms? (TOMD: 12–13)

For the inferentialist, the contentfulness of a concept involves its rational relations with other concepts: applying one concept in a judgement provides reasons for applying or not applying others. This is a normative affair, since applying one concept in a judgement may oblige, permit or preclude the application of others. To say that the conceptual norms governing the application of concepts in judgements are *determinate* is to say that on any occasion in which a judgement features as the premise or conclusion in a material inference, it is settled in advance of the act of judging whether the material inference is a good one or not. In other words, even if the judgement in question is entirely novel, in the sense that no one has ever applied the concept in that set of circumstances, or attempted to draw these conclusions from it, it is already established in advance of so doing whether the application or inference is appropriate or not. The historicist complains that while the inferentialist conception of rationality assumes that there are such determinate conceptual norms, it does not appear to feel the need to tell an explanatory story about them.

One can recast this complaint in terms of a distinction between the institution and administration of these determinate conceptual norms. For the inferentialist, to be rational is to play the game of giving and asking for reasons. In playing the game, Brandomian linguistic practitioners *administer* determinate conceptual norms, sanctioning performances of themselves and others in light of their implicit grasp of these norms. Furthermore, they can render these norms in explicit form, and thus as appropriate targets of critique and challenge. Through these interactions they constantly improve their own grasp, and the grasp of others, on the conceptual norms so administered. It is through these administrative procedures that they allow these determinate conceptual norms to have a grip on them. The historicist complaint is that these practitioners take the *institution* of these norms for granted, and nothing in the inferentialist conception of the game of giving and asking for reasons explains how determinate conceptual norms can be instituted.

At various points in MIE, Brandom does talk of the institution of determinate conceptual norms, notably in the context of a discussion of the seventeenth-century German thinker Samuel Pufendorf, from whom he derives the following lesson:

> Our activity *institutes* norms, *imposes* normative significances on a natural world that is intrinsically without significance for the guidance and assessment of actions. A normative significance is imposed on a non-normative world, like a cloak thrown over its nakedness, by agents forming preferences, issuing orders, praising and blaming, esteeming and assessing. (MIE: 48)

As a result of the "disenchantment of the natural world" accompanying the rise of modern science, we cannot turn to a meaningless natural world for determinate norms. Instead, we must turn towards ourselves, "meaning-generating subjects" (MIE: 49), and recognize that it is our activities that institute determinate norms. The historicist complaint is that nothing more is said to explain the relationship between our meaning-generating activities and the determinate norms they institute.

It is all too easy to hear this complaint as focused on a supposed "moment of institution" in which the norms that bind are brought into existence, so that the challenge posed is to explain how this transition from a norm-less world to a norm-full one is achieved. Although Brandom's rhetoric occasionally makes it seems as if there were such an act of throwing the normative cloak over a non-normative world, this is not his considered opinion, and rightly so.[2] It is hard to cash out this metaphor of a moment of imposition in a way that makes sense. One core difficulty is that if this moment of institution itself is not subject to norms, it appears to be nothing more than a "random leap in the dark", and it is hard to see how such anything instituted by such an arbitrary act can be reasonable.[3]

The challenge posed by the historicist, however, is not this one regarding a moment of institution. As I understand it, for Brandom there is no act of instituting that is separate from the act of administering. The social practice of administering the norms, applying them in judgements and keeping score on judgements made, determines their contents and so institutes them. What the historicist demands is an explanatory account of how playing the game of giving and asking for reasons can institute determinate conceptual norms, akin to the explanatory account how playing the game of giving and asking for reasons administers these norms that is provided by the inferentialist.

How does the historical conception overcome this deficiency?

Consider the historicist's challenge in light of the gerrymandering problem raised in Chapter 5. Suitably recast in terms appropriate to the current context, the problem is that for any finite set of administrative performances, be they actual performances or dispositions to perform, it is possible to conjure up an infinity of mutually exclusive norms for which that set of administrative performances would be an instantiation. If our administrative processes institute conceptual norms, therefore, it is hard to see how they could be determinate. As Brandom asks, "How does what we have actually done with the terms, the judgements we have actually made, settle what we ought to do with them in novel cases?" (TOMD: 13).

The historicist's response distinguishes between considering the process of administering conceptual norms as a temporal one and as a historical one. In considering the administrative process as temporal, one focuses on a sequence of consecutive time-slices of playing the game of giving and asking for reasons, one following the other over time. In considering the administrative process as historical, one focuses as well on the authority structure exercised by past instances of playing the game on future ones, and on the authority of future instances of playing the game on past ones. It is through a consideration of this historical process that one can understand how the process of administering such norms is said to institute them.

In order to develop this idea, Brandom asks us to consider a legal analogy involving applications of case law in a common-law model. All a judge has to go on in making a decision according to the common-law model are past cases, which she applies to the case at hand. (This differs from a statutory-law model in which the judge can appeal to statements of principle or rules of application.) In making a decision, the judge will select certain prior cases as relevant precedents, and attempt to extract considerations that apply to the current situation. In so doing, the judge accords authority to those past decisions she is drawing on, and in making her judgment, she exercises authority over future judges who may be constrained by it.

One may be inclined to say that in this model past judgments constrain present judgments, and present judgments constrain future ones. Constrain perhaps, but not determine. Since the current judge has a certain degree of latitude about which cases to treat as relevant precedents and why, past judgments constrain but do not determine present judgments, and present judgments constrain but do not determine future ones. In this way, she exercises a certain authority over past judgments, and future judges exercise a certain authority over her. One can think of this in terms of petitioning for recognition of authority: the decisions of past judges petition her for recognition, and her own judgment, once made, will petition future judges for recognition. The authority of the judgment depends on the petition being successful. There is, therefore, one direction of authority running from past through present to future, though whether this is authoritative or not depends on a converse direction of authority from future through present to past. The current judge's relationship with future judges is, like her relationship with past judges, one of mutual recognition. In making a decision, she recognizes the authority of both past and future judges, and in this way, "the authority of the past over the present is administered on its behalf by the future" (TOMD: 233).

Illustrative of the complexity of the process of mutual recognition as this legal analogy may be, one may be excused for wondering about its relevance to our question. Granted there is a sense in which making these judgments, those that are treated as precedential by future judges and made in light of the authority of past judgments, both institutes and administers norms. The norms so instituted are not, however, determinate norms. In the case just described, it was conceded that past judgments do not determine present ones; there are always similarities and differences between past cases and present that permit, in fact require, the judge to choose which cases to treat as precedential, and in what way. In this practice, there are no determinate norms, in the sense that past judgments involving a concept do not settle in advance whether the application of that concept in a judgment is appropriate in current or future circumstances.

Let us ask this question, however, from the point of view of the judge herself. What would it be for her to treat a prior judgment as determining in advance how it is correct to judge in this case? The answer is that she recognizes the prior judgment as precedential by using it to justify her current judgment. In so doing, the current judge recognizes the authority of the prior judge; she treats that decision as an appropriate one. By recognizing the prior judgment as precedential, she not only treats it as constraining her current judgment, she also treats it as determining in advance what the decision ought to be in the current case. Brandom calls this an act of *rational reconstruction*. In the common-law tradition, all that can be appealed to in justifying a current decision are past decisions treated as precedential. Appealing to a past decision is a kind of rationalization, as the past decision selected as precedential and the present decisions are taken to rationally fit together. In taking a past decision as precedential, she is making past and present part of an ongoing tradition. Whether this is a *rational* tradition that is made, however, depends, in turn, on future judges taking it as such, by including it in their own rational reconstructions.

Here is a key challenge facing this proposal: how can the act of taking a norm to be determinate make it so? In taking a judgment as precedential, the current judge treats it as determining the norms applicable in her current case. From this *retrospective stance*, therefore, the norms instituted appear to be determinate. Future judges have some latitude as to whether to recognize this current judgment as precedential, however strongly one petitions them to so do. From this *prospective stance*, therefore, the norms instituted do not appear to be determinate. Which stance is correct? The historicist wants to answer that both are. To do this, the historicist needs to provide a way of thinking about the notion of determinateness that is itself perspectival, in the sense captured by the difference between the prospective and retrospective stances. Developing such a conception of determinateness is, therefore, a central challenge facing the historicist. I call this a challenge rather than an objection: like the obstacles to be overcome in an army assault course, this task is clear from the outset, and success of the historicist project will be measured in the way it is negotiated.

Does the historical conception require an emendation of inferentialism or does it merely mandate a supplementation?

Although Brandom calls the legal case an analogy, it is best to think of it as a simplified model, in the same way that the gameplaying practice outlined in Chapter 2 is a model. In both instances, we are provided with a description of the authority and responsibility structure implicated in a set of moves in a social practice, whose actual performance would constitute the kind of practice we are trying to understand. A legal model is useful, because it allows us to consider a somewhat familiar example of the process of instituting and administering norms. In addition, since the common-law model stipulates that the only appropriate justification for a judgment are prior judgments, it is clear that all that can institute such norms are prior judgments. Lastly, the legal practice is simplified in the sense that it need not involve claims with specifically empirical content, even though the judgments are constrained by other judgments. To introduce empirical content would require the introduction of the authority and responsibility structure of reliability inferences into the practice, thereby treating some practitioners as able to make some judgments non-inferentially. The legal case allows us to ignore these complications in responding to the historicist's challenge.

Our brief description of the historicist conception makes it clear that it is a proposed supplementation and not a proposed correction of the inferentialist conception. The supplementation, however, appears to take a particular form. The historicist does not merely add another conception of rationality to stand alongside the inferentialist one, but attempts to broaden the perspective from which the playing of the game of giving and asking for reasons is viewed, to include a historical, and not just a temporal, frame.

Whilst this suggestion permits the inferentialist to embrace the historical conception without altering its detail, it is worth stressing that the historicist's challenge to the inferentialist does not require embracing historicism. I do not just mean that there may be alternative ways to respond to the historicist's challenge, but that the inferentialist may not need to respond. That is, the inferentialist could reject the claim that an explanatory story needs to be told about the institution of determinate conceptual norms, while continuing to deliver the rich and detailed inferentialist account regarding the process of administering these norms. This kind of theoretical quietism may not sit comfortably with Brandom's intellectual sensibilities, but the historicist has to do more to persuade the inferentialist that the task needs to be undertaken than merely pointing towards a perceived explanatory silence. As we have seen throughout Brandom's work, his response to this kind of complaint is to undertake the proposed explanatory task until it yields the kind of insight that will persuade an opponent that this is an explanatory task worth undertaking. "The proof", Brandom likes to tell us, "is in the pudding" (RPC: 236). Unlike the inferentialist conception, however, there is as yet insufficient historicist pudding to taste, let alone swallow, although Brandom is hard at work assembling the Hegelian raw ingredients.

We began this book by suggesting that an introduction to Brandom's philosophy is somewhat premature, since it is currently showing signs of change. We are now in a position to end by putting this point more carefully. Brandom's earlier work, especially MIE, provides a novel and detailed inferentialist conception of rationality, in terms of the social practice of the administration of conceptual norms, playing the game of giving and asking for reasons. His current work, especially his Hegel-inspired writings, aims to provide a further historicist conception of rationality, which develops an account of the relationship between these administrative practices, and the institution and development of determinate conceptual norms. The focus of this book has been on Brandom's inferentialist conception of rationality. One of the dangers in writing a book about the Mighty Living lies in the constant threat of the need for a sequel.

Notes

Introduction

1. An additional reason not to undertake this project is that Brandom himself has provided his own introduction, in the form of a short book entitled *Articulating Reasons* (henceforth AR). For a variety of reasons, I concur with a reviewer of that work that AR is "more helpful for those conversant with his approach", and does not "serve well as a first point of contact with Brandom's thinking" (Peregrin 2001: 51). The review suggests that "it would indeed be desirable to have a concise and comprehensive introduction to the Brandomian doctrines".
2. Cf. Žižek (2002: xi): "There are philosophical books, minor classics even, which are widely known and referred to, although practically no one has read them page by page (John Rawls's *Theory of Justice*, for example, or Robert Brandom's *Making It Explicit*) – a nice example of interpassivity, where some figure of the Other is supposed to do the reading for us."
3. This quoted phrase is from Brandom (RPC: 238). Some of the frustrations of the phobe stem from a failure to appreciate the conjectural nature of some of the motivating claims, albeit a failure encouraged by a tendency to imply assertoric force at a stage when conjectural would be more apposite.
4. "[The project] is animated by the ideal of the systematic philosophers of old: the invigorating clarifying prospect achievable by laying alongside our ordinary ways of talking or thinking an alternate idiom in which everything can be said" (MIE: xxiii).
5. Rorty's omission from the text of MIE – he disappears entirely after the dedication, not even featuring in the index – is surprising. We shall explore one central area of influence in Chapter 8.
6. The wording here is adapted from Franks (2005: 1).
7. Following Brandom (MIE: 545–7), the superscripts denote ^{s}scare quotes^{s}. See p. 157 for a formal discussion.

Part I: Sapience (Introduction)

1. This is implied in RDAH: 238.
2. See, for example, AR: 157.

3. Cf. TOMD: 217. It will emerge that Brandom treats such mutual recognition in a constitutive vein, as constituting community membership. This means that my status as a sapient being is not something I can achieve on my own, and neither is yours. The status of being a sapient being is thus essentially a social (I–Thou) achievement, the joint product of a social division of labour between us.
4. For a detailed empirical study of actual parrots see Pepperberg (1999). Her loose and inconclusive discussion as to whether Alex, her African Grey parrot, has a language (critically discussed by Fitch *et al.* (2002: 1143)) could be seen to reveal the shortcomings of ignoring the issue of the practical import of such demarcational questions.

Chapter 1: Parrots

1. This question is repeated throughout Brandom's writings. See, among others, 1983: 644; 1985: 32; MIE: 88, 122; AR: 17, 48, 108, 191; TOMD: 349–53; BSD II: 16.
2. See AR: 14, 17; BSD II: 17.
3. "Before a man makes any proposition, he is supposed to understand the terms he uses in it, or else he talks like a parrot . . ." (E: 4.8.8).
4. This reading helps overcome an oft-made criticism of Locke at this point (see, e.g., Bennett 1971: 5) that he lacks sufficient evidence for the claims made here about parrots. Locke, on this reading, is not trying to establish the claim about parrots. Rather he is using a widely assumed exemplar of purported difference to try to understand what the purported difference reveals. (This is not, of course, to deny anthropocentric tendencies elsewhere in Locke, or to read anachronistically into his text the kind of methodological phenomenalism we shall consider here.)
5. Brandom goes so far as to contend that, as long as one attempts to describe the scene using a purely physicalist vocabulary, the responses are "virtually indistinguishable" (MIE: 276; TOMD: 350). As will emerge in the ensuing discussion, the contrast with a physicalist vocabulary here is a normative vocabulary, and not a supernatural one.
6. As an anonymous referee pointed out, describing the rule that the behaviour of the litmus paper is subject to as a "norm" is highly questionable. Brandom's discussion of this in MIE (30–32) is bound up with Kantian themes, and the terms "norms" and "rules" are used interchangeably (e.g. "natural beings, who merely act according to rules, that is, regularly, are capable of acknowledging norms only by obedience to them" (MIE: 32)).
7. MIE: 59–62, 629–30. (I have adapted the terminology somewhat.)
8. "We might imagine a normative practice, according to which red things are *appropriately* responded to by making a certain noise. This would still not be a conceptual matter" (AR: 17).
9. "The fundamental speech act – the one whose presence is necessary and sufficient for the practices involved to qualify as *linguistic* practices – is *assertion*" (1997b: 150). "Specifically *linguistic* practices are those in which some *doings* have the practical significance of *sayings*. The core case of *saying* something is making a *claim*, *asserting* something" (BSD II: 16).
10. "Asserting cannot be understood apart from inferring" (MIE: 158) "*[A]sserting* and *inferring* are internally related practices" (BSD II: 16).

11. The utterances of children are considered in KSOR: 896.
12. The term "logocentric" is intended to be provocative, because Brandom here explicitly embraces what is normally hurled as a term of abuse: "We philosophers should be proud to acknowledge and affirm our logocentrism" (BSD II: 18). By logocentrism in this context I do not mean the privileging of speech over writing, but the claim that, *pace* Rorty or Derrida, one should privilege reason-giving over other things one can do with language. Brandom's central defence of this claim seems to involve pointing to just how much of linguistic practice can be recreated by taking this as a basic assumption. Price (2004) offers a broader defence that can fruitfully be harnessed in tandem with Brandom's project.
13. The clearest discussion of this account is in TOMD: 348–67. There Brandom attributes the claim to Sellars, although (a) the attribution has been hotly contested (see McDowell 1998a; 2002a: 279–81), and (b) it is clear that the two-ply account is endorsed by Brandom. Cf. Brandom (2002a).
14. As usual, Brandom's account of a phenomenon – in this case observation – begins with an account of the speech acts (observation reports) used to express it.
15. As the term "system" betrays, I am drawing on some automaton-theoretic terminology to characterize these abilities.
16. Cf. Haugeland (1985: 54). In those systems that will be of greatest interest to us, there will be some kind of feedback mechanism operating between reading and writing (see especially BSD III: 36–8; BSD VI: 3–5. Cf. MIE: 528–9). This means that the system can alter its responsive dispositions based on the outcome of past doings, so that not every response to an identical stimulus-input type will be the same in every case. In a Test–Operate–Test–Exit (TOTE) cycle we have an interlinked and open-ended sequence of feedback-governed performances, with the results of one performance affecting the subsequent performance. (The notion of a TOTE cycle was popular in psychology in the transition from behaviourism to cognitivism. Miller *et al.* (1960) treated the TOTE cycle as the basic theoretical unit of psychology, forming the core of purposive behaviour; Brandom, of course, would not treat the cycle in terms of actual envisaged goals, or in terms of action.)
17. This example is a reference to Brandom's account of the difference between theoretical and observational objects. Drawing on Sellars, Brandom contends that the distinction is methodological and not ontological as it depends on the RDRD abilities of the observer. As a result, "physicists with the right training can noninferentially report the presence of mu mesons in cloud chambers" (TOMD: 363). Or, as he says elsewhere, the "candidate stimuli one might have the ability to discriminate can include such species as poetry that qualifies as lyrical, actions that are cruel, remarks that are witty or telling, historical events that illustrate the superiority of liberal political arrangements, and so on. And the responsively elicitable performances could include anything one had the ability to do: painting the well-composed pictures, toeing the Party line, riding a bike, standing the right conversational distance from someone, and so on" (BSD II: 6–7). To be observable is for the stimulus in question to be able to be "read" in this sense; "nothing real is in principle beyond the reach of observation" (TOMD: 363).
18. The phrase, and the claim, are due to Sellars (1997).
19. Brandom (1997c: 126). Again, the context is a discussion of Sellars.

20. The next two paragraphs are influenced by the discussion in Wilson (1995). Talk of "inner life" here is, of course, vague and provocative. Minimally, to have an inner life in the sense intended here is to paraphrase Nagel (1974), for the question "what is it like to be a parrot?" to make sense. For Locke, the intimate connection between mindedness and the entertaining of ideas, as well as the quite literal internal nature of such ideas, gives the phrase "inner life" a stronger and more vivid reading.
21. For example, perception involves having "some Idea . . . *present in the Understanding*" (E: 2.9.4) and Locke explicitly allows that members of the animal kingdom are able to perceive things, stating: "This faculty of *Perception* seems to me to be that, which *puts the distinction betwixt the animal Kingdom, and the inferior parts of Nature*" (E: 2.9.11). Even the claim, made in our context, that parrots have articulate sound reveal that they do have ideas, for Locke notes in his discussion of the modes of sound that every articulate sound is an idea (E: 2.18.3).
22. Bird tunes are discussed explicitly to show that such birds are able to contemplate and retain this simple idea in memory (E: 2.10.10). Locke allows that some non-human animals are able to discern this idea as distinct from one another and even compare such ideas there, creating the Idea of relation, albeit imperfectly (E: 2.11.4).
23. Locke seems to think of the particulars received from sensation (particular ideas) as determinate repeatables, but of the concepts that we form through abstraction (abstract ideas) as determinable repeatables. See Sellars (1997: 58–9). Locke is extremely concerned with explaining how we move from determinate to determinable. Notoriously, he is surprisingly unconcerned with how we are able to entertain determinate repeatables from the token unrepeatables given in sensory experience. This could explain how Locke easily suggests that non-human animals can reason with particulars, as it is somewhat easier to make sense of this if the particulars they are saddled with in sensation are repeatable types and not just tokens.
24. None of the discussions of parrot talk in the *Essay* mentions the lack of general terms or the ability to abstract as a reason for denying language to such creatures. Immediately after he has distinguished between words and language at the beginning of Section 3, Locke proceeds to discuss general signs (E: 3.1.3). This seems to be after language is already in play; the lack of general signs in a language is an "inconvenience" for language users rather than an essential feature of language use. (This distinction is echoed in the relation between Part 2 ("Of Signification of Words") and Part 3 ("Of General Terms") of Book III.) The reason that is proffered focuses on the contention that such sounds are used without any "connexion between the sound and the idea" (E: 3.2.7).
25. This contrast between imitation and rational deliberation is a contested one, with a long history, that still persists in contemporary discussions. See Heyes & Papineau (2006) for a critical discussion of the use of the dichotomy in contemporary psychological literature. (As an aside: their way of mapping the contemporary issues rests on a conception of folk psychology that is blind to the Brandomian notion of a linguistic practice.)
26. There are two aspects of Locke's thinking that explicitly feature in Brandom's work as a foil, neither of which is mentioned here: Locke's account of communication (discussed in Chapter 7) and his naturalism (e.g. AR: 35).

27. TOMD: 349. See also AR: 23.
28. Cf. Hacking (1975: 43–53).
29. There is, of course, a related and much broader sense of representationalism that is resolutely Lockean. Locke's ideas are signs that signify or represent something other than themselves. It is this representational dimension of Lockean ideas that so bothers his critics: it both worryingly provides the image of the subject as passively surveying the representations just given to it in perception, and raises epistemic concerns by placing intermediaries between mind and world.

Chapter 2: Rational beings

1. For example AR: 190 and BSD IV: 28.
2. As Brandom tells us, "[c]laims about the relations between meaning and use have a clear sense only in the context of a specification of the vocabulary in which that use is described . . . The specification of use employed here is neither so generous as to permit semantic or intentional vocabulary nor so parsimonious as to insist on purely naturalistic vocabulary. Instead, it makes essential use of *normative* vocabulary. The practices that confer propositional and other sorts of conceptual content implicitly contain norms concerning how it is correct to use expressions" (MIE: xiii).
3. "The first step in the project is accordingly the elaboration of a pragmatics . . . that is couched in the practical scorekeeping *attitudes* of attributing and acknowledging deontic *statuses* of commitment and entitlement . . . The next step is to say what structure such a set of social practices must have in order to qualify as specifically *discursive* practice" (MIE: xiv). The constraint here, developed below, is that the first step is conceptually independent of the second.
4. Claims involving such normative terms are part of normative vocabulary although they need not have normative force in the sense of themselves prescribing or prohibiting something.
5. This is clearest in Rödl (2000) and Dowell (2006), from whom I have taken the phrase.
6. Compare: "The explanatory program thus requires that these normative idioms do not depend for their intelligibility on any of the semantic or psychological concepts that are to be explained by means of them" (Rosen 1997: 163). Cf. Rosen (2001).
7. This is a central theme of BSD, in particular.
8. In this kind of reductive explanation, we are neither translating the terms of one vocabulary into the other, nor claiming that one is derivable from another. See BSD I: 31, developed below.
9. As Dowell (2006) correctly points out, Brandom's own description of the model, in Chapter 3 of MIE, makes use of intentional and semantic vocabulary, creating the suspicion that such terms are smuggled into the model illicitly, or that Brandom's explanatory ambitions are not as lofty as he makes out. We return to these suspicions in Chapter 4.
10. This point is made convincingly by Rödl (2000). In a footnote to MIE, Brandom states: "[p]art of what is distinctive about the approach is that . . . what are here treated as semantic primitives are themselves explained in terms of a prior pragmatics, which in turn appeals to *normative* primitives, themselves made available by mapping the theoretical idiom onto our

ordinary talk" (MIE: 681, n. 6). My point here is that even though there may be a mapping between ordinary talk and the theoretical idiom, the mapping is not a direct translation of one to the other, and it is important to treat the idiom introduced as theoretical.

11. This is an interpretation of a claim made by linguists pointing to the context-sensitivity of normative terminology. See, for example, Kratzer (2002), cited approvingly in Wedgwood (2006).
12. Cf. Rödl (2000: 344), who, in a similar manner, introduces the notion of basic correctness, modelled on a Habermasian notion of an Ur-concept.
13. The rules of the game will define what is relevant. No two tokens will be identical in all respects; after all, there will always be something that distinguishes them as tokens. Although this will be developed later on, it should be stressed at the outset that, despite the impression in the text, the tokens here are best thought of as acts of tokening, and the types are best thought of as equivalence classes of possible performances similar in some specified sense. This idea is developed in Chapters 5 and 6.
14. The awkward relationship between belonging and a commitment, implied in these sentences, is discussed below.
15. Disavowing, querying and responding will be developed further below.
16. In addition, one also becomes entitled to any counter-type that is a committive consequence of a counter-type to which one is entitled.
17. Or successfully mount a counter-challenge. See below.
18. This is an important point in the ensuing discussion, as it is possible for a player to be entitled to two incompatible counter-types, as long as she is not committed to both. See below.
19. In light of this, one needs to modify the account of disavowals proffered earlier, according to which the removal of a counter from before the gameplayer results in the removal of the counter from the player's commitment-box, as well as the counters that are its committive consequences from that gameplayer's commitment-box, unless those counters are the committive consequence of another counter-type(s) that still features in the gameplayer's commitment-box and has not also been disavowed. In light of the addition of both entitlements and incompatibilities to the model, the act of disavowing becomes more complex. In adding a counter-type to the commitment-box, one removes counter-types that are incompatible with it from the entitlement-box. So, in disavowing, one not only removes from the commitment-box the disavowed counter-types, one also restores those counter-types that were previously removed from the entitlement-box. Not all disavowals are successful; for example, in a situation in which the person disavows one counter but continues to put forward another counter that is incompatible with the disavowal, the scorekeeper will not restore those counter-types to the entitlement-box.
20. In a fuller description of a game one would have to take into account the role of auxiliary counter-types too. See Chapter 6.
21. Thus, one adds to the entitlement-box the permissive consequences of entitlements to those commitments that are actually undertaken, whilst one adds the committive consequences of entitlements without commitments. This allows one to be entitled to two counter-types that would be incompatible if commitment to both were undertaken.
22. In a game with more players, an additional element must be considered. If player A places a counter in front of her in what is, according to the

scorekeeper, the presence of player B, and B has, according to the scorekeeper, no incompatible counter-types in her commitment- and entitlement-boxes, then the scorekeeper will add that counter-type played by A (and all the other various consequences) to B's entitlement-box.

23. I have been forced to confront this objection more carefully after reading MacFarlane (forthcoming), to which the following discussion is indebted.
24. This echoes Brandom's own description when he says: "these counters, which are distinguished by bearing the player's mark, being on his list, or being kept in his box, constitute his score" (BSD IV: 28).
25. MIE: 183. Likewise, "Talk of deontic statuses is . . . traded in . . . for talk of the attitudes of taking or treating people as committed or entitled. Deontic statuses are revealed as scorekeeping devices used for identifying and individuating deontic attitudes" (MIE: 648). "*[A]ll* one can do with a commitment (or entitlement) in the model presented here it to take up a deontic attitude towards it . . . To understand them, one must look at actual practices of keeping score, that is, at deontic attitudes and changes of attitude" (*ibid.*: 194).
26. In addition, A'ing makes certain moves inappropriate that were appropriate prior to the A'ing – a part of the responsibility undertaken by the gameplayer.
27. Cf. RPC: 238. "The question is whether or not such a response would be a *mis*-understanding."
28. Pagin's concerns here do raise a challenge for proponents of the assurance view of testimony (e.g. Ross 1986; Hinchman 2005; Moran 2005). Brandom has been cited as a proponent of this view, a suggestion I reject for reasons alluded to in the text, and made explicit in Wanderer (forthcoming).
29. I have learnt to think this way from a paper by Kukla & Lance, delivered at the Space of Reasons Conference held in Cape Town, South Africa in 2004. They say far more about these distinctions than there is room for here.
30. Brandom explicitly includes such overhearing in MIE: 186. By the hearer–overhearer contrast, I do not mean just the distinction between addressee and ratified participant in the conversation, but the difference between addressee and any eavesdropper whomsoever. This further discussed in Chapter 7.
31. There is a third sense of I–Thou sociality, according to which a speech act such as asserting is to be treated as specifically second-personally addressed. This is discussed in Chapter 7.

Chapter 3: Logical beings

1. The ellipses indicates that a system following a straight-schedule algorithm will continue until the list is complete no matter what the result of the performance, as there is no feedback mechanism from the result of an exercise of the primitive ability that could tell the process to halt once it has achieved a particular goal. Introducing a feedback mechanism, so that the next step is dependent on the results of previous steps, involves another type of algorithm: a branched-scheduled algorithm, so called because it includes conditional branches in its list. Systems that are capable of following branched-schedule algorithms can alter their responsive dispositions depending on the outcome of past doings, so that not every response to an

identical stimulus-input type will be the same in every case. Cf. Haugeland (1985: 68).

2. The discussion of these cases is inevitably replete with qualifiers. As Brandom rightly concedes, "the question of which practices-or-abilities are and which are not substantively algorithmically decomposable is an empirical question, not the sort we can confidently answer from our armchairs . . ." (BSD III: 13).
3. As the qualifier indicates, the following discussion of explication is tentative. I find Brandom's own exposition of this crucial aspect of his theory unclear. In particular, the concept of explication seems to undergo changes in focus and nuance in his writings over time, although these alterations are not explicitly noted. What follows is an attempt to discern a central conception from among these alterations.
4. See Lance & O'Leary-Hawthorne (1997). Their rich discussion, especially the interpretation and critique of Brandom, merits further consideration.
5. This explicating description is itself subject to critique and sanction. See the discussion of normative phenomenalism versus phenomenalism about norms in Chapter 4.
6. The conditional introduced here is the two-valued conditional, which treats an inference as good so long as it does not have instances of true premises and a false conclusion. Although Brandom does not mention this, it seems possible to beef up the notion of the conditional introduced to get different conditionals, by holding out for a stronger conception of what makes an inference good. The method of introducing these alternative conceptions would be the same, namely response substitution.
7. Negation can be introduced in a similar manner. In the mini-game, B would respond to the tokening by A of the counter-type q by removing entitlement to the counter-type s. In our description of the game, it was said that this was treating certain claims as incompatible with others, in the sense that commitment to one claim precludes entitlement to the other. In order to be able to keep a score that recognizes such relations, the scorekeeper must be able to sort pairs of claims into those that are incompatible; B treats q and s as such an incompatible pair. It is then possible to introduce the negation by elaborating on this ability to sort pairs of moves into those that are incompatible via response substitution on these basic read–write abilities. Once he has mastered negation locution (together with the conditional), B could say: "if something is q then it is not s"; by substituting this for responses he can already write in situations that he can already read. Negation thus makes explicit the implicit ability to treat two claims as incompatible.
8. The example being considered is a case of direct (*oratio recta*) rather than indirect (*oratio obliqua*) saying, a difference in logical vocabulary that Brandom marks by distinguishing between "says . . ." and "says that . . .". In both one ascribes an assertion of something to a gameplayer. The something that is asserted by this gameplayer fills the space following the locution. In the case of direct saying that we are considering, the scorekeeper says what it is that the gameplayer asserted by direct quotation, so what follows the "says . . ." locution is a token of the same lexical type as that asserted.
9. Where the "says . . ." operator is followed by a token of the same lexical type as B's original claim ("A says p").
10. This should not be treated as an extra condition over and above elaboration and explication – it is part of what is meant by the latter.

11. This sentence gestures informally at the very formal notion of a conservative extension. See MIE: 123–5, drawing on Dummett's (1973) account (cf. discussion in Weiss 2002: 108–22). There are technical reasons for such a stipulation: it is required to overcome the possibility of a runabout inference ticket: see Prior (1960) and Belnap (1962). Brandom's conception of the role of logical locutions provides an independent motivation for such a stipulation.
12. It is somewhat misleading then that Brandom tends to use light or seeing metaphors when talking about such logical abilities. See references to the "searchlight of explicitation" (MIE: 641) that brings our practices from the "dim twilight" (*ibid.*: 384) into "light of day" (*ibid.*: xix, also 384) or, as above, into the "well lit discursive marketplace" (*ibid.*: 403). Or even more explicitly, "[t]he broadly inferential scorekeeping proprieties that otherwise remain implicit in the shadows of the practical background, are brought into the full, revealing light of explicit, public propositional awareness" (*ibid.*: 641). It is less misleading if one bears in mind the conception of experience as situated transactional learning noted in Chapter 1 and developed in Chapter 8.
13. This is a central theme of McDowell's critique of Brandom, a theme that will resurface in various places, and in various forms, in this book (cf. McDowell 2002b, 2005b). An anonymous referee suggests that this line of critique can be traced back to Sellars, and I have used the language of self-correction here to reflect this. No doubt Brandom would challenge this interpretation of Sellars.
14. I am indebted to an anonymous referee for this way of putting matters.
15. Laurier (2005), especially as interpreted by Brandom in RPC.
16. A more formal discussion of the Brandomian concept of truth is undertaken in Chapter 8.
17. Cf. Davidson (1975).
18. These themes are further developed in Chapters 7 and 8.
19. Brandom calls such an explanatory approach "phenomenalist" (MIE: 291) for, like the classical case of phenomenalism, that which is represented is explained in terms of the act of representing. I have tried to avoid this term in the text, however, as Brandom notoriously uses it in a variety of ways. For example, here phenomenalism involves the claim that instead of focusing on what a particular property is, we should focus on what it is that one is doing in taking someone to have that property, i.e. in ascribing it. Elsewhere the phenomenalist is described as being interested in what a particular property is, where being that property consists in being correctly taken to have such a property (e.g. MIE: 291 and the discussion in Shapiro 2004: 142–3). On yet other occasions, phenomenalism is glossed in terms of a supervenience claim, to the effect that facts about having a particular property supervene on facts about what things are taken to have such a property (e.g. MIE: 292). Such claims do not seem to be equivalent. (I return to this in Chapter 4.)
20. There are obvious parallels between this approach and a performative analysis of truth claims on which Brandom explicitly draws and develops.
21. As Shapiro (2004) points out, although Brandom does not mention this example explicitly, one can adopt a similar methodological approach towards another much-debated philosophical concept, that of meaning. As a result of A placing p before her, B places p before him. By treating A's performance as an asserting, B treats A as authorizing his own commitment to p and would defer to her if challenged regarding his entitlement to p. B's

tokening of p is a performance of the same type as A's tokening, even though they are, of course, distinct performances. If B did not treat his performance as being of the same type as A's, it would not be appropriate to defer to A to provide an entitlement in this regard. Let us, then, introduce a range of possible tokening performances that B would treat as appropriate to defer to A, as a result of her original tokening of p. Performings within this range may differ from A's tokening of p in a whole host of respects, but they are all performances that B treats as authorized by A's tokening of p, such that if B were to perform in such a manner it would be appropriate to defer to A to justify the performance. What this means is that we have generated a group of performance types that all share this common deferential potential. If, for example, B were to defend his putting forward of the counter-type x by deferring to A as a result of her putting forward counter-type p, B is treating counter-types p and x as related by this relationship of deferential potential. Now let us introduce into this practice a locution that could make explicit B's treating of certain performances as having this shared deferential potential, the "means that . . ." locution. When challenged as to how he can defer to A with regard to x when A never asserted x, B says that x means that p. In saying this, B could justify his tokening x by explicitly deferring to A's tokening of p. Furthermore, it licenses anyone else to token x on A's authority. To say that B treats x as having the same meaning as p is to say that anyone who is authorized to token p is, in the very same manner, authorize to token x. If so, we have explained meaning ascriptions in terms of how these can be used to entitle others to various claims. (Cf. Lance & O'Leary Hawthorne 1997: 4–8 for the contrary claim that Brandom does not offer an account of meaning claims.) Shapiro's suggestion has important implications for the notion of deferral in testimonial cases – see Wanderer (forthcoming).

22. It is interesting to compare the philosophical methodology I have been attributing to Brandom with a widely discussed methodology that falls under the heading of genealogy. The approach was, of course, made famous by Nietzsche – although the version of this I wish to consider for the purposes of the contrast is that utilized by Edward Craig regarding the concept of knowledge (Craig 1990). On his approach, one begins by imagining a cooperative social group of language-speaking human beings who seek true beliefs in order to survive, but do not yet have the full-blown concept of knowledge. One then provides some insight into the function and value of the concept of knowledge by telling a plausible narrative regarding how the full-blown concept may have come about from proto-concepts used in this "epistemic state-of-nature". Using this method, Craig provides a "practical explication" of the concept of knowledge, according to which the concept arises from the need to identify or flag good informants – those who will tell the truth about a particular subject of enquiry. For both Brandom and Craig, one begins with an imagined practice that is arrived at by removing features familiar to our own practice, until we are left with a stripped-down alternative, involving beings just barely recognizable as proto-versions of ourselves. In both cases, one explicates the practical role of some central concept via a narrative of emergence of a target concept from these proto-practices. Both facilitate functional accounts of concepts that may seem resistant to them. Given these methodological similarities, it is unsurprising that there is a great deal of similarity between the resultant accounts of knowledge arrived at by Brandom and Craig. (Both explicitly proffer such methodologies as a

successor notion to the traditional method of philosophical analysis. See BSD I: 23 and Craig 1990: 7.) There are differences, however. Craig's overall concern is to explain why we have the concept of knowledge that we have. As the phrase "state of nature" betrays, genealogical accounts tend to have naturalizing goals. For Brandom this just means that the vocabulary used to describe the doings in question are "natural" – possibly in that they feature in the vocabulary of the natural sciences. To achieve this, Craig begins with a *prima facie* plausible hypothesis as to what the practical point of the concept may be, and then uses the state-of-nature scenario as a way of considering what a concept with the hypothesized goal would look like. Brandom's overall concern differs. He aims to explore the relations between two sets of linguistic abilities: those necessary to make any assertions whatsoever, and those required to deploy the "knows that . . ." locution. To achieve this, he begins with the former abilities and considers how to introduce these into the practice. The point of Brandom's methodology is structural, and is not, as Craig's is, purely functional.

23. Note that this is something that B could not say with just the conditional locution, which only allows him to say that one claim follows from another.

Chapter 4: Us

1. Although Brandom provides this as a gloss on Davidson's conception of rationality, he both endorses it and incorporates it into his own model on the following page (TOMD: 6). It also features tacitly in the discussion of the collapse of levels at the conclusion of MIE (MIE: 643–4).
2. This is the third of the three questions posed at the opening of Chapter 2.
3. See MIE: 28–9 and, especially, 645–7.
4. In the last (italicized) sentence of the previous quotation from MIE, Brandom seems to equate normative space with the normative practices of giving and asking for reasons. This does not cohere with other aspects of his work discussed earlier, although it does leave the impression that Brandom is pursuing the stronger response considered and rejected here.
5. A similar claim is made in Whiting (2006). It should be noted that Brandom does not use the case of gerrymandering to motivate the claim that interpretation begins at home, but argues for this on independent grounds, based on the essentially perspectival nature of semantic content. These concerns, however, could not be directly introduced into the discussion here without begging the question. The point here is that even if we could establish that interpretation begins at home, it would be of little use in ruling out the possibility of the anthropologists.
6. For example Gibbard (1996); Shapiro (2004: 142–3); Rödl (2000).
7. "The claim that this formal characterization in terms of inferentially articulated normative statuses, and the material one in terms of mapping onto our own practices, are two ways of picking out the same practices is a bold and potentially falsifiable empirical claim. I do not claim to have demonstrated in MIE, the truth of the conjecture that these two notions of rationality in fact coincide" (TOMD: 8–9). Talk of "two conceptions of rationality" in this quotation masks the difficulties that such an admission raises, since the whole point of the challenge is that there is no reason to think that the game-playing practices provide any conception of rationality.

8. This response is clearest in RPC: 239–40.
9. The cost–benefit analysis at the local level, according to which one is better off treating someone as one of us if one can, may well explain the psychological motivation behind such unwarranted projection.
10. "The extent to which crucial characteristic features of linguistic expressions of many different categories can be reproduced is the best possible reason to conclude that the (mere) intuition that the scorekeeping practices on which they are based could have the complex consequential structure of commitment and entitlement inheritance described, while still being just a game . . . is mistaken" (RPC: 240–41).
11. It is possible, however, to combine this with a normative claim made towards the end of MIE so that "one *ought* to adopt the discursive scorekeeping stance whenever one *can* adopt it" (MIE: 644). The reason for this is largely instrumental; the benefit of engaging in conversation far outweighs not doing so. As a result of this commitment, even this weaker response suggests that Martian anthropologists ought to treat our gameplayers as rational beings. This is still weaker than the first defence, which says they must, and not just ought, do so.
12. Cf. Gaita (2000: 157–86); the quoted phrase is taken from p. 180.
13. By tooling-up, I mean the process of acquiring, via elaboration, the abilities to deploy new vocabularies. Brandom uses this phrase in a related sense (see BSD III: 55), although the idea of language as a tool is critically discussed in PP and thus should be used here with care.
14. Cf. MIE: 112 and, especially, FNNF: 373.
15. Rosen (1997: 170), Rödl (2000) and Dowell (2006) all challenge Brandom's explanatory reductive ambitions in a related sense.
16. Early on in MIE, Brandom tells us that "part of what is distinctive about the approach is that what are treated as semantic primitives are themselves explained in terms of a prior pragmatics, which in turn appeals to normative primitives, themselves made available by mapping the theoretical idiom onto our ordinary talk" (MIE: 681, fn. 6). We have already noted, in Chapter 2, the distance between the normative primitives and those of our ordinary talk. It is, however, possible to read this footnote as endorsing the explicatory reading of the project advocated here, in which the starting point is our ordinary talk.

Part II: Inferentialism (Introduction)

1. This is meant as stipulative, and follows Brandom (e.g. PP: 41). Admittedly, this is not how the terms "semantics" and "pragmatics" are often used. (See Szabo 2005 for an overview of more orthodox views.)
2. More formally, it claims that a theory of meaning should take the form of an axiomatic theory, whose recursive axioms generate theorems in the form of specifications of truth conditions for every sentence in the language. If we begin with a finite base of clauses that specifies the referent of primitive expressions in a language (for example, axiom 1: The reference of "Mandela" is Mandela; axiom 2: For all x, x satisfies "is lawyer" if and only if x is a lawyer), then one can use a theory of truth to generate the truth-conditional theorems (for example, A: "Mandela is a lawyer" is true if and only if Mandela is a lawyer) that can be used to state the meaning of the sentence. The key is

to realize that the relations between the left- and right-hand sides of A is not a relation between sentences; the expressions on the right-hand side of the theorem are used, not mentioned.

3. MIE: 284–5; 1997b: 142–3. Brandom is also dissatisfied with accounts of the representational primitives proffered in R1 (MIE: xvi, 6–7, 93–4, 132). Since he does not explain the source of the dissatisfaction in detail, I have ignored it here. (It is sometimes implied that the requisite account has not been given; it is sometimes implied that it has been given but is inadequate as it fails to establish the relations between such primitives and the use of the expressions to which they are applied. The latter concern may not worry the representationalist who also rejects what I call "neo-pragmatism" in Chapter 5.)
4. Denying that it can be used to *explain* meaning is not to the same as denying that it can be used to *explicate* meaning. Brandom contends that the latter remains open for the inferentialist, so that he can use the powerful machinery of a truth-conditional meaning theory (albeit in a suitably modified form), while pursuing an inferentialist theory of meaning.

Chapter 5: Sentential semantics

1. This assumption will be modified significantly in Chapter 6 to include asymmetric anaphoric structures.
2. It will help to simplify matters if we work with the fantasy (which sustained an empire) that English is the only language. Brandom's semantic theory, of course, acknowledges that a sentence possesses semantic content only contingently, and can be attributed to sentences in other languages too. This is incorporated into an inferentialist theory via the notion of deferential potential mentioned in Chapter 3.
3. It is not surprising, therefore, that an anti-holist such as Fodor extends this image further in his talk of belief-boxes: the "bearer-with-content" image almost ceases to be metaphoric on his picture. The comments in the text raise a number of potential difficulties regarding holism that are not addressed here. See chapter 6 of TOMD for an extremely complex discussion.
4. See, for example, Fodor (2003: 14–26) and Williams (2004), from whom I have taken the terms. Use of the phrase "Homeric struggle" to describe a basic divide in philosophy of language and mind is drawn from Strawson (2004: 132).
5. See PP: 43–4; BSD I: 14. The constraint is sometimes expressed more strongly, to the effect that the explanatory goal of semantic theory is exhausted by its potential contribution to pragmatic theory. Even if some neo-pragmatists may endorse the stronger version too, the weaker version noted in the text has greater intuitive plausibility, and will suffice for our purposes.
6. Compare: "Cartesians do not deny that it's the uses we put our concepts to that makes them worth the bother of having or studying them. What Cartesians deny is just that our putting our concepts to uses that we do is *constitutive* of the concepts or our having them" (Fodor 2003: 21).
7. This constraint is discussed clearly in Shapiro (2004: 144–6) and Dowell (2006: 153–5). "Relevant aspects" are those pertaining to the pragmatic features of a minimal Brandomian linguistic practice described in scorekeeping terms. There is, however, more to pragmatics than this, even for Brandom (see Wanderer forthcoming).
8. See PP: 44–6; BSD I: 14.

9. Quoted phrases are from PP: 45.
10. This differs from the readings of Brandom's inferentialism in Dowell (2006). Dowell treats Brandom as identifying meaning with use, and thereby sees him as fulfilling the constraints in this all-too-easy manner. She correctly notes (2006: 155, fn. 30) that, on her reading, the constraint of semantic pragmatism yields an unusual sense of explanation. I take this as evidence that one should resist such a reading.
11. "Any use of the term commits the user to the inference that is curled up, implicitly, in it" (Brandom 2001b: 76).
12. Brandom terms this "weak inferentialism" (e.g. AR: 219).
13. For example AR: 220.
14. MacFarlane (2000: 36–41) calls this way of picking out logical form a decoy, in that it draws attention away from the real target.
15. As Brandom puts it, the fixed vocabulary could be zoological or theological vocabulary, thereby allowing one to define the notion of good zoological or theological form (MIE: 105).
16. "The point here is that whilst we are using the Fregean notion of invariance under substitution to define formality, it is not being used as a way of demarcating the logical" (BSD II: 29).
17. In this work, I have chosen to concentrate on Brandom's account of cognitive structure, empirical and otherwise. His account of practical structure, alluded to in this paragraph, is mostly ignored (cf. MIE: 222 for these terms). This omission is for reasons of space alone, and is not an indication that its role is secondary in the overall system. Having said that, the ideas regarding practical structure are, to my mind, insufficiently developed in MIE, especially relative to the account of cognitive structure. The clearest discussion of practical structure is in chapter 2 of AR, to which the interested reader should turn.
18. The thought experiment is due to Putnam (1979).
19. MIE: 119, 332. Those familiar with the twin-earth literature may wish to apply the label "long-arm inferential role theory" to Brandom's position. (An inferential role theory is one that explains the meaning of linguistic expressions in terms of the functional role those expressions play in thinking and speaking. Short-arm versions claim that the content associated with a content-bearer is determined by its relation to other content-bearers within a thinker's head, whilst long-armed versions allow for the functional role to include relations with objects and properties in the external world.) Although Brandom's inferentialism here is world-embracing, this way of making the division is misleading at best, as it implies a division between word and world that, as shall see, Brandom wishes to overcome. Cf. Greenberg (2005).
20. Their practical engagements with water, including the ability to read water stimuli and write sentences involving "water" in response, are world-involving. As we shall show later on, it is because we treat their performances as such that we can treat the semantic content associated with their sentences as potentially outrunning their actual and potential dispositions to apply such concepts.
21. Terms such as "deductive entailment" are normally reserved for the formal case. I use them here for reasons of familiarity. In the material case, Brandom refers to these as commitment- or entitlement-preserving, for reasons that, if not already apparent, are spelt out below.
22. See Brandom (2005a) and BSD III and V for a further indication of the

extent of the difficulties caused for the inferentialist by the admittance of non-monotonicity into strong inferentialism. This is an extremely difficult area that requires further work.

23. Given the non-monotonicity of material inferences, we should probably rephrase the case of commitment-preservation to say that an inference from a set of premises X to a sentence p is commitment-preserving if S is committed to X then she is committed to p. Likewise, in the case of entitlement-preservation, we should say that an inference from a set of premises X to a sentence p is entitlement-preserving if S is committed and entitled to X then she is *prima facie* entitled to p.
24. See MIE: 636; FNNF: 359–60.
25. Everyday talk of understanding employs both visual and tactile metaphors. Cf. Lakoff (1987).
26. See Harman (1984), discussed in TOMD: 193.
27. The Harman point raises a number of extremely difficult questions regarding the relationship between logic and reasoning that are, of course, not solved by the move made in the text.

Chapter 6: Subsentential semantics

1. "[I]t is coherent to interpret a community as using . . . sentences but not subsentential expressions, while it is not coherent to interpret any community as using subsentential expressions but not sentences" (MIE: 399).
2. We shall be assuming throughout this chapter that discerning subsentential structure that can play an indirect inferential role will suffice to be able to explain the ability to understand and produce an indefinite number of novel sentences. There is a considerable body of literature disputing/defending this claim, notably Fodor & Lepore (1991; 2001); McCullagh (2003); and, especially, Brandom BSD V, which will not be discussed here.
3. Brandom seems to simply assume that one can discern such subsentential parts (e.g. AR: 131), although he claims that such an assumption need not be made (see MIE: 688, n. 26). Whether one can make do without such an assumption depends on how one understands Brandom (1987), and its relationship to MIE. I do not pretend to have achieved such an understanding.
4. As Fodor & Lepore (2001: 474) point out, it may turn out that the syntactic categories that emerge here may not correlate with those of traditional grammatical theory.
5. On occasion, Brandom misleadingly says that all three of these (being *substituted in*, being *substituted for* and *substitutional frame*) are all roles that an expression could play (MIE: 368). The looseness here stems from the fact that Brandom is sometimes talking of what are called simple predicates (such as "spoke out against the current government's HIV-AIDS policy") and sometimes of what are called complex predicates (such as "α spoke out against the current government's HIV-AIDS policy"). (See Dummett 1973: 24–33 for the distinction on which Brandom draws.) Unlike complex predicates, simple predicates could be seen as the raw ingredients of the substitutional process and, as we shall see, can be involved in substitutions as opposed to frame replacements. In the text, I shall limit myself to complex predicates. (The fact that simple predicates are similar to singular terms in this sense causes problems for Brandom's claim that one can distinguish singular terms from predicates in terms of their syntactic, as well as their

semantic, roles, as this seems to be the case only for complex predicates that are identifiable only after singular terms have been discerned (see McCullagh 2005: 215–19).)

6. Brandom is explicit about this, and talks of substitution inferences "in a broad sense" which includes both substitutions and frame replacements. He calls the former "basic", and the latter "derived", substitutional variation (MIE: 371).
7. There is an important qualification to the above account. Consider the inference from (8) "President Thabo Mbeki believes that the first democratically elected president of the Republic of South Africa spoke out against the current government's HIV-AIDS policy" to (9) "President Thabo Mbeki believes that the author of *Long Walk to Freedom* spoke out against the current government's HIV-AIDS policy". Substituted-in sentences (8) and (9) seem to be substitutional variants of each other, in that one moves from one to the other by substituting the definite description "the author of *Long Walk to Freedom*" for the definite description "the first democratically elected president of the Republic of South Africa". The appropriateness of such a substitution, however, does not stem from the substitutional commitment attributed as a result of a commitment to the appropriateness of the SMSIC from (1) to (2). (One may be prepared to accept the substitution from (1) to (2) but not from (8) to (9), if one does not believe that Mbeki believes that the author of *Long Walk to Freedom* is (=) the first democratically elected president of the Republic of South Africa.) Brandom excludes such cases by limiting the general pattern to occurrences of such subsentential expressions to when these occur within an extensional context (see MIE: 690, fn. 37). In Brandomian terms, such occurrences of the expression have *primary* substitution-semantic occurrence, and SMSICs only relate such primary occurrences of the expressions. Since the context of the occurrence of these definite descriptions in (8) and (9) is intensional, the expressions do not have primary semantic-substitutional significance, and are thus not governed by the SMSIC from (1) to (2). This limitation requires Brandom to proffer a prior account of the distinction between intensional and extensional contexts. This may seem difficult for the inferentialist, as the typical way of making such a distinction appeals to denotation and truth values that do not feature here. (Typically, extensional contexts are said to be those where coreferential terms can be interchanged, while preserving the truth value of the sentence in which they occur.) Brandom certainly attempts to make this distinction in terms of the notion of designatedness (MIE: 346–60) although McCullagh (2005) has argued that Brandom lacks the resources to make the distinction.
8. In fact, we shall focus only on Brandom's account of "purported singular reference". A fuller discussion should also be able to account for the success of such purport. Brandom allows for this by introducing the notion of an existential commitment, itself understood as a form of substitutional commitment. This will not be pursued further here. Cf. MIE: 440–49.
9. More generally, since the example is one of preservation of commitment alone, to say that a substitution is reversible, or symmetric, is to say that if a transformation involving substitution of one term for another preserves a semantically relevant status (such as commitment or entitlement) irrespective of the sentence frame, then inverse transformations will preserve that same status, irrespective of the sentence frame.

10. There has been some scepticism as to whether this way of distinguishing between singular terms and predicates works (e.g. Graham 1999; Oliver 2000; Fodor & Lepore (2001); McCullagh 2005).
11. We need to add an account of their substitution-structural role to make these necessary and sufficient. According to the full account, a singular term is a syntactically significant term that, in syntactic terms, is substituted for and, in semantic terms, enters into reversible substitutional inferences. One of the undoubted highlights of MIE, that will not be rehearsed here, is an "expressive deduction of the necessity of this structure" (MIE: xxii), an argument to the effect that this pairing of syntactic and semantic conditions must be the case for logical, self-conscious beings such as ourselves. See MIE: 376–84.
12. This is actually a reciprocal claim, although we shall focus only on one direction here. In a discussion of this claim, Pippin contends that this sense-dependence claim "lacks bite" and is "anodyne" (Pippin 2005: 384). Whether one experiences something as having bite depends on the diet one is used to. Such claims are hardly standard fare, or even palatable, within contemporary anglophone philosophy.
13. Brandom (2005a: 431). The claim of reference-dependence between claiming and fact is only crazy for some regions of facts. In other words, there are some facts that cannot be said to antedate our practices of claiming. An obvious example: the fact that I am claiming that p cannot be said to pre-date the social practice of claiming. One can distinguish regions of facts by the types of vocabulary used to state the facts. The claim that "junior lecturers ought to follow the demands of their Head of Department" is, if true, a normative fact, as it requires normative vocabulary to state it. It is hardly crazy to reject the claim that there were such normative facts before there were discursive practices.
14. Cf. Williamson (2004: 110) for a similar suspicion, directed at McDowell.
15. Brandom calls this a kind of substitutional triangulation. Focusing on the case of singular terms, two distinct claims at the sentential level purport to be about the same object (the three vortices of the triangle) when the terms used to index the transformations have a symmetric substitutional inferential significance. In our example, the italicized subsentential terms are singular terms since they have such symmetric substitutional significance that could be made explicit by the non-trivial identity claim: "that rabbit is (=) Jessie".
16. A central argument in MIE, that will not be rehearsed here, goes further to claim that, for any language that has the expressive resources of the conditional or negation, unpacking the notion of fact will lead one to see that the notion of fact must have the basic structure of attributing properties and relations to objects. In this sense, facts are about objects. Note: even if this argument is successful, it does not undermine the explanatory priority of facts over objects. First, while there is an explanatory route from unpacking the notion of facts to unpacking the notion of objects, there is no converse route. Secondly, the argument leaves open the possibility of facts without objects, albeit a world that we would be significantly impoverished in talking about.
17. This foreshadows Brandom's account of the expressive role of the predicate "refers" as an anaphoric-pronoun-forming operator. This is discussed further in Chapters 7 and 8.

18. In saying the case shows how to form an anaphoric chain, I do not mean that it states the psycholinguistic mechanisms by which such chains are formed in practice, but that the example illustrates just what it is that is achieved when the mechanisms function correctly (cf. MIE: 457).
19. The terms "anaphoric" and "recurrence" will be used interchangeably, even though there is a difference between them: anaphora is an asymmetric kind of recurrence. Brandom treats anaphora as the more basic recurrence structure (cf. MIE; 471–2).
20. "There are two varieties of substitutional equivalence. These are *intra*term and *inter*term, or de jure and de facto equivalences of tokenings. The former are (taken to be) binding on all interlocutors; the latter vary from doxastic repertoire to doxastic repertoire, according to the particular substitutional commitments undertaken by or attributed to an individual. Each attributor takes recurrence to bind all, in keeping track of significances of identificatory commitments and invocations of them by term use. But the identificatory or substitutional commitments themselves vary from individual to individual" (MIE: 452).
21. Here we follow Brandom (in turn following Chastain 1975) in using "#" quotes to mark off discourses containing multiple sentences, potentially by different users.
22. Brandom boldly asserts that we should treat rigidity as an anaphoric phenomenon (cf. MIE: 468–72). Non-rigid expressions are incorporated into such an anaphoric account by distinguishing between basic predicates and compounds of these, drawing on Brandom's account of quantifiers in substitutional terms (see MIE: 434–49 and 471). The tentative tenor of his discussion of these points in MIE concedes that far more is needed to follow through the details of such a claim. For example, an account of the pragmatic significance of a scorekeeper treating a term as a rigid designator should be offered.
23. Cf. Weiskopf & Bechtel (2004: 50–51).
24. I am drawing here on Sellars' (1958: 306–7) distinction between labelling and describing.
25. The reason for stressing this stems from Fodor's recent rejection of pragmatist approaches to concept possession, which he sees as "the defining catastrophe of analytic philosophy of language and philosophy of mind in the last half of the twentieth century" (Fodor 2004: 30). For Fodor, pragmatism is characterized as an approach that treats mastery of the concept X in terms of the having of sorting and inferring abilities involving the concept; in contrast, Fodor argues that these abilities are neither necessary nor sufficient for concept possession. Fodor includes Brandom as a pragmatist (whom he "disagrees with about everything . . . under the sun" (Fodor 2003: 23)); although the comments here make clear that Brandom is not a pragmatist about concept possession in Fodor's sense.

Chapter 7: Communication

1. Versions of the challenge first arise in the context of discussions of Quine's (1951) endorsement of "semantic" holism.
2. The phrase is taken from MIE: 510.
3. All these alternatives are explicitly considered by Brandom. Cf. Scharp (2003) for a similar list.

4. Cf. Fodor & Lepore (1991: 17).
5. Cf. Fodor & Lepore (2001).
6. See, for example, Boghossian (1994) and Horwich (1998).
7. Fodor & Lepore (2001). The response here is that of Horwich (1998).
8. Quine (1951) and the discussion in MIE: 634–5.
9. For example MIE: 195–6, 596; AR: 174.
10. "The proposal is accordingly not to *analyze* belief in terms of commitment but to discard that concept as insufficiently precise and replace it with clearer talk about different sorts of commitment" (MIE: 196).
11. This is a common philosophical distinction that Brandom is utilizing here in a somewhat idiosyncratic manner. A *res* is a thing; a *dictum* is a saying.
12. Davidson (1984: 206–37). Brandom's discussion is in MIE: 534–9.
13. As Rouse (2002: 217) puts it: "there is a formal sense in which sameness of conceptual content is preserved despite different collateral commitments and their divergent inferential significance". This formal sameness is marked by "a trackable isomorphism among inferential roles revealed by the transformations that different discursive scorekeeping perspectives make upon one another, not any substantially shared content".
14. Brandom (MIE: 596) also allows for the possibility that some commitments we just come with, by default as it were.
15. Cf. MIE 600 for the local–global distinction. Can the scorekeeper apply this distinction to himself in the present? The structural account of objectivity requires that the distinction be available even in such a case, yet it is puzzling how one can achieve this in practice prior to mastery of the ascriptional locutions. This is not a problem for Brandom's account of objectivity *per se*, although it does undermine his contention that we should treat such ascriptional locutions as logical locutions that have the function of making explicit what was already implicit in the doings of rational beings prior to their mastery over such locutions. See Laurier (2005) and Brandom's response in RPC.
16. I have in mind here the rich historical accounts of the concept by Daston & Galison (2007).
17. Haugeland (1982), cited approvingly in, for example, TOMD 48.
18. Brandom's endorsement of the stronger institution claim is discussed in the conclusion. Haugeland too endorsed the stronger claim about self-constitution, although he appears to have changed his mind about this in more recent work – e.g. Haugeland (1998: 4–5) – critiquing Brandom on just this aspect in Haugeland (1998: 358, n. 14). (Thanks to an anonymous referee for pointing this out.)
19. In MIE: 601–7, Brandom offers a series of proofs that the scorekeeping process described in the book is such that, from the local perspective of the scorekeeper, none of the following conditionals holds: (a) for every proposition p, if p is true then everybody claims that p; (b) for every proposition p, if everybody claims that p then p is true; (c) for every proposition p, if p is true, then I claim that p; and (d) for every proposition p, if I claim that p then p is true. Brandom concedes that "there is clearly lots of room for dispute as to whether what is constructed [in MIE] is enough objectivity – whether it is the right sort of objectivity, or all the objectivity we need in order to understand, say, the use of concepts in the mature natural sciences" (FNNF: 356).
20. Cf. Schneewind (1998) for a rich historical account of the development of this Enlightenment thought.
21. See also Brandom (1979) for an early expression of this point.

22. Concerns about coercion are raised by Pippin (2005, esp. 390–96). Concerns about alienation are raised by McDowell (e.g. 1999, 2002b: 303; 2005b).
23. It is not merely that the extant discussion of the autonomy thesis in Brandom's writings is underdeveloped. Additionally, the discussion is (a) bound up with issues of Hegelian exegesis and (b) focused primarily on the constitutive question. We return to the latter in the conclusion.
24. By the hearer–overhearer contrast, I do not just mean the distinction between addressee and ratified participant in the conversation, but the difference between addressee and any eavesdropper whomsoever. (Cf. Goffman 1981: 131 discussed in Clark & Carlson 1982: 332.)
25. I arrived at this way of thinking about the notion of the second-personal by reflecting on the work of Langton and Hornsby on illocutionary silencing (e.g. Hornsby & Langton 1998; cf. Bird 2002).
26. This is a somewhat awkward point to express as we have followed Brandom in treating recognition as recognition in practice. If so, in refusing to recognize an act, one both recognizes it in practice (a performance) and refuses to acknowledge the address (a non-performance). The response of silence here expresses both performance and non-performance at once.
27. The characterization of I–Thou relations in MIE is primarily negative: its functions is to mark the rejection of accounts of the sociality of linguistic practice based on I–We relations that construe the notion of the social in terms of a broader linguistic community, of which the speaker is a part.
28. I pursue this line of thought more fully in Wanderer (forthcoming).

Chapter 8: [s]Losing the world[s]?

1. The phrase "Representationalist Totalitarianism" is taken from VP: 170.
2. See Menand (2001: 361, cited in Price 2004) and, of course, Rorty (1979).
3. Similarly, Price (forthcoming) worries that Brandom's position intends "not so much to deliver Dewey's coup de grâce to representationalism, as an old fashioned coup d'état – to take over the representationalist empire intact, by rebuilding its walls on properly pragmatic foundations".
4. A similar question is raised by Price (2004; 2008), although the formulation here differs in an important respect.
5. The image is McDowell's (e.g. 1994: 11). Cf. Brandom's criticism in 1996: 244, fn. 5.
6. For reasons that will emerge later, it is more precise to say that such practices are *potentially* world-involving, for Brandom allows the possibility of a linguistic practice lacking empirical content.
7. The prosentential theory of truth does not originate with Brandom (see Grover *et al.* 1975). He modifies the account and applies it to the case of reference.
8. Brandom (2002c) is a clear expression of this point.
9. Rorty (1998: 136; 2000: 185; cf. Rorty 1982: 13).
10. This is a common Rortyian theme. See, for example, Rorty (1988: 21).
11. It is only *prima facie* entitlement since S (or anyone else) may have collateral commitments that are incompatible with that one. If, for example, S has information that G lacks about the non-standard lighting conditions operating when G makes his observational report, S can still treat G as a reliable reporter of redness, while not endorsing his observational report. S could

treat G as a reliable reporter of red things and thus treat him as entitled to such a report, even if he were to explicitly disavow his own reliability and tell her not to rely on his claim.

12. For example Lance (1997: 182); Loeffler (2005: 63).
13. See also MIE: 225; BSD VI: 13.
14. Inferential relations constrain, but do not dictate, inferential processes. Notice that in trying to rectify my incompatible commitments, I am at once trying to work out what the right concepts are, and what claims are true. These are not to be separated in terms of meanings and beliefs, but form a part of a solitary process. We explore some implications of this in the conclusion.
15. Cf. VP: 167 and Rouse (2002: 102).
16. See Rouse (2002: 206–7), which seems to imply the contrary.
17. This critique stems from McDowell (1994). The specific discussion of Brandom includes McDowell (1996; 1998b; 2002a; 2005a; forthcoming).
18. One reason for McDowell's concerns would be metaphilosophical: his quietistic aversion to theoretical construction in philosophy ensures that the talk of constraints and theories in what follows is unMcDowellian.
19. McDowell provides the following analogy for this sense of exculpation: "if someone is found in a place from which she has been banished, she is exculpated by the fact that she was deposited there by a tornado. Her arriving there is completely removed from the domain of what she is responsible for; it is not that she is still responsible, but there is a basis for mitigating any sanctions" (McDowell 1994: 8).
20. See also MIE: 333 and 686 fn. 58 for an expression of this agreement.
21. Apparently incorrectly – see Biederman & Shiffrar (1987).
22. I have been influenced here by MacFarlane (2004), who argues that McDowell needs to explain why he thinks that the use of mathematical concepts is not an empty game. In the course of the argument, he notes that an inferentialist alternative account of content will seem plausible in absence of such an explanation. Macbeth (forthcoming) also highlights the differences between the accounts of conceptual content offered by Brandom and McDowell, although she draws them even further apart than the reading offered here.
23. Brandom appears to be aware of this complaint himself, and sets to counter it by providing a historico-inferentialist justification for the kind of selective historical reconstructions of positions he undertakes. See Brandom (2004), reprised in TOMD.

Conclusion: Towards a historical conception of rationality

1. The primary sources for the historicist conception to date are Brandom's discussions of Hegel, especially TOMD (178–234); 2005b; 2006; 2007b.
2. Cf. Pippin (2005: 391, 392).
3. Both the problem, and the quoted phrase, are McDowell's (2005b: 35). Cf. McDowell (2002b: 276).

References

References to works by Brandom

This is a list of Brandom's writings that are referred to in the book, apart from those listed in the Abbreviations on pp. x–xi. A full bibliography of Brandom's writings is available at www.pitt.edu/~rbrandom/publist.html

1976. "Truth and Assertibility". *Journal of Philosophy* **78**(6): 137–49.

1979. "Freedom and Constraint by Norms". *American Philosophical Quarterly* **16**(3): 187–96.

1983. "Asserting". *Noûs* **17**(4): 637–50.

1985. "Varieties of Understanding". In *Reason and Rationality in Natural Science*, N. Rescher (ed.), 27–51. Lanham, MD: University Presses of America.

1987. "Singular Terms and Sentential Sign Designs". *Philosophical Topics* **15**: 125–67.

1994. "Unsuccessful Semantics". *Analysis* **54**(3): 175–8.

1996. "Perception and Rational Constraint: McDowell's Mind and World". In *Perception*, E. Villanueva (ed.), 241–59. Atascadero, CA: Ridgeview.

1997a. "Replies". *Philosophy & Phenomenological Research* **57**(1): 189–214.

1997b. "From Truth to Semantics: A Path Through Making It Explicit". *Philosophical Issues 8: Truth, Sociedad Filosofica Ibero-Americano* 141–54 and 199–214.

1997c. "Study Guide". In *Empiricism and the Philosophy of Mind*, W. Sellars (ed.), 119–81. Cambridge, MA: Harvard University Press.

1998. "Perception and Rational Constraint". *Philosophy & Phenomenological Research* **58**(2): 369–74.

2001a. "Reason, Expression, and the Philosophic Enterprise". In *What is Philosophy?*, C. P. Ragland (ed.), 74–95. New Haven, CT: Yale University Press.

2001b. "Modality, Normativity, and Intentionality". *Philosophy and Phenomenological Research* **63**(3): 587–609.

2002a. "Non-Inferential Knowledge, Perceptual Experience, and Secondary Qualities: Placing McDowell's Empiricism". In *Reading McDowell: On Mind and World*, N. H. Smith (ed.), 92–105. London: Routledge.

2002b. "When Philosophy Paints Its Blue on Gray: Irony and the Pragmatist Enlightenment". *Boundary 2* **29**(2): 1–28.

2002c. "Explanatory vs. Expressive Deflationism about Truth". In *What Is Truth?*, R. Schantz (ed.), 103–19. Berlin: De Gruyter.
2004. "Hermeneutic Practice and Theories of Meaning". *SATS – Nordic Journal of Philosophy* **5**(1): 5–26.
2005a. "Sketch of a Program for a Critical Reading of Hegel: Comparing Empirical and Logical Concepts". In *Internationales Jahrbuch des Deutschen Idealismus / International Yearbook of German Idealism, Vol. 3, 2005: Deutscher Idealismus und die analytische Philosophie der Gegenwart / German Idealism and Contemporary Analytic Philosophy*, K. Ameriks (ed.), 131–61. Berlin: De Gruyter.
2005b. "Responses to Pippin, Macbeth and Haugeland". *European Journal of Philosophy* **13**(3): 429–41.
2006. "Kantian Lessons about Mind, Meaning, and Rationality". *Southern Journal of Philosophy* **44**, Supplement, 49–71.
2007a. "The Structure of Desire and Recognition". *Philosophy & Social Criticism* **33**(1): 127–50.
2007b. "Inferentialism and Some of Its Challenges". *Philosophy & Phenomenological Research* **74**(3): 651–76.

Works by other authors

Beebe, J. 2003. "Attributive Use of Prosentences". *Ratio* **XVI**: 1–15.
Belnap, N. D. 1962. "Tonk, Plonk and Plink". *Analysis* **22**: 130–34.
Bennett, J. 1971. *Locke, Berkeley, Hume: Central Themes.* Oxford: Clarendon Press.
Biederman, I. & Shiffrar, M. M. 1987. "Sexing Day-Old Chicks: A Case Study and Expert Systems Analysis of a Difficult Perceptual-Learning Task". *Journal of Experimental Psychology: Learning, Memory, and Cognition* **13**(4): 640–45.
Bird, A. 2002. "Illocutionary Silencing". *Pacific Philosophical Quarterly* **83**(1): 1–15.
Boghossian, P. 1994. "Inferential Role Semantics and the Analytic/Synthetic Distinction". *Philosophical Studies: An International Journal for Philosophy in the Analytic Tradition* **73**(2–3): 109–22.
Chastain, C. 1975. "Reference and Context". In *Language, Mind and Knowledge*, K. Gunderson (ed.), 194–269. Minneapolis: MN: University of Minnesota Press.
Clark, H. H. & Carlson, T. B. 1982. "Hearers and Speech Acts". *Language* **58**(2): 332–73.
Craig, E. 1990. *Knowledge and the State of Nature: An Essay in Conceptual Synthesis.* Oxford: Clarendon Press.
Daston, L. & Galison, P. 2007. *Objectivity.* New York: Zone Books.
Davidson, D. 1975. "Thought and Talk". In *Mind and Language*, S. Guttenplan (ed.), 7–23. Oxford: Oxford University Press.
Davidson, D. 1984. *Inquiries into Truth and Interpretation.* Oxford: Clarendon Press.
Dowell, J. L. 2006. "Making It Totally Explicit". *Philosophical Papers* **35**(2): 137–70.
Dummett, M. A. E. 1973. *Frege: Philosophy of Language.* London: Duckworth.
Fitch, W. T., Hauser, M. D. & Chomsky, N. 2005. "The Evolution of the Language Faculty: Clarifications and Implications". *Cognition* **97**(2): 179–210.
Fodor, J. A. 1992. *Holism: A Shopper's Guide.* Oxford: Blackwell.
Fodor, J. A. 2003. *Hume Variations.* Oxford: Clarendon Press.

Fodor, J. 2004. "Having Concepts: A Brief Refutation of the Twentieth Century". *Mind and Language* **19**(1): 29–47.

Fodor, J. & Lepore, E. 1991. "Why Meaning (Probably) Isn't Conceptual Role". *Mind and Language* **6**(4): 328–43.

Fodor, J. & Lepore, E. 2001. "Brandom's Burdens: Compositionality and Inferentialism". *Philosophy & Phenomenological Research* **63**(2): 465–81.

Franks, P. W. 2005. *All or Nothing: Systematicity, Transcendental Arguments, and Skepticism in German Idealism.* Cambridge, MA: Harvard University Press.

Gaita, R. 2000. *A Common Humanity: Thinking about Love and Truth and Justice.* London: Routledge.

Gibbard, A. 1996. "Thought, Norms, and Discursive Practice: Commentary on Robert Brandom, Making It Explicit". *Philosophy & Phenomenological Research* **56**(3): 699.

Goffman, E. 1981. *Forms of Talk.* Oxford: Blackwell.

Graham, P. J. 1999. "Brandom on Singular Terms". *Philosophical Studies: An International Journal for Philosophy in the Analytic Tradition* **93**(3): 247–64.

Greenberg, M. 2005. "A New Map of Theories of Mental Content". *Philosophical Issues* **15**: 299–320.

Grover, D., Camp, J. & Belnap, N. D. 1975. "A Prosentential Theory of Truth". *Philosophical Studies* **27**: 73–124.

Habermas, J. 2000. "From Kant to Hegel: On Robert Brandom's Pragmatic Philosophy of Language", H. Cooke (trans.). *European Journal of Philosophy* **8**(3): 322–55.

Hacking, I. 1975. *Why does Language Matter to Philosophy?* Cambridge: Cambridge University Press.

Harman, G. 1984. "Logic and Reasoning". *Synthese* **60**: 107–28.

Haugeland, J. 1982. "Heidegger on Being a Person". *Noûs* **16**: 16–26.

Haugeland, J. 1985. *Artificial Intelligence: The Very Idea.* Cambridge, MA: MIT Press.

Haugeland, J. 1988. *Having Thought: Essays in the Metaphysics of Mind.* Cambridge, MA: Harvard University Press.

Heyes, C. & Papineau, D. 2006. "Rational or Associative? Imitation in Japanese Quail". In *Rational Animals*, M. Nudds & S. Hurley (eds), 187–95. Oxford: Oxford University Press.

Hinchman, E. S. 2005. "Telling as Inviting to Trust". *Philosophy and Phenomenological Research* **70**(3): 562–87.

Hornsby, J. & Langton, R. 1998. "Free Speech and Illocution". *Legal Theory* **4**(1): 21–37.

Horwich, P. 1998. *Meaning.* Oxford: Clarendon Press.

Kratzer, A. 2002. "The Notional Category of Modality". In *Formal Semantics: The Essential Readings*, P. Portner & B. Partee (eds), 289–323. Oxford: Blackwell.

Kretzmann, N. 1968. "The Main Thesis of Locke's Semantic Theory". *Philosophical Review* **77**: 175–96.

Kukla, R. & Lance, M. 2004. "Yo vs. Lo". Paper delivered to Space of Reasons Conference, University of Cape Town, South Africa.

Lacey, N. 2004. *A Life of H. L. A. Hart: The Nightmare and the Noble Dream.* Oxford: Oxford University Press.

Lakoff, G. 1987. *Women, Fire, and Dangerous Things: What Categories Reveal About the Mind.* Chicago, IL: University of Chicago Press.

Lance, M. 1997. "The Significance of Anaphoric Theories of Truth and Reference". In *Truth*, E. Villanueva (ed.), 181–98. Atascadero, CA: Ridgeview.
Lance, M. & O'Leary Hawthorne, J. 1997. *The Grammar of Meaning: Normativity and Semantic Discourse*. Cambridge: Cambridge University Press.
Laurier, D. 2005. "Pragmatics, Pittsburgh Style". *Pragmatics and Cognition* **13**(1): 141–60.
Locke, J. (1689/1975). *An Essay Concerning Human Understanding*, Peter H. Nidditch (ed.). Oxford: Oxford University Press. **[E]**
Loeffler, R. 2005. "Normative Phenomenalism: On Robert Brandom's Practice-Based Explanation of Meaning". *European Journal of Philosophy* **13**(1): 32–69.
Macbeth, D. 2008. "An Antinomy of Empirical Judgment: Brandom and McDowell". *Pécs International Conferences in Philosophy series.*
MacFarlane, J. 2000. "What Does it Mean to Say that Logic is Formal?" Unpublished PhD thesis. University of Pittsburgh.
MacFarlane, J. 2004. "McDowell's Kantianism". *Theoria: A Swedish Journal of Philosophy* **70**(2–3): 250–65.
MacFarlane, J. Forthcoming. "Pragmatism and Inferentialism". In *Reading Brandom: On Making It Explicit*, J. Wanderer & B. Weiss (eds). London: Routledge.
McCullagh, M. 2003. "Do Inferential Roles Compose?". *Dialectica: International Journal of Philosophy of Knowledge* **57**(4): 431–8.
McCullagh, M. 2005. "Inferentialism and Singular Reference". *Canadian Journal of Philosophy* **35**(2): 183–220.
McDowell, J. 1994. *Mind and World.* Cambridge, MA: Harvard University Press.
McDowell, J. 1996. "Reply to Gibson, Byrne, and Brandom". In *Perception*, E. Villanueva (ed.), 283–300. Atascadero, CA: Ridgeview.
McDowell, J. 1997. "Brandom on Representation and Inference". *Philosophy & Phenomenological Research* **57**(1): 157–62.
McDowell, J. 1998a. "The Woodbridge Lectures 1997: Having the World in View: Sellars, Kant, and Intentionality". *Journal of Philosophy* **95**(9): 431–92.
McDowell, J. 1998b. "Reply to Commentators". *Philosophy & Phenomenological Research* **58**(2): 403–31.
McDowell, J. 1999. "Comment on Robert Brandom's 'Some Pragmatist Themes in Hegel's Idealism'". *European Journal of Philosophy* **7**(2): 190.
McDowell, J. 2002a. "Responses". In *Reading McDowell: On Mind and World*, N. H. Smith (ed.), 269–305. London: Routledge.
McDowell, J. 2002b. "Knowledge and the Internal Revisited". *Philosophy and Phenomenological Research* **64**(1): 97–105.
McDowell, J. 2005a. "Self-Determining Subjectivity and External Constraint". In *Internationales Jahrbuch des Deutschen Idealismus / International Yearbook of German Idealism, Vol. 3, 2005: Deutscher Idealismus und die analytische Philosophie der Gegenwart / German Idealism and Contemporary Analytic Philosophy*, K. Ameriks (ed.), 21–37. Berlin: De Gruyter.
McDowell, J. 2005b. "Motivating Inferentialism: Comments on Making It Explicit (Ch. 2)". *Pragmatics and Cognition* **13**(1): 121–40.
McDowell, J. Forthcoming. "Brandom on Observation". In *Reading Brandom: On Making It Explicit*, J. Wanderer & B. Weiss (eds). London: Routledge.
Menand, L. 2001. *The Metaphysical Club.* New York: Farrar, Straus & Giroux.

Miller, G. A., Galanter, E. & Pribram, K. H. 1960. *Plans and the Structure of Behavior*. New York: Holt, Rinehart & Winston.
Moran, R. 2006. "Getting Told and Being Believed". In *The Epistemology of Testimony*, J. Lackey (ed.), 272–306. Oxford: Clarendon Press.
Nagel, T. 1974. "What is it Like to be a Bat?". *Philosophical Review* **83**: 435–50.
Oliver, A. 2000. "Pink Elephants". *London Review of Books* 22 November: 35–6.
Pagin, P. 2004. "Is Assertion Social?" *Journal of Pragmatics* **36**(5): 833.
Pepperberg, I. M. 1999. *The Alex Studies: Cognitive and Communicative Abilities of Grey Parrots*. Cambridge, MA: Harvard University Press.
Peregrin, J. 2001. "Review: R. Brandom: Articulating Reasons". *Erkenntnis* **55**(1): 121–7.
Pippin, R. B. 2005. "Brandom's Hegel". *European Journal of Philosophy* **13**(3): 381–408.
Price, H. 2004. "Immodesty Without Mirrors – Making Sense of Wittgenstein's Linguistic Pluralism". In *Wittgenstein's Lasting Significance*, M. Kölbel & B. Weiss (eds), 179–205. London: Routledge.
Price, H. 2008. "One Cheer for Representationalism?" in *The Philosophy of Richard Rorty*, ed. R. Auxier, Chicago, IL: Open Court.
Prior, A. N. 1960. "The Runabout Inference-Ticket". *Analysis* **21**: 38–9.
Putnam, H. 1979. *Philosophical Papers*. Cambridge: Cambridge University Press.
Quine, W. V. 1951. "Main Trends in Recent Philosophy: Two Dogmas of Empiricism". *The Philosophical Review* **60**(1): 20–43.
Rödl, S. 2000. "Normativität des Geistes versus Philosophie als Erklärung: Zu Brandoms Theorie des Geistes". *Deutsche Zeitschrift fuer Philosophie* **48**(5): 762–9.
Rödl, S. 2005. "Transcendental Deduction of Predicative Structure in Kant and Brandom". *Pragmatics and Cognition* **13**(1): 91–107.
Rorty, R. 1979. *Philosophy and the Mirror of Nature*. Princeton, NJ: Princeton University Press.
Rorty, R. 1982. *Consequences of Pragmatism: Essays, 1972–1980*. Minneapolis, MN: University of Minnesota Press.
Rorty, R. 1988. "Representation, Social Practise, and Truth". *Philosophical Studies: An International Journal for Philosophy in the Analytic Tradition* **54**: 215–28.
Rorty, R. 1997. "What Do You Do When They Call You a 'Relativist'?". *Philosophy and Phenomenological Research* **57**(1): 173–7.
Rorty, R. 1998. *Truth and Moral Progress: Philosophical Papers*. Vol. 3. Cambridge: Cambridge University Press.
Rorty, R. 2000. "Reply to Brandom". In *Rorty and his Critics*, R. Brandom (ed.), 183–90. Oxford: Blackwell.
Rosen, G. 1997. "Who Makes the Rules Around Here?". *Philosophy & Phenomenological Research* **57**(1): 163–71.
Rosen, G. 2001. "Brandom on Modality, Normativity and Intentionality". *Philosophy and Phenomenological Research* **63**(3): 611–23.
Ross, A. 1986. "Why do we Believe what we are Told?". *Ratio: An International Journal of Analytic Philosophy* **28**: 70–89.
Rouse, J. 2002. *How Scientific Practices Matter: Reclaiming Philosophical Naturalism*. Chicago, IL: University of Chicago Press.
Scharp, K. 2003. "Communication and Content: Circumstances and Consequences of the Habermas–Brandom Debate". *International Journal of Philosophical Studies* **11**(1): 43.

Schneewind, J. B. 1998. *The Invention of Autonomy: A History of Modern Moral Philosophy*. Cambridge: Cambridge University Press.
Sellars, W. 1958. "Counterfactuals, Dispositions, and Causal Modalities". In *Minnesota Studies in the Philosophy of Science, Volume II: Concepts, Theories, and the Mind–Body Problem*, H. Feigl, *et al.* (eds), 225–308. Minneapolis: University of Minnesota Press.
Sellars, W. 1997. *Empiricism and the Philosophy of Mind*. Cambridge, MA: Harvard University Press.
Shapiro, L. 2004. "Brandom on the Normativity of Meaning". *Philosophy & Phenomenological Research* **68**(1): 141–60.
Smith, N. H. 2002. *Reading McDowell: On Mind and World*. London: Routledge.
Stout, R. 1999. "The World of We". *Times Literary Supplement* no. 5016: 35.
Strawson, P. F. 2004. *Logico-linguistic Papers* (new edn.). Aldershot: Ashgate.
Szabo, Z. G. 2005. "Introduction". In *Semantics versus Pragmatics*, Z. G. Szabo (ed.). Oxford: Clarendon Press.
Wanderer, J. Forthcoming. "Brandom's Challenges". In *Reading Brandom; On Making It Explicit*, J. Wanderer & B. Weiss (eds). London: Routledge.
Wedgwood, R. 2006. "The Meaning of 'Ought'". In *Oxford Studies in Metaethics, Volume 1*, R. Shafer-Landau (ed.), 127–60. Oxford: Clarendon Press.
Weiskopf, D. A. & Bechtel, W. 2004. "Remarks on Fodor on Having Concepts". *Mind and Language* **19**(1): 48–56.
Weiss, B. 2002. *Michael Dummett*. Chesham: Acumen.
Whiting, D. 2006. "Between Primitivism and Naturalism: Brandom's Theory of Meaning". *Acta Analytica: Philosophy and Psychology* **21**: 3, no. 40, 3–22.
Williams, M. 2004. "Context, Meaning, and Truth". *Philosophical Studies: An International Journal for Philosophy in the Analytic Tradition* **117**(1–2): 107–29.
Williamson, T. 2004. "Past the Linguistic Turn?". In *The Future for Philosophy*, B. Leiter (ed.), 106–28. Oxford: Clarendon Press.
Wilson, M. D. 1995. "Animal Ideas". *Proceedings and Addresses of the American Philosophical Association* **69**(2): 7–25.
Žižek, S. 2002. *For they know not what they do: Enjoyment as a Political Factor*, 2nd edn. London: Verso.

Index